William Graham Campbell

The Apostle of Kerry

Or, the Wonders of the Irish General Mission, being the Life and... Third Edition

William Graham Campbell

The Apostle of Kerry
Or, the Wonders of the Irish General Mission, being the Life and... Third Edition

ISBN/EAN: 9783337125264

Printed in Europe, USA, Canada, Australia, Japan

Cover: Foto ©Lupo / pixelio.de

More available books at **www.hansebooks.com**

THE APOSTLE OF KERRY;

OR,

THE WONDERS OF THE IRISH GENERAL MISSION,

BEING THE

LIFE AND LABOURS

OF THE

REV. CHARLES GRAHAM;

TOGETHER WITH THOSE OF THE CELEBRATED

GIDEON OUSELEY,

WHO TRAVELLED WITH MR. GRAHAM ON THE ABOVE MISSION FOR MANY YEARS.

ALSO TWO APPENDICES,

CONTAINING ONE OF MR. GRAHAM'S SERMONS, AND ALSO ONE OF MR. OUSELEY'S IRISH HYMNS, CAMP MEETINGS, &c.

"And the hand of the Lord was with them, and a great number believed and turned unto the Lord."—ACTS XI. 21.

BY THE REV. WM. GRAHAM CAMPBELL,
Irish General Missionary, and near Relative of Mr. Graham.

THIRD EDITION

TORONTO:
THE WESLEYAN METHODIST CONFERENCE BOOK-ROOM,
KING STREET EAST.
1869.

TORONTO:
PRINTED AT THE WESLEYAN CONFERENCE OFFICE,
KING STREET EAST.

DEDICATION.

This Volume

IS INSCRIBED TO

THE REV. WILLIAM ARTHUR, A.M.,

Principal of the Methodist College, Belfast,

AS A TOKEN OF PERSONAL ESTEEM,

AND ALSO

ON ACCOUNT OF THE DEEP INTEREST WHICH FOR MANY

YEARS HE HAS TAKEN IN THE

IRISH MISSIONS.

PREFACE.

"Lead on, O Lord, and I will follow Thee ;
E'en though my path a rugged one may be,
Still I will onward press,
While Thine Almighty arm my steps uphold
To cherish, keep, and bless."

To the Christian it is always a pleasurable as well as a profitable task to trace the hand Divine in directing and controlling the various evolutions of human affairs, especially in those things connected with the salvation of men and the extension of the Redeemer's kingdom. It was well and wisely observed by Flavell, that "those who diligently watch the Providence of God shall never want for a Providence to watch." The rise and progress of Methodism, and its chosen instruments, furnish a large chapter in the volume of a special Providence. The venerable Wesley occupies a prominent place therein, as well as his remarkable brother, Charles, "the bard of Methodistic song." Nor has it been less so in its wonder-workings, as seen in the preparation and raising up of suitable agencies for the regeneration of Ireland. It has been often said, that "emergencies make the men ;" we would rather say, that

"God makes the men, and providential emergencies call them forth;" or, to use the language of a great poet,

"Divinity shapes our ends."

It was so in patriarchal, in prophetic, and more remarkably so in the early history of Christianity; also in the origin and progress of the Reformation of the sixteenth, and not less so of the eighteenth century, in the marvellous history of Methodism. It is specially the design of the author, to make prominent and emphatic the remarkable dispensation of God's unerring and benevolent Providence in raising up the subject of this memoir, and at such a time! In fact, almost everything about him partakes largely of the sentiment so often and so familiarly expressed, speaking of the Most High,—

"He nothing does or suffers to be done,
But we ourselves would do, could we but see
The end of all events as well as He."

There are *many* good people whose history and memoirs could only at best interest a local or a family circle; there are others whose career partakes so much of marvellous incident, and so much of the rich displays of Divine grace, as to make their history of world-wide importance. In this light, we would consider the history of Mr. Graham to stand. Men have been raised up in all ages, since the rise of Christianity, who seemed to tread in the foot-prints of apostles and martyrs; men who "conferred not with flesh and blood" to impart immortal benefits on their country, and upon mankind in general; perhaps never more so than during the latter part of the past and the beginning of the present century. Men who won for themselves a name in the annals of our churches, which will excite the admiration of generations yet to come. As our work is closely connected with what is technically called "The Irish General Mission," we will be excused for naming three of those worthies who laboured on Irish soil, and in the Irish language, to an extent almost beyond conception, namely, Thomas Walsh, Charles Graham, and Gideon Ouseley—men head and shoulders above their fellow-labourers, and who, like David's "three worthies," endangered their lives again and again, in drawing the water of life from a richer fountain than that of the **well of** Bethlehem; and then, aloud, inviting their perishing countrymen, in the language of Isaiah, "Ho! every one that thirsteth, come ye to the waters; and he that hath no money; come ye, yea, come, buy wine and milk, without money and without price." These men were prepared by the Hand Divine to become leaders in the van of the missionary corps, or what Dr. William Crook calls, in his *American Methodism,* "*Legio Tonans*—the Thundering Legion," willing—

"To spend and to be spent, for them
Who had not yet their Saviour known."

They **were** also called "**Cavalry Preachers;**" but **better** even, for euphony's sake, **they had** been called "**Calvary Preachers;**" for this they were in the highest sense of the word. That was their watchword—the secret, the source, and the centre of their power and success. They sang—

"Vouchsafe us eyes of faith to see
The Man transfixed on Calvary;
To know Thee who Thou art."

Hence success and revivals were the constant rule of their labours; the want of them the exception. "Not, indeed, the mountain torrent," says Dr. Dixon, in his *Life of Miller,*

a*

"but the steady and onward flow of the majestic river, spreading bloom and beauty in its course along the adjacent soil." Such moral triumphs and victories constrain us to predict that when the laurels of Waterloo shall have mouldered into dust, and the deeds of Trafalgar lie deep beneath the sable wave of oblivion, the toils and triumphs, the conflicts and conquests, of those deathless names of missionary fame, shall be had in everlasting remembrance not only in the archives of the Church militant but in those of the Church triumphant as well.

It is, therefore, incumbent on us to rescue and redeem as much as possible of their history, in order to stimulate the zeal, to challenge the faith, and to rouse the energies of the Church of the present, and to transmit the same down to the latest generation. To clear away, if possible, the difficulties which surround their names by ignorance and neglect, as Layard did the mounds which accumulated round the famous sculptures of Nineveh, and then exhibited them to the admiration of the world, in their fairest proportions. In the grave-yard of many an obscure village, moulders the unhonoured remains of numbers of those heralds of the cross—

> "Whose hearts were pregnant with celestial fire;
> Whose hands the rod of empire might have swayed,
> Or waked to ecstasy the living lyre."

During the period in which men live who have been eminent for usefulness, the public is rarely led to examine the slow gradations by which that usefulness becomes matured; it will therefore be our pleasing duty to supply this deficiency, at least in some degree, concerning one of the above evangelistic lights—so small at its commencement, but so clear and steady during a long period of more than half a century—we mean Mr. Graham. Of Mr. Ouseley, also, we will be able to speak largely, and considerably from documents unpublished before. On Thomas Walsh we will not enlarge more than to say, that he was one of the earliest fruits gathered in from the Irish harvest-field, through the instrumentality of one of the very first preachers Mr. Wesley sent to this country. His conversion took place in the street in Limerick, while Robert Swindles preached from Matt. xi. 28, "Come unto me all ye that labour and are heavy laden, and I will give you rest." Thomas was a respectable Roman Catholic young man, who lived at a distance, but came into Limerick that day. He was intended for the priesthood. The Word reached his heart, and from that time he became a "burning and a shining light," and died, as it has been quaintly but truly said, "An aged man, at twenty-eight." A considerable portion of the materials at the command of the writer was left by Mr. Graham himself; other portions by his son, and the remainder,—the result of hard catering among the living and the dead,—by the author, who stands in relationship to the subject of this memoir, as maternal grand-nephew.* It is upwards of thirty years since he was first urged to undertake this task, which he did then attempt, but for want of time on the

---

* The author expresses his obligations for the advantages he derived from the following works :—*The Memorials of Mr. Ouseley*, by (now the late) the Rev. W. Reilly ; Dr. Steven's *History of Methodism in the Eighteenth Century* ; Dr. Smith's *History of Methodism* ; Rev. Wm. Smith's *Consecutive History of Methodism* ; Rev. R. Huston's *Life of Mr. Tackaberry, and Lecture on "Ouseley and Graham,"* and the *Minutes of the Irish Conference*, in 3 vols., published in Dublin.

laborious posts of duty assigned to him, he had to abandon it again and again. And even now, the same cause might justify the postponement for some future season, during which he might have more leisure; but as so much attention has been lately directed to this General Mission agency, both by the persecution which the writer met with during the past year, in the town of Granard, as well as the interest taken in its success, in this country and in America, he considers a further delay would not serve the cause in which Mr. Graham and others so nobly laboured. And although the work has been hastily written, and mostly so when others were enjoying the balm of "Nature's sweet restorer," yet he ventures to send it forth, and will feel more than repaid if but the heart of some drooping missionary is cheered in his hallowed toil; and if it shall, in the slightest degree, contribute to promote the interests and perpetuate the agency of "The Irish General Mission."

These circumstances will, it is hoped, apologise for any errors,* and now, sincerely praying that the same missionary

---

* The following ingenious and eloquent apology for faults of this kind is given in Peter Martyr's "Common-Places," a book which was published in 1574. The original spelling is preserved:—

"There is no garden so well trimmed but hath some weeds; **no silver so well tried** but hath some drosse; no wine so well fined but hath some leeze; **no honie so well** clarified but **hath some dregs**; finallie, no human **action,** but hath some defect: mervell not then, (good readers,) that this volume, **consisting** of so manie leaves, lines, and letters oftentimes varied, both in **forme** and matter, a fault or two doo escape; were the corrector's care never so great, his diligence never so earnest, his labour never so continual, his eies never so quick, his judgment never so sound, his memorie never so firm; brieflie, all his senses never so active and livelie. Such faults, **therefore,** as are passed, being but few in number, if it please you, in reading favourablie to **amend.**"

flame which burned with such fervour in the breast of this devoted prophet of the Lord, and of his associates in this great enterprise, may be more fully coveted and realized by himself and all his brethren in the ministry, this humble volume is committed to Him without whom nothing is strong, or wise, or holy, or good, but with whose favour the feeblest effort can a "lasting blessing prove." The writer also hopes the sermon in the Appendix, will be acceptable to many, and also the Irish Hymn, with its humble translation, together with the account of American Camp Meetings, and the Rev. R. Wallace's death, &c. The author must here express himself as laid under renewed and lasting obligation to his constant and respected friend, the Rev. W. Arthur, A.M., for his kind permission to dedicate this memoir of Mr. Graham to him. If a higher mark of respect could be offered—it would be gratefully tendered to our honoured countryman. We will now conclude these prefatory remarks with the lines which will be found at the end of Mr. Ouseley's master-work on the Romish controversy, called *Old Christianity* :—

"Go forth my artless book, in Jesus' name
  I cast thee on the waters ;
    Go thy ways,
  And if, as I believe, thy meaning's good,
  The world shall find thee
    After many days."

W. G. C.

BLACKROCK, DUBLIN, *August* 20, 1868.

PREFACE TO THE SECOND AND THIRD EDITIONS.

The writer has to apologize for not having made some prefatory remarks on the *Second* Edition of this work, in which several improvements and corrections were made; but having to leave Europe for America, while that Edition was passing through the press, in Dublin, he could not conveniently notice it. Another Edition is now called for both in Canada and in the States; and at the suggestion of some of his respected friends, he has in this Edition (third) lessened the quantity of poetry and some of the other parts not directly bearing on either the Memoirs or the General Mission. By this means the Author is enabled to introduce a more lengthened account of Mr. Ouseley's early life, labours, and successes, together with many marvellous anecdotes. These will be found in chapters 8 and 23. The Author knew Mr. Ouseley personally, and often travelled and laboured with him. It is also his pleasure to say that Mr. Ouseley was instrumental in some of his earliest convictions, and he hopes that a fuller length portrait of that great man will yet bless the Church of God and the world. It is not for the Author to say how far this has been attempted in this volume—especially in this Edition.

In fact it is impossible to write the life of either Graham or Ouseley apart; they can never be separated, and never will, in time or eternity, for they were lovely and loveable in life and in death. One is almost led to ask, "Shall we e'er behold their like again?"

The Author now returns his grateful acknowledgments to the following names for their truly kind, timely, and flattering opinions of the work—in fact, some of them too much so, at least for publication :—The Rev. the President of the British Conference, for 1868-69, the Rev. R. Hall; also the ex-President, the Rev. Mr. Bedford; the Rev. Charles Prest, and the Rev. W. M. Punshon;* the Rev. Dr. Scott, Belfast; the Rev. Messrs. James Tobias, J. W. McKay, and McMullen; the Editors of the *Irish Evangelist*, *Watchman*, *Recorder*, New York *Christian Advocate*, and the Toronto *Christian Guardian*;† Bishops Morris, Baker, and Scott, of the United States; also Drs. Stevens, Durbin, and Wneydon. There are many both in

---

* The following is just to hand :—

"TORONTO, March 13, 1869.

"MY DEAR MR. CAMPBELL,—I like your book very much. I had read it before it was my own. There is a raciness in the man and in the style which suit each other Graham was an arrow of the Lord, and you have worthily portrayed him.

"With kindest regards,

"I am, my dear sir,

"Yours very truly,

"W. M. PUNSHON.

"Rev. W. G. Campbell."

† "It is bound in good style, printed on good paper, and in beautiful type. As to composition, there is not a dull page or a tedious chapter in the whole book."—REV. DR. JEFFERS.

Canada and in the States who still remember the two great **Irish** Missionaries, Graham and Ouseley, to whom this American Edition will be acceptable. The writer has spared no pains to make this volume as interesting as possible; **and he has great pleasure** in stating that the getting up of the work does great credit to the Methodist Book Room, at Toronto—a Book Room which does credit to the country for the orthodox and evangelizing tendency of its numerous **periodicals and** publications, under the supervision of the Rev. Mr. Rose.

W. G. Campbell.

Toronto, March 17, 1869.

INTRODUCTION.

"Let others boast their ancient line,
In long succession great;
In the proud list let heroes shine,
And monarchs swell the state.
Descended from the King of kings,
Each saint a nobler title sings."

THE term "Apostle," as connected with the title of this book, and applied to Mr. Graham, requires explanation. We use it only in a secondary or conventional sense. It has been frequently so used by churches in all ages, especially in reference to missionaries who first introduced the Gospel into new places; for instance, Swartz was called the Apostle of India; Brainard, the Apostle of the North American Indians; Judson, the Apostle of Burmah, and it has been often so used among ourselves, as in the case of John Crook, who was called "The Apostle of the Isle of Man," &c. The term ἀποστολος literally signifies "a messenger" or envoy—ἀπο, from, and στελλω, to send—"I send a message," on a confidential errand. The word was anciently used to signify a person commissioned by a king to negotiate important affairs, then it was used synonymously with the word "herald." The apostles were first called *disciples*, to denote that men must be *first taught* of God before they are *sent* of God. (See Dr. Clarke on Matt. x. 2, and Rom. i. 1.) It is applied to our Lord (see Heb. iii. 1) in a peculiar and pre-eminent sense, as "The sent of

God ;"—also applied to the twelve apostles in a *special* sense, and in which there can be no successors. It was necessary for them to *see* our Lord, to *witness* His death, resurrection, and ascension; to *write* the Scriptures, and to *work* miracles; hence the modern "*apostolical succession*" boast is, as Archbishop Whately said, "a fable;" but in spirit, in labours, in success, and especially in the conversion of sinners, it may be justifiable; and in this sense it is so used by us. In fact the word *Bishop* might, with equal propriety, be applied to Mr. Graham, for such he was, in the strictest sense of the term. It is used synonymously with the word *Elder*, or *Presbyter*, in Acts xx. 17, 28: they were required "to feed the flock of God," and to *oversee it*—not the ministers.

> " Not all the hands of all mankind,
>   Can constitute one *overseer;*
> But spirited with Jesus' mind,
>   The heavenly messengers appear.
> They follow close, with zeal divine,
>   The *Bishop* great, the *Shepherd* good ;
> And cheerfully their lives resign,
>   To save the purchase of His blood."—*Wesley.*

The writer would now record another name,—that of the Rev. Edward Hazleton, who may well be called "The Apostle of Donegal." He was instrumental in the conversion of the gifted Dr. Elliott, of America, the author of the work entitled *Roman Catholicism*. In the Minutes of 1855, which record Mr. Hazleton's death, it is said,— "Hundreds will be the crown of his rejoicing in the day of the Lord Jesus." His last words were, "The will of the Lord be done." He deserves a lengthened record. The writer would say the same of many more of his beloved fathers, such as the Revs. W. Ferguson, M. Tobias, William

Stewart, George Burrows, and H. Deery, &c. It would fail him to speak of about one hundred more of those standard bearers who passed away to mansions in the skies since he entered the ministry, in 1831. What a glorious "shining front" of God's nobility from the Irish battle field there displays the "unutterable name!" Whatever may have been their pretensions on earth, they have now realized the truth of Tennyson's *(Poet Laureate)* lines:—

> "'Tis only noble to be good;
> Kind hearts are more than coronets,
> And simple faith than Norman blood."

The name *Graham* signifies, in the Danish language (from which it is derived), "The commander of an army," and one might almost venture to say, that it was never more appropriately applied, in the *best* sense of the term, than to the subject of this memoir; for, since the days of the apostles, perhaps no man gathered in, and conducted onward, a greater number of "The Sacramental Host,"—the Wesleys and Whitfield excepted,—than Charles Graham, as the following pages will testify. With them, he also might truly exclaim:—

> "O the fathomless love that has deigned to approve
> And prosper the work of my hands!
> With my pastoral crook I went over the brook,
> And, behold, I am spread into bands!"

The large families of the Grahams now spread over England, Ireland, and Scotland, are all of Danish extraction, and have descended from the renowned *Græeme*, the son of Scioldus, the King of Denmark. It also appears that Fergus II., King of Scotland, was married to the daughter of this Græeme about the year 404. He is said to have accompanied his son-in-law to Scotland, taking with him his whole family, and became a general in the king's army. Charles Graham's ancestor came directly from Scotland at the time of the Revolution, and fought gallantly under King William. He afterwards settled down at Drumahair, about six miles from Sligo; the ruins of the old mansion are said to remain there still. The head of the family, being a Scotch laird, was in the habit of returning yearly to Scotland for his rents, but one of those occasions proved to be his last. It was supposed he was either drowned or murdered. He was never heard of afterwards. He left a widow and four orphan sons to deplore his loss, and that in a strange land. One of those sons was the grandfather of Charles Graham. Alas! how uncertain are the fairest prospects on earth, confirmed by every day's experience. What is our life? It is but a vapour.

"The path of glory leads but to the grave."

The aged lady was truly pious, as will be seen. She reared her children industriously and well, and also her grandson, the father of Charles; but while we may here trace Mr. Graham's family through a long line of ancestral respectability, it will be our more pleasing duty and privilege to trace him to a higher, a richer, a nobler parentage, by which alone he could claim a title to "A never-fading crown." And, after all, what are wordly distinctions and and an earthly name, even royalty itself, especially in the time of worldly reverses, and in the hour of death? But, above all, what will they avail in "that day for which all other days were made?"

"True happiness is not the growth of earth,
The search is useless if you seek it there;
'Tis an exotic of celestial birth,
And only blossoms in celestial air."

CONTENTS.

	Page
INTRODUCTION	vii

CHAPTER I.
Early Life and Conversion—Mr. Wesley's opinion on Dress, &c. 1

CHAPTER II.
Becomes a Local Preacher—Entertains Views on the Limited Atonement—Deliverance—Mr. Wesley's Visits to Sligo, &c. 14

CHAPTER III.
Marriage—Entire Consecration to God—Sanctification 22

CHAPTER IV.
Interview with Dr. Coke—Bartholemew Campbell's Conversion at Lough Derg—Mr. Graham's Appointment to Kerry, &c. 28

CHAPTER V.
Preparation for and Entrance on the Kerry Mission—Its Evangelization 37

CHAPTER VI.
Evangelization of Different Parts of the Co. Cork—St. Patrick a Protestant 48

CHAPTER VII.

Appointments to Enniskillen, Parsonstown, Mountrath and Longford 58

CHAPTER VIII.

Irish General Mission—Conversion of a Convict on the Morning of the day on which he was hung in Longford—Mr. Ouseley's Early Life and Conversion.................................... 70

CHAPTER IX.

General Mission Continued—Marvellous Labours and Successes.. 104

CHAPTER X.

General Mission—Great Conflicts and Conquests—Conversion of Terrence M'Gowan of Maguire's Bridge, &c................... 127

CHAPTER XI.

General Mission—Opinion of Conference, and of Dr. Coke, &c... 144

CHAPTER XII.

General Mission—Extensive Revival—Great Persecution in Kilkenny—Increase on the three years, 10,473, &c 152

CHAPTER XIII.

Graham and Ouseley Separate—Lorenzo Dow—Remarkable Conversions in Clare and Wexford................................ 161

CHAPTER XIV.

Conversion of an Episcopalian Clergyman in Naas—Lord Sidmouth's Bill upset 170

CHAPTER XV.

Dr. Coke's Death—Mr. Noble's Conversion—Various Appointments—Discussion on the Sacrament—Asked to go to India 182

CHAPTER XVI.

Marvellous Deliverance of Rev. James Rutledge—Accused of Rebellion—Conversion of Young Graham in Dublin, &c...... 192

CHAPTER XVII.

Rev. John Feely's Letter—A Roman Catholic Convert—Letters, &c 202

CHAPTER XVIII.

Letter from Mission House, London—Wesley on Sanctification, &c 211

CHAPTER XIX.

Feeley's Character of Ouseley—Ouseley's of Feely—Unity, &c. 221

CHAPTER XX.

Last Appointment to Wexford—Various Letters, &c............... 235

CHAPTER XXI.

Last appointment of Mr. Graham—Illness in Athlone—Mr. Ouseley's letter—Mr. Graham's last letters to his Son, &c. 239

CHAPTER XXII.

Sickness and Triumphant Death—Visit of Rev. John Feely—Conversion of a Roman Catholic—Remarkable Revival in Antrim through the instrumentality of Mr. Feely in 1858... 245

CHAPTER XXIII.

Mr. Graham's Character—Mr. Ouseley's character, and marvellous Anecdotes—Labours and successes—Tablet, &c..... 256

CHAPTER XXIV.

Concluding Chapter—Opinion of Author on the General Mission—Evangelization of Ireland, &c............................ 283

APPENDICES.

APPENDIX A.

Mr. Graham's Sermon, and Ouseley's Irish Hymn, translated by the Author into verse .... 289 *Page*

APPENDIX B.

Camp Meetings—Mrs. Cook's and the Rev. Jas. Shaw's description—Rev. R. Wallace's Death, and Tablet in Centenary Chapel, Dublin 305

THE APOSTLE OF KERRY.

CHAPTER I.

EARLY LIFE AND CONVERSION.

"*God is love.*"—1 JOHN iv. 8.

" Love found me in the wilderness, at cost
 Of painful quests, when I myself had lost;
 Love on its shoulders joyfully did lay
 Me, weary with the greatness of my way,
 Love lit the lamp, and swept the house all round,
 Till the lost money in the end was found;
 'Twas Love whose quick and ever watchful eye
 The wanderer's first step homewards did espy;
 From its own wardrobe Love gave word to bring
 What things I needed—shoes, and robe, and ring."

THE town of Sligo, near to which Mr. Graham was born, and in which, twenty years later, he was "born again," is a good Irish sea-port, in the province of Connaught, and is situated on the north-western coast of the island. It lies in the centre of a vast basin, formed by surrounding mountains. The Atlantic flows into it, and forms a commodious and beautiful harbour for ships of large tonnage. The town is also rich in a variety of ancient ruins, some of which are in a fine state of preservation. The neighbourhood abounds in all the elements of picturesque scenery. It is relieved from the monotony of other parts of Ireland by an agreeable diversity of wood and water, of mountain range and fertile valley, all of which render it what may be truly called *romantic*—including the bold, the beautiful, and the sublime. Lough Gill, close by, can compare in beauty, for its size, with any lake in Ireland, and may be called the "Killarney of Connaught." The town is distinguished in Irish history for having given battle in 1798 to General Humbert, who commanded the French army, and who had to succumb to Marquis Cornwallis, a few days after, in the County Longford. It also suffered much from the civil wars of 1640 and 1641, to which we must refer again. But while these attractions of place and scenery may be interesting to tourists, historians, or antiquaries, they are still more so to the admirers of the footprints of Providence and of grace, inasmuch as they are associated with the names of many of the illustrious dead, who served both the Church of God and their country, and especially as being the birth-place of the subject of our Memoir. They witnessed his early days, his rising manhood, his conversion to God, and particularly his early evangelistic labours, for at least some twenty years of his hallowed career.

Mr. Graham was born on the 20th August, 1750, at a village called Tullinnagrackin, within two English miles of the town of Sligo, on the south or Dublin side, and, to use his own language, "of parents who where punctual, honest, and kind, but as to vital piety, it was neither known nor thought of." They conformed to the service of the Church of England, as they had no place of worship in the locality belonging to that of their forefathers—the Church of Scotland. His father was reared by his own grandmother, the ancestral lady already alluded to, who, like another *Lois*, instructed him well in the theory of divine truth until he became at least a good textuarist. But his knowledge, alas, was all in vain as far as decision for Christ was concerned.

> "Knowledge, alas, 'tis all in vain,
>   And all in vain our fear;
> Our stubborn sins will fight and reign,
>   If love be absent there."

The state of morals in that neighbourhood then, and indeed one might justly say all over the land, was most deplorable. An episcopalian clergyman writes of the period thus—"Every sin might be practised with impunity; the country was degraded, ignorant, and corrupt; and after the celebration of divine worship (on the Sabbath), both in the church and Roman Catholic chapel, away went all, accompanied by priest and parson, either to the chase or to the merry dance-ring, so well described by Goldsmith in his *Deserted Village*—

> 'And still as each repeated pleasure tired,
>   Succeeding sports the mirthful band inspired."'

An aged Wesleyan minister, the Rev. Matthew Lanktree, wrote of this era also in the following mournfully graphic language:—"Blasphemy, Sabbath-breaking, and drunkenness, were awfully predominant; party spirit, pitched battles, sanguinary conflicts, nocturnal devastations, and private murders, were the order of the day. At fairs and markets they fought like furies, until bloodshed and battery marked the conquest. The very amusements displayed equal barbarity. Song-singing, card-playing, and dancing were regarded as among the innocent things; but Sabbath-breaking was awfully prevalent, especially on pattern (patron) days (alluding to days devoted to the patron saint of some well—such as "Saint John's Well," &c., no doubt in reference to Bethesda of old): on those days drinking, riot, and every evil work abounded; but the wakes (that is, *waking the dead*) were the most profane, **ludicrous, and obscene. At one** time a prayer for the repose of the dead; at another time a *keen* (Irish cry for the dead), sometimes rising to **a** wail **by** the mourning women, perhaps half drunk; and then the smoking, drinking, **and** jokes by the aged, while the young were allowed **to** revel in all manner of folly." It was the misfortune of young Graham **to** be surrounded **by all** these associations **in** his youth, for they **were equally prevalent both among** Protestants and Roman Catholics. **The lad was sent to school when** young, **but** remained only long enough **to** read, **to write, and to make** up some accounts. This was the *maximum* of **common-rate** education among the middle-classes in those **days,** and happy **was** the **youth** who attained **even** to this **standard.** He left **school at fourteen,** and became the fond **companion** of his father **on the** farm, and accompanied him **to fairs** and **markets,** "to take the old man safely home." After his return **from** school—which he **was then** too glad to leave, but which **he** greatly regretted **in after-life—we** may describe him in **the** following lines **of** *Willis,* **an** American poet—

> "A noble boy,
> A **brave,** true-hearted, careless **one,**
> **Full** of unchecked, unbounded **joy,**
> **Of** dread of books, and love of **fun,**
> And **with a** clear and ready smile,
> Unshadowed **by a** thought of guile."

This *youth,* now called **by** the over-fondness of both parents **their** "dear Charles," **soon** began to learn the evil habits and corrupt practices of those around him. His father's society was greatly courted, as he was both generous and hospitable himself. The son was thus early inducted into all the convivialities of foolish company, and he soon became a learned disciple in the school of Bacchus, where all the arts of hell are freely taught. Self-will and obstinacy, as well as quarrelling and gambling habits, were all acquired, until the *mastery* was fully obtained; and, although young in years, the sentiment of Wordsworth was truly verified—

"The child is father to the man."

The parents were now unable to restrain the habits of the young Tyro. Their own indulgence tended to strengthen them. Still his father would sometimes reprove him, and frequently repeated portions of those Scriptures which he himself had learned in early life from his good old Scotch grandmother. His "dear Charles" would promise amendment, but as frequently—

"Disappointment smiled at hope's career."

As to family and private devotions they were never named, unless by an occasional repetition of the following doggrel lines after lying down at night:—

> "There are four corners on my bed,
> There are four angels round me spread.
> Matthew, Mark, and Luke, and John,
> Bless the bed that I lie on,
> And if I die before I wake,
> I pray to God my soul to take."

This was the *sum total* of the devotional piety of those days, and many of the Protestants were as superstitious as the Romanists in invoking saints and angels. "Alas! where there is no vision the people perish." And we might ask, were things better in England where the following superstitious notions were entertained in regard to the destiny of children who were born on certain days?

> "Monday's child is fair of face;
> Tuesday's child is full of grace.
> Wednesday's child has toil and woe;
> Thursday's child has far to go.
> Friday's child is loving, giving;
> Saturday's child works hard for a living.
> Sunday's child, the seventh day,
> Is happy, lucky, wise and gay!"

A trying circumstance now occurred which greatly alarmed this young desperado, namely, that of the death of his father. His sickness was protracted, but it appears from what Mr. Graham states afterwards, that the affliction was sanctified, and he had a pleasing hope that "mercy to his rescue flew;" for in recording the event his words are, "I believe he died in the favour of God, and with His praises on his lips." The old man was led by the Spirit of God, through the light of the truth received in early life, to see his lost condition. He earnestly sought and happily found redemption in the blood of the Lamb. Oh, the infinite advantages of a religious training! And how true the saying, "Train up a child in the way he *should* go, and when he is old he will not depart from it!" It was so in this case, although he did depart from it "for many long rebellious years." The solemn event of his death affected young Charles very deeply, at least for a time; but he consoled himself, that as he obtained his father's blessing before he died, all was well, and he resolved to cease from evil; but his promises were "like the morning cloud and early dew," and were as easily and speedily broken as Samson's withes; for scarcely had his father been more than a few days interred, when the historical phrase might be adopted, that "Old Adam was too strong for young Melancthon." Off he plunged again into greater excesses than before. Restraint was out of the question, and he became "desperately wicked." The spirit of Scotch clanship and hero worship came upon him with all the power of a ruling passion. He became a noted pugilist, and his motto was "to conquer or to die." His companionship was entirely in character, and its members might be truly called what he himself afterwards designated the notoriously ungodly, "Sons of Belial." What were called "the Sligo Bucks," a class of the most reckless and vicious characters of the age, were in full swing. Indeed, it seemed to be then the rage of the day for each town to turn out "bands" vieing with each other in deeper crimson; but those in Sligo and "the Mallow Rakes" excelled. Nor was young Graham and his companions a whit behind. He drank in iniquity as water, and, to use his own expression, "I might truly be called *legion*, for no chains could bind me." Reminding one of John Newton's description of himself—

> "Legion was my name by nature,
> Satan raged within my breast;
> Ne'er was sinner ever greater,
> Ne'er was mortal more oppressed."

Yet the Spirit of God did not cease to strive with him, for sometimes the alarming portions of Scripture which his father taught him would now and again flash across his wayward mind; but like unwelcome and forbidden intruders, they were resisted again. Yet, unwearied, Love Divine pursued him, as the following circumstance will fully prove,—an event which considerably contributed in putting a drag on the wheel of his corrupt nature, if not the actual *turning*-point in his history. A respectable Protestant woman had died in the neighbourhood, whose brother was a local preacher in the town of Sligo. It appears he was formerly one of Graham's companions in folly and in crime. Graham attended the wake with a number of his associates, and, according to wonted custom, they began, at a certain time of the evening, to indulge themselves in foolish sports. The local preacher interposed and mildly rebuked them. They insisted on their accustomed rights, but he was firm to his purpose. They bitterly retorted, and said—" Perhaps we will get to heaven as soon as yourself." "That may be," said he; "but unless you *live* the life of the righteous, your hope of heaven will be as vain as that of Balaam, who said,— 'Let me die the death of the righteous, and let my last end be like unto his;' but, alas! how did he *live?*" This was a nail fastened in a sure place. Young Graham went home chafed in his mind, but resolved to search the Bible all through, until he found out what was recorded of Balaam. The result was, he found that Balaam "loved the wages of unrighteousness," and was afterwards found dead among the slain in battle. (Numbers xxxi. 8.) "From this moment," says he, "the scales began to fall from my eyes." But he was not thoroughly awakened yet to a deep sense of his guilt and danger, although he began " to feel after God." The husband of the deceased woman just referred to became anxious about the salvation of young Graham. On the following Sabbath he called and prayed in his mother's house, after which Graham asked him from what book did he learn that fine prayer? The friend responded, and said that he had not learned it from any book, and that prayer was the gift of God. This greatly stunned young Graham, for he never heard an extemporaneous prayer before. This friend had himself lately joined the Methodists, and was truly converted. He then invited young Graham to accompany him to hear a Methodist preacher in Sligo. He did so, but it was a leader who conducted the service; most likely Andrew Mabin, of whom we will have to speak hereafter. The first impression on this new hearer's mind was that of *wonder* at the plain dress of the congregation, so different from any he had ever witnessed; the Methodists of those days—especially the female portion of them—carried out St. Peter's injunction,—"Whose adorning let it not be that outward adorning of plaiting the hair, and of wearing of gold, or of putting on of apparel." (1 Peter iii. 3.) On which Mr. Wesley remarks,—"Three things are here forbidden—1st, *plaiting* (or curling) the hair; 2ndly, *wearing* gold (by way of ornament); 3rdly, putting on costly (or gay) apparel. These, therefore," says he, "ought never to be allowed, much less defended by Christians." How far this contrasts with the present race of Methodists and other professing Christians, let conscience and usage declare. Neatness and cleanliness are always to be admired, and there was no person a greater advocate for these virtues than the venerable man named. His motto was, with good old Herbert,—

"Let thy mind's sweetness have its operation
Upon thy person, clothes, and habitation."

And we would merely add, that these three things will generally guide in regard to dress—namely, *age, circumstances,* and *position.* At all events young Graham's mind was deeply impressed with the modest apparel of the first Methodist congregation he had ever witnessed. Small matters of this character may be overruled so as to contribute to great results. It is said of the celebrated William Bramwell, that on one occasion, when travelling in a stage-coach with a strange gentleman, the conversation turned on prayer,

1*

when Bramwell said to his companion, "I believe, Sir, you never pray." The stranger asked him why he said so. "Because," said Mr. B., "I see no sign of it on your knees." The gentleman had the curiosity to look at the knees of Mr. Bramwell's trousers, and saw them threadbare with frequent and long kneeling. It is stated that this simple circumstance led to the gentleman's conversion. The friend already referred to invited Graham again to accompany him on the following Sabbath to Sligo. The Rev. Francis Wrigley preached from Matt. vii. 21,—"Not every one that saith unto me, Lord, Lord, shall enter into the kingdom of heaven, but he that doeth the will of my father which is in heaven." Under this sermon he was completely broken down. The interrogatory mode of application prevailed among the Methodist preachers of those days, and often with marvellous results, as was the case in this instance. "Is there any person here," said the preacher, "guilty of such and such crimes?"—*particularizing* a number of them. Graham's conscience smote him at once, or rather the Holy Spirit applied the word, and it would appear that he cried out *audibly*, "I am the man." The following Scripture was literally fulfilled:—"He was convinced of all, he was judged of all, and the secrets of his heart were made manifest," &c. (1 Cor. xiv. 24, 25.) He went home with the barbed arrow of conviction deeply infixed. He might surely say, in Doddridge's description of Colonel Gardiner,—

> "My conscience felt and owned the guilt,
>   And plunged me in despair;
> I saw my sins His blood had spilt,
>   And helped to nail Him there."

This awful but hopeful struggle began. "The strong man armed kept his palace," but not now "in peace." Still he refused to let the captive go! An alarming dream, in which all his sins stood out before him in dread array, "and which," says he, in his record of this fearful scene, "caused me great horror of mind." He awoke, no doubt, exclaiming, "O wretched man that I am, who shall deliver me from the body of this death?" Truly *wretched*, helpless, and distressed, he ceaselessly groaned—

" The sinner's only plea,
  ' God be merciful to me.'"

He penned the following penitential confession, which may be compared to Ezekiel's roll of lamentation, and mourning, and woe:—"I took my full swing of pleasure, and neither vows nor good purposes could stand before the power of temptation. I regarded neither God, or man, or demon, or kindred, except my mother, who had often cause to weep over me. When I went abroad I seldom returned without a fight, and at different times my wickedness endangered my life." The recollection of all this lay like a millstone on his heart. Thus he continued for a full fortnight, in all the agony of woe. At length the hour of deliverance arrived. He went to Sligo, and heard the sweet sound of Gospel grace again, very likely from the same minister under whom he was awakened. In the middle of the sermon, while the preacher was directing the convinced penitent to the Lamb of God, faith sprung up in his heart, " the Sun of Righteousness arose with healing in his wings," and joy and gladness filled his weary and heavy laden spirit. He writes, "I believe on that occasion I received the justifying grace of God, for I felt my trouble disperse like mist before the rising sun." We may well adopt Cowper's language on the way of salvation by faith:—

> "O how unlike the complex works of man,
> Heaven's easy, artless, unencumbered plan;
> Legible only by the light they give,
> Stand the soul-quickening words, 'Believe and live.'"

This auspicious event took place on the 17th of March, 1770, and in the twentieth year of his age. He returned to his house like the publican "justified," to tell to his overjoyed mother what God had done for his soul. At once the spirit of grace and supplication was poured upon him, and immediately he commenced family prayer, and bid fair for worlds on high. One is constrained to wonder that a career so *reckless* and *prodigal* could be pursued so long with any kind of proper attention to his farm and to his mother's comforts; but-now she forgot all her pain, and toil, and care, and, better still, she very soon became herself the subject of penitential sorrow and heartfelt joy. He writes of her distress thus:—"She watered her couch with her tears, and mingled her drink with her weeping;" but ere long she, too, found "the pearl of great price," and that to the no small joy of "her dear boy." This event took place while he was engaged one morning in family prayer. She never lost the conscious sense of the Divine favour until she finished her happy course. Both mother and son now went on their way rejoicing, and all around shared in their joy.

But, alas! like many young converts, imagining his mountain so strong that he "could never be moved," and ignorant of Satan's devices, soon, by unwatchfulness, he lost the light of God's reconciled countenance, and became the subject of very deep distress. However he fled at once to "the horns of the altar." He wrestled there for three days and nights, scarcely partaking of either food or sleep; and if his agony was poignant before, it was sevenfold more so now. He thought he committed the unpardonable sin against the Holy Ghost, and, like David, he literally "roared by reason of the disquietness of his heart." He might truly say,— "The pains of hell got hold upon me." Like Peter, he "wept bitterly;" but when his strength had well nigh failed, like another wrestling Jacob, God appeared in his distress, and he exclaimed :—

> "O what shall I do my Saviour to praise,
> So faithful and true, so plenteous in grace;
> So strong to deliver, so good to redeem
> The weakest believer that hangs upon him?"

If his peace "flowed as a river" before, it flowed as a torrent now. It was "joy unspeakable, and full of glory." Besides he was doubly watchful and circumspect. From this time, I believe, he never for an hour lost the sweet sense of sins forgiven during his after-life of fifty-four years. The painful ordeal through which he now passed he recorded most faithfully, and he hoped it would be a warning to young beginners to hearken to our Lord's admonition: "Watch and pray, lest ye enter into temptation." If the enemy can succeed in getting the young believer to depend on self, and thus push him off his guard, he will soon tempt him to question the genuineness of his conversion. We would strongly recommend in such cases an immediate application to some experienced Christian friend for prayerful sympathy and counsel. The writer was well nigh casting away his own confidence in the beginning of his Christian course for want of such advice.

> "Happier we each other keep,
> We each other's burden bear;
> Never need our footsteps slip,
> Upheld by mutual prayer."

CHAPTER II.

BECOMES A LOCAL PREACHER—CONFLICT AND VICTORY.

> "He now begins from every weight set free,
> To make full trial of his ministry;
> Breaks forth on every side and runs and flies,
> Like kindling flames that from the stubble rise;
> Ranges through all the city, **lanes, and streets,**
> And seizes every prodigal he meets;
> Where'er the ministerial spirit leads,
> From house to house the heavenly fire he spreads."

"AND when thou art converted (restored), strengthen thy brethren," said our Lord to Peter; so it was now with this young restored disciple of Jesus. Being "strong in the Lord, and in the power of His might," he began to speak boldly and indiscriminately to every one whom he met, about "Christ and Him crucified." He also began to hold prayer meetings here and there. New scenes of usefulness presented themselves to him day by day, and verifies what Charles Wesley said of Whitfield. He very soon became the object of attraction and esteem; but he had not the slightest idea at the time, of a wider circle of labour than his own immediate neighbourhood afforded. His highest ambition seemed to be that of a *local* preacher —a lay order among the Wesleyans—and even this he regarded in a very responsible point of view. The following circumstance gave him both light and encouragement as to the Divine will in this matter, as well as proved the truth of the following Scripture—" Unto the upright there ariseth light in darkness."

One day, while pondering in one of his fields on the responsibility of this office, and how he might best promote the Divine glory, and withal feeling his own utter insufficiency, just then he felt a strange sensation coming over him, and in a moment, as if wrapt up in vision, he thought he saw a person approach him, who threw his mantle over him, and then immediately vanished. At once he thought of Elijah casting his mantle on Elisha. (See 1 Kings xix. 19.) This greatly strengthened him, and confirmed him in a thorough conviction that God would open some door of usefulness before him, which presently presented itself thus: —A local preacher, who was unable to attend his appointment, sent to request Mr. Graham to do so for him. He was rather nonplussed for a moment, as he had not hitherto preached from a regular text; but while beginning to hesitate, and making it a subject of prayer, the following passage came powerfully to his mind,—" Woe is me if I preach not the gospel; for a dispensation of the gospel is committed unto me." This was enough: he saddled his horse, and off he went, assured that God would not send him on this "warfare at his own charge." His own words are, " My heart was filled with holy fire, which was the anointing of the Holy Ghost." Both himself and the people were greatly blessed that night. He became now what might be called, "a local evangelist," but still attending to his agricultural pursuits. Just at this time some heavy trials awaited him. A division took place among the Methodists in Sligo. The greater part united with a Mr. Mabin, a merchant of influence, and the chief man in the society. He separated from Mr. Wesley, and sent for a Calvinistic minister to Scotland, who took possession of the little chapel. The Methodists had to remove to another place. Mr. Mabin sent for Mr. Graham, and held out the hope of his being immediately called to the work of the ministry. Being very unsuspicious, and glowing with a holy passion for the salvation of souls, he yielded to the thought for the time being; obtained the books which bore on the "five points" of Calvinism; read them with avidity; and, for a short time, embraced the doctrine of "a limited atonement." He earnestly prayed for Divine direction, and was soon afterwards led to change his purpose, and remain with the people of his early choice. A severe fever, which periled his life, together with a conversation, or rather a controversy, which he had with the Rev. Mr. Thomas, a Wesleyan preacher, greatly contributed to strengthen his resolution. The subject of discussion was, the convenant which God made with Eli, and the rejection of himself and family, which went to show, that though the convenant *seemed* to be absolute, yet there must have been an implied condition, inasmuch as the convenant was changed. "Show me," said Graham, "a single passage in all God's book where he ever broke his covenant, (for 'it is ordered in all things and sure,') and I will submit." "O yes," said Thomas, "here it is,"—repeating the following passage, which sounded like thunder in his ears (see 1 Sam. ii. 30): "Wherefore the Lord God of Israel saith, I said indeed that thy house, and the house of thy father, should walk before me for ever: but *now* the Lord saith, Be it far from me; for those that honour me I will honour, and they that despise me shall be lightly esteemed." Graham writes, "I was down at a blow"—alluding to one of his pugilistic expressions. He thought to recover, but, said he, " I was completely foiled." From this time he resumed his full sphere of usefulness in the Methodist society. All through this ordeal he retained the life of God in his soul, but he was greatly grieved at the reception Mr. Wesley met with from his old friends in Sligo on his next visit. Mr. Wesley records it thus in his Journal :—"Mr. K—— and family would scarcely look at me, although the last time they would almost pull out their eyes for me, but now—

> 'They wondered at the strange man's face
> As one they ne'er had known.'"

And again, "My old friend, Andrew Mabin, did not own me; however, a few did, and we seem by all this late bustle and confusion to have lost nothing." Among those *few*, was Mr. Graham, who was then labouring away with double energy. His own words are, "I was determined to 'spend and to be spent' in the cause of my Master, and I thought I should have no hindrance, for His word was as fire in my bones." In fact, the burden of souls lay so deeply on his spirit as to swallow up every other desire. His feeling was, " Give me souls or else I die." Richard Baxter writes in his *Reformed Pastor*, " I never knew a minister much owned of God unless he had a desire bordering on unhappiness to see the fruit of his labours." It was truly so with Mr. Graham. " The desire for the conversion of souls," said John Howe, " is nothing else but a spiritualized humanity." " The zeal of the Lord had eaten him up." He was greatly strengthened by Mr. Thomas' experience—the preacher to whom allusion has just been made. He gave the following statement to Mr. Graham :—" I have known God since I was nine years of age, and if I knew a better way than what I have followed among the Methodists I would embrace it."

The deplorable state of the community around, deeply affected Mr. G., especially the Roman Catholic portion of it. Those with whom he could religiously associate were very few and far between, unless those who feared God in Sligo, but the divisions and controversies there, were withering. He warned the Romanists wholesale wherever he met them, "to flee from the wrath to come." This procedure soon brought upon him the ire of the priests, who began to proclaim him from the altars, and told the people to avoid him as a "*demon*," "a false prophet," and a "madman." The old game was up at once. One of these reverend gentlemen, apparently kinder than the rest, "pitied the young man," and resolved to try his hand in recovering this outcast from the sacred fold of Rome. Accordingly he sent for young Graham, but the interview was of a very short duration.

The priest said, "I sent for you, Mr. Graham, because I pity you to be spending your time in striving to pervert my people; and you know that ours is the true Church, and out of the Church of Rome there is no salvation.

"I know no such thing," said Mr. Graham; "for if you can show me one in your whole parish who is not on the way to hell I will join your Church at once."

"On the way to hell?" said the priest.

"Yes," said Mr. Graham.

"Do you mean that my father is on the way to hell? How can you make use of such an expression?"

"I ask you, Sir," said Mr. Graham, "is sin the way to hell?"

The priest said, "Yes."

"Well, then," said Graham, "I don't know one in your whole parish who is not committing sin from day to day." This was quite enough, the inference was awfully conclusive.

The priest pronounced him "incorrigible," and regretted that he had anything to do with such a rough customer! Before they parted, Graham administered the following sharp reproof—"I fear, Sir, God never sent you to preach the Gospel, for if He did you would profit the people." They then parted, and the priest took good care never to send for him again.

They afterwards met at a funeral, and the priest accosted him, with an infidel sneer, by saying, "Your Bible, Sir, might as well be *Roderick Random* as anything else."

"Sir," said Graham, "you appear more like a buffoon than a teacher of religion."

The record does not say whether they ever met again. However, he set his face as flint against this dire system, and verified the Scripture declaration—"The righteous are as bold as a lion." As might be expected, a great revival of religion soon spread like fire around the land, and Graham "waxed stronger and stronger." Many were brought to a saving knowledge of the truth. Most likely this was the first extensive *revival,* as known by that name, with which the Sligo circuit was visited! Still his labours were circumscribed, for he had his farm to mind, and his mother's needs to supply. Like Paul, he wrought "with his own hands," and was "chargeable to no man." He also applied himself to reading, and soon became "a workman that needed not to be ashamed, rightly dividing the word of truth." We might apply those expressive words in a remarkable sense to him.

> "'Stablishes the strong, restores the weak,
> Reclaims the wandering mind, binds the broken heart,
> And trains by every rule
> Of holy discipline to glorious **war**,
> The sacramental host of God's elect."

Nor was he long allowed to pass on unmolested. He had soon "to endure the contradiction of sinners against himself," like his Divine Master! It was commonly reported that the Methodists acted on the *non*-resistant principle, and that they never retaliated! This led to the report being tested in Mr. Graham's case. As he was going one Sabbath morning to meet a class at some distance, a stalwart Romanist, who was likely instigated by altar denunciations, came up to him and struck him on the side of the head, or rather on his cheek. Graham, who was well known formerly to fear the face of no man, but now blending the harmlessness of the dove with the meekness of wisdom, and *literally* acting on the Scripture injunction in Matthew v. 39, as laid down by our blessed Lord, "turned the other side," and said, "Now strike me on this side," which he did. Mr. Graham merely replied, "It will be a mercy if you are able to lift that arm on this day week." On that day week, to the consternation of the whole country, the man was buried. From that time, preachers and class leaders were allowed to pass that way unmolested. But when violence did not succeed, busy slander assumed its venomous sting, and tried its unhallowed game. Going to meet his class on another occasion, he found a large kitchen crook on the road, and took it up to leave it at the next house for the owner, whose "flitting" had passed by some short time before. He was met by a man who immediately raised the report, "Graham stole the crook;" and this passed as a by-word, or a nickname, on the Methodists for years, until it was a little altered into "Ouseley stole the crook." The writer remembers the slander. But "through evil report and through good report" Graham pursued the even tenor of his way, "rejoicing that he was counted worthy to suffer anything for Christ." Dr. Young, in his *Centaur not Fabulous*, says, "Envy has under its banner hatred, calumny, treachery, with the meagreness of famine, the venom of pestilence, and the rage of war." But Dryden's translation of Ovid's description of *Envy* is more terse—

> "She never smiles but when the wretched weep,
> Nor lulls her malice with a moment's sleep;
> Restless in spite, while watchful to destroy,
> She pines and sickens at another's joy;
> Foe to herself, distressing and distrest,
> She bears her own tormentor in her breast."

One would almost imagine that Ovid had a presentiment of the *envy* which was to characterize professing systems of the Christian religion in after-times. We should rather say antichristian, for their motto has been "to bite and devour one another," "an inscription," says Richard Watson, "only worthy to be written on the gates of hell." May it soon give way to one truly worthy of the sacred name and cause of Him after whom we are called—namely, "See how these Christians love one another!"

> "Ye different sects, who all declare,
>   Lo! "Christ is here," lo, "Christ is there;'
>   Your stronger proofs divinely give,
>   And show me where the Christians live."

CHAPTER III.

FILIAL ATTACHMENT—MARRIAGE, AND ENTIRE CONSECRATION TO GOD.

> " Go and toil in any vineyard,
>   Do not fear to do or dare—
> If you want a field of labour,
>   You can find it anywhere."

HAVING now spent some time in the capacity of a local preacher, and with great acceptance, yet having his maternal parent to provide for, who was far advanced

> "In age and feebleness extreme,"

he could not think of taking a wider sphere which would separate them, especially as his father gave her in charge to him. But still he had some inward impression that God might at a future day require him to give himself wholly to the work of the ministry. In the meantime he took counsel, and asked in prayer for Divine direction—for in everything "he made his requests known to God"—relative to changing his condition in life. In this step he resolved to abide by the Scripture standard—" Be not unequally yoked with unbelievers" (2 Cor. vi. 14), well knowing that "a prudent wife is of the Lord." (Prov. xix. 14.) He states, "If God ever heard prayer, He did it in this matter." He directed him to the house of a respectable and pious family, below Sligo, of the name of Phillips, and there he found the wife of his choice in Miss Phillips, of whom he speaks thus: "She is truly a helpmeet for me, and proves a blessing to my soul. Thank God for giving me one as my partner who is an heir of glory." The account he gives of her early conversion is nearly as remarkable as his own. She was aroused from her sinful slumber by an awful dream of the solemn transactions of the final judgment. She earnestly sought, and speedily found redemption in Christ, and became a "burning and shining light." She now entered into all the views of her husband relative to the salvation of souls, and encouraged him forward in his happy toil:—

> "True bliss, if one can reach it, is composed
> Of hearts in union, mutually disclosed,
> When one in spirit, interest, and design,
> Each girds the other to the race divine."

His marriage seems only to have itensified his desire for more publicly and more frequently proclaiming the glorious Gospel—the grace of God. Whenever he was called away to any distance to fill preaching appointments, she well supplied his lack of home duties, as far as directions relative to the farm and business affairs were concerned. Indeed, the love of souls became so much his ruling passion, that he entertained the idea of emigrating, especially as his mother had passed away about this time. He says of her death,—"She died triumphantly happy, and blessing the day she was ever born." Never did greater love exist between mother and son; for while he rejoiced in her complete victory over death, yet he mourned for her "as one mourneth for his mother." We may truly say of her as Charles Wesley wrote on his mother—

> " In sure and certain hope to rise,
> And claim her mansion in the skies;
> A Christian here the flesh laid down,
> The cross exchanging for a crown.
> Meet for the fellowship above,
> She heard the call, ' Arise, my love.'
> ' I come,' her dying looks replied,
> And lamb-like as her Lord she died."

In speaking of his intention to emigrate, his feelings are thus expressed:—" I cared not at this time where my sun went down, so that God would make me the instrument of plucking sinners as brands from the eternal burning." Both husband and wife sent up to their cry to God to be guided aright in this matter. The result was, a richer baptism of the Spirit, and a willingness to wait for clearer light. He knew his being married presented an obstacle to his being called out into the regular work of the Methodist ministry in this country, as there was a strict rule then, as now, in the Conference, on that subject. The Lord, however, answered in another way, in giving him to see the absolute necessity of entire sanctification, or what he generally called "a clean heart." And as there was much written and spoken on this subject at this time, he resolved not to rest short of the blessing, that he might be the better able to recommend it to others. His continual cry, as well as that of his good wife, was, " Create in me a clean heart, O God, and renew a right spirit within me." "Just as I arose one morning," he writes, "the Lord visited me in a most remarkable manner, and forcibly impressed these words of the 103rd Psalm on my mind,—' Bless the Lord, O my soul: and all that is within me, bless his holy name. Bless the Lord, O my soul, and forget not all his benefits: who *forgiveth* all thine iniquities; who *healeth* all thy dis-

diseases.'" He again says :—"In that solemn moment, I found such a change pass on my soul as I had been unacquainted with before—a change which filled me with 'joy unspeakable and very full of glory'—I could from that hour say, that 'I walked all the day long in the light of his countenance :'—

'Not a cloud to arise or darken the skies,
Or hide for a moment the Lord from my eyes.'"

In the last part of the above passage two blessings are included; first, "Who forgiveth all thine iniquities," and, secondly, "*Who healeth all thy diseases*." It was this second blessing he sought and now found : the entire sanctification of his nature. "My cup was full," he writes, "and running over ; and so unspeakable was my joy, that it lifted me above all earthly things. Wherever I came, the people had little rest; for where I slept I was either preaching, praying, or praising God aloud continually." He might surely adopt the following lines of Lorenzo Dow, the American preacher:

"I praised the Lord both night and day,
And went from house to house to pray ;
And if I met one on the way,
I always something found to say,
About this heavenly union."

He was now like a flame of fire, and all the Sligo Circuit seemed to partake of the influence, and vast numbers were led to seek, and happily found, the same heavenly treasure. To this wonderful work, no doubt, Mr. Wesley refers in one of his next visits to Sligo :—"Upon inquiry, I found there had been for some time a real revival of religion here. The congregations have considerably increased, and the Society is nearly doubled."—Vol. iv. page 117. On the same page of this Journal Mr. Wesley writes :—" I now received an intelligent account of the famous massacre at Sligo, a little before the revolution. One Mr. Morris, a Popish gentleman, invited all the chief Protestants to an entertainment, at the close of which, on a signal been given, **the men he had prepared** fell upon the Protestants, and **left not one** of them alive." In another part of his **Journal** he records :—" I have just read a history of the Irish **rebellion of 1641**, during which 200,000 Protestants were butchered in cold blood, and for which God has still a controversy to settle with this country."

Mr. Graham was now made more extensively useful than ever, and he was very anxious to know the full will of God concerning him. It would appear as if he was not sufficiently experienced to enter on the great work of evangelizing the land. His own unfitness—at least in his own estimation—made him tremble. The Lord applied this passage, " I will send by whom I will send." But "*holiness* of heart" was his constant theme. D'Aubigné states that Luther sought this, and found it, but called it under another name, namely, " A second conversion." D'Aubigné also tells us that he sought it himself, and found it, three hundred years after Luther. Baxter, Fletcher, Wesley, William Carvosso, and Thomas Walsh professed to have obtained it as a *distinct* blessing. So did Lady Maxwell, Mrs. Fletcher, and Mrs. Rogers obtain it. Boardman, an American writer, calls it, " The higher life ;" Dr. Peck calls it " The central idea of Christianity ;" another calls it " Christian purity ;" Mr. Wesley calls it " Christian perfection ;" Mrs. Palmer, of America, says, " It is laying the will on the altar ;" Mr. Fletcher calls it " Perfect purity,

—to be obtained by faith in the virtue of the atonement." His language is very strong, but appropriate,—

> "My heartstrings groan with deep complaint,
> My flesh lies panting, Lord, for Thee ;
> And every limb and every joint
> Stretches for perfect purity."

These lines express Mr. Graham's feelings when seeking the above blessing. He never did anything by the half-measure system. What he saw to be right and his duty, he did it with all his heart. Every faculty of his soul was now filled with pure and entire love to God and man. His constant feeling and language in everything was,—

> "Father, thy only will be done."

CHAPTER IV.

PREPARATION FOR THE EVANGELIZATION OF KERRY.

> "Yes! in every doubt and sorrow,
>   Let my heart exultant say,
> I will trust Him with to-morrow,
>   I will trust Him with to-day;
> I will trust for food and raiment,
>   I will trust His gracious care,
> And attend a humble claimant
>   At the bounteous gate of prayer."

In the happy state described in the foregoing chapter, Mr. Graham continued to labour on, "in season and out of season," for many years. At length Doctor Coke visited Sligo, and was on the look-out for agents who understood the Irish language, in order to send the Gospel to the Irish-speaking population. He sent for Mr. Graham, and when the Doctor asked him if he could preach in the Irish language, he said, "I cannot, as I never attempted it, although I can speak it well." The Doctor wondered very much; but Mr. Graham meekly said, "Doctor, do you think that every Christian man who speaks English can preach in English?" The Doctor saw the force of the observation, and was struck with the candour and honesty of the man and of the Christian. Both were disappointed; but the right time was not yet come. On his return home after this interview with the Doctor, he thought he would attempt to write out a sermon in the Irish language, which he did; and after reading it to some of his friends, they encouraged him to preach it, and they would gather Romanists and Protestants to hear it. He consented, and a vast concourse assembled, who were delighted with this, his first effort in their own beloved language. He writes thus in reference to it:—" Truly, God was present, and made it a blessing; it was a softening, melting time. The Romanists declared they never heard anything like it, and encouraged me to come and preach for them again. Accordingly, I appointed the day, and came home much refreshed and encouraged, believing that God had yet something for me to do in this country." He made a third attempt, but the priest took the alarm, and proclaimed that he was "a wolf in sheep's clothing," and forbade any of his flock to go near him. But the Lord opened another door at some distance, where all appeared hopeful for a time, and many heard the Word of life in their own loved tongue. Even here a new persecution arose, for the Episcopalian ministers began, as well as the priests, to oppose this " new sect;" but there was no discharge from this war. Still, " Woe is me if I preach not the gospel" sounded in his ears. All this time the Lord was preparing him for harder conflict in another part of the country. He had a very remarkable dream, the purport of which was that he should go far to the south-west of the kingdom, and there proclaim the message of life; but that he must be full forty years of age before he could go. Like Moses, he was not yet qualified for the arduous enterprise. This must have occurred at least three years before he went to the County Kerry, as he was then in his 37th year. During this interval some strange circumstances transpired. The Rev. John Black was appointed to the Sligo Circuit in the year 1789. Shortly after he arrived, he called on Mr. Graham to say that he invited a good brother of the name of Bartholomew Campbell, or familiarly called Bartley Campbell, to come to the Circuit and assist him; that he was rather a little eccentric, as he was formerly a Roman Catholic, and was converted in Lough Derg, in the County Donegal, and went by the name of "The Lough Derg preacher." Mr. Graham merely said that any eccentricity might not serve the good cause. Mr. Black said he could not draw back. So the matter rested. But in a few days, Mr. Black was no more; he was drowned below Sligo, having gone beyond his depth in bathing. The record (in part) in the Minutes for 1790 is, in answer to the question, "Who has died this year?" ANSWER—"John Black, a young man of excellent spirit, clothed with humility, and high in grace. His talents promised very extensive usefulness. As he was one day bathing in the sea, he got beyond his depth, and was drowned. 'How unsearchable are His judgments, and His ways past finding out!'"

Campbell came to Sligo according to arrangement, but how was he affected when he found Mr. Black dead, whom h was coming to assist! Mr. Graham took the stranger by the hand, and brought him through the Circuit. Very soon the report spread abroad that "he was converted in 'Lough Derg,'" which attracted multitudes to hear him from all quarters, and especially Romanists. This was the very thing to serve Graham, who was just prepared to preach to them in the Irish language, little imagining that he was thereby preparing for his arduous work in the County Kerry, to which he was appointed at the following

Conference. These two evangelists, who might well be styled "Boanerges," or "Sons of Thunder," laboured away as flames of fire for nearly a year, and the Lord wrought mightily with them by moral signs and wonders following. Great numbers of Romanists and Protestants were truly converted to God. Invitations reached them from all parts of the country, and from neighbouring Circuits. They complied with a very pressing one from the Rev. Thos. Barber, of the Longford Circuit, where they laboured with very great success. After some time Campbell returned to his own neighbourhood, in the County Tyrone, having filled the mission for which Providence sent him.

Before we give a further account of Bartley's conversion, we will first introduce a description of the lake and the island, including the origin of its superstitious attraction.

The celebrated Lough Derg is about two miles long, and, from its irregularity, about fifteen miles in circumference. It is situated in the County of Donegal. From the town of Donegal it is five miles distant, and about three from Pettigo. A more solitary place for devotional purposes could not possibly be selected, being in the centre of a wild and mountainous tract of country, on whose surrounding hills not a trace of vegetation is to be seen; adding to its gloomy solemnity. It is well adapted for religious contemplation. The mind is excited to an obliviousness of worldly cares, feeling, as Selkirk describes Juan Fernandez, "out of humanity's reach." In the lake are several islands; the one resorted to by "the pilgrims" is about half a mile from the shore, and called "St. Patrick's Purgatory." It is only 126 yards long and 42 broad. The cave is seventeen yards long and two yards wide, and so low that a tall man could not stand erect in it. The floor is the natural rock, and scarcely any light enters the place. This is one of the places for devotion. There are two chapels, a good house for the clergy, and a few cabins have been erected.. These nearly occupy the whole extent of the surface of the island. The "stations" commence on the first of June, and end the 15th of August, during which time multitudes of "pilgrims" of both sexes are seen flocking to it from all quarters to do penance. From ten to twelve thousand annually resort to it, each person paying sixpence for being ferried into the island, which is done by a man who keeps boats for the purpose, and to whom the ferry is let at £260 per annum. When pilgrims arrive in the vicinity of the holy lake, they take off their hats and shoes, and go bareheaded and barefooted, always carrying beads, a staff, or a cross in their hands. The time generally taken to perform "a station" is three days, unless in cases of extraordinary turpitude, when it requires six or nine. They commence by asking the Prior's blessing at St. Patrick's altar, say one Paternoster ("Our Father," or the Lord's Prayer); one Ave Maria ("Hail Mary);" and one Creed. Rising up, they kiss the stone of the altar, and then proceed into the chapel, where they say three Paternosters, ten Ave Marias, and seven creeds. They then go round one of the chapels seven times, saying ten Ave Marias again, and seven Paternosters every round. Thrice they surround and kiss a large stone cross, fixed in the centre of a bed, saying the same number of prayers as before. This course must be repeated every day. The last twenty-four hours of the "station" must be spent in one of the chapels, called "the prison," during which time no food is allowed the pilgrims but oaten bread and "wine;" but the wine is only the water of the lake made lukewarm, and is said to have the property of real wine. Sleep is denied them, and if any drowsiness appears they get a friendly twitch of a rod from persons appointed for that purpose. In this last place (the prison) they say a decade, that is, ten Paternosters, ten Aves, and ten Creeds. A dip in the water was formerly necessary to complete the purgation, but is dispensed with latterly, because of its injurious effect. There is a burying ground on an island close by, called "The Saints' Island," for those who die when on station, which, through privation and fatigue, frequently happens.

It was to this place poor Bartley resorted to expiate his guilt! He had to come forty Irish miles. The following account of the circumstances attending his conversion is taken from Dr. Stevens' work on Methodism, who, it appears, transcribed it from Reilly's *Life of Ouseley:* "He went through the required ceremonies, and received absolution from the officiating priest, but his conscience was more disquieted than ever. Before he left he once more applied to the priest, to know if there was any comfort for him.

" 'Did I not give you absolution?' said the priest.

" 'You did, father,' said Bartley.

" 'And do you deny the authority of the Church?' said the priest.

" 'By no means,' said poor Bartley; 'but my soul is in misery. What shall I do! Oh, what shall I do!'

" 'Do!' said the priest, 'why, go to bed and sleep.'

" 'Sleep!' exclaimed the bewildered pilgrim, 'no, father; perhaps if I did I might awake in hell.'

"The priest threatened him with the usual pastoral punishment. The awakened penitent hastened to a retired spot, threw himself on the ground, and with tears and groans prayed to God for light; and, like another Luther, who found peace as he was walking on his knees up Pilate's steps at St. Peter's, Bartley soon found peace, so well described by Cowper,—

> " 'I was a stricken deer, that left the herd
> Long since ; with many an arrow, deep infixed,
> My panting side was charged, when I withdrew
> To seek a tranquil death in distant shades.
> There was I found by One who had himself
> Been hurt by the archers. In his side he bore—
> And in his hands and feet—the cruel scars.
> With gentle force soliciting the darts,
> He drew them forth, and healed, and bade me live.'

He now began to exhort the pilgrims to look to Jesus, that they too might obtain the same peace of **mind.** The priest being alarmed, drove him from the place. Bartley returned home **'rejoicing in the God of** his salvation,' **and was ever afterwards known as 'the Lough Derg pilgrim and preacher.'** He became a witness for what he called ' the jewel' of the soul, which he ceased not to proclaim to priest and people wherever he went. He became remarkably useful, and was a great favourite with Dr. Coke. He heralded him from place to place, as an official would a judge of assize, and with amasing influence, obtained crowds to hear the Doctor." Henry **Moore,** in his *Autobiography,* states that he admired Bartley's simple but devout character ; that he had a strong understanding, and great ardency of spirit ; that **he perfectly understood the Irish language, and became a means** of great good to the Roman Catholics, from whom he **separated.** "He walked," says Mr. Moore, "a hundred miles to see me when I was stationed in Dublin. He gave me an account of the work of God in those parts near the place where he lived. I admired **' the grace of** God in him,' and rejoiced for all the good that he had received from the Lord, and for what He had enabled him to do, considering his uncultivated mind; and I was amused with some of his strong expressions. At any meeting where no conversions took place he called it a 'sham fight.'"

Mr. Graham remained on the Longford Circuit, at the earnest request of Mr. Barber, until the Conference,—allowing wife and farm to do for themselves. Mrs. Graham wrote to him thus:—"Dear Charles—Go and labour away for God, and I will abide by the stuff, and share the last penny with you to sustain you in all your expenses." "This," says he, "was as fresh oil to the wheel, and I bounded as a hart." On the Longford Circuit he had full scope for all his talents, preaching daily in English and Irish, with great acceptance and success. Mr. Barber gave him "the right hand of fellowship," and "magnified the grace of God in him;" and in order to bring his case before the Conference, he had the preachers of the district to hear him, and they unanimously recommended him, regarding his case as an extraordinary one. The Conference received him, notwithstanding his being married, and appointed him to the County Kerry. Dr. Coke was President that year (1790), and knowing Mr. Graham well, he rejoiced greatly in the appointment. He was then forty years of age, less by a month, but fully that by the time he reached Kerry, thus literally fulfilling his dream. It appears that the claims of the County Kerry were again and again pressed on the attention of the Conference; but they were postponed from year to year, for want of a suitable agent who understood the Irish language. Mr. Barber wrote to Mr. Graham at Longford about his appointment, on which the latter remarks:—"It made my heart tremble, hearing there was neither Circuit nor Society there. All my faith was exercised, but I opened my mouth to the Lord, and I dare not draw back." He repaired at once to his native place, near Sligo, to prepare for this long and perilous journey, which he did with all speed, reminding one of the conduct of Ezra, whom Mr. Graham and his good wife imitated, for "they sought of the Lord a right way for themselves and their little ones, and he was entreated of us." He entered on this enterprise with great anxiety and timidity, verifying the truth of the following lines :—

> "How willing is the man to go
> Whom God hath never sent;
> How timorous, diffident, and slow,
> God's chosen instrument."

CHAPTER V.

ENTRANCE TO KERRY.

"Soldier, go, but not to claim
   Mouldering spoils of earth-born treasure;
Not to build a vaunting name;
   Not to dwell in tents of pleasure.

"Thou hast sterner work to do;
   Hosts to cut thy passage through;
Close behind thee gulphs are burning,
   Forward; there is no returning."

It may be truly said of Mr. Graham, and of the journey on which he was entering, that, like Abraham, "he went out not knowing whither he went," and "he journeyed *southwards*," as well. In leaving his native place he expresses his feelings thus:—"Trusting in the faithfulness of that God who had already led me through scenes of suffering, I took my leave of my native country with a small hope of ever returning to it again, hearing such reports of Kerry, and that the inhabitants thought very little of a man's life, especially that of a Methodist preacher." He and his wife and two children arrived safely at Limerick, where they were received with all cordiality by the Methodist Society, of whom he speaks in unbounded terms of gratitude. It appears he preached for them, and that they appreciated both himself and his work. Having settled his little family there, he started, on the third day after his arrival in Limerick, for Kerry. He rode on horseback, and had eighteen miles of a bad mountain road to pass over, besides eighteen miles more on the coach road. On the mountains over which he passed, it was said, there were deeds of bloodshed repeatedly committed. He, however, passed over without any interruption, and arrived in Castle Island in the evening, after a ride of some forty English miles, and thus reached within ten miles of Tralee, the county town of Kerry. He was no sooner settled in the humble hotel of the town, intending to stop for the night, than it was noised abroad that a "false prophet" had come to town. Immediately the priest gathered a mob, and came to the inn, and insisted on their putting out the stranger, which, of course, had to be done to please "his reverence" and his brave band of "defenders of the faith," like the saints at Granard in 1867! It was then late in the evening, and the stranger knew not the country. Alas! where were even the common rights of humanity? Or did they ever hear, "I was a stranger, and ye took me in?" Or had they ever heard of the parable of the good Samaritan? Out he had to go; and thus thrust into the street, he wandered off on the road to Tralee. Such are the tender mercies of Rome. No wonder if his worst fears of Kerry would haunt him with the idea of their being fully realized. The only thing which can be said is, that the mob did not molest him. When about half way to Tralee, he called at a farmer's house, and told his tale of disappointment. At once he was invited to come in. He found his host to be a staunch Protestant, who sent out and gathered a congregation for the missionary, for it was upon this condition that he promised to remain.

The congregation soon assembled, and on that night *possession* was taken of Kerry. The word preached was with power. The man of the house was deeply affected, and next morning, when Mr. Graham was leaving for Tralee, Mr. Groves said, "Sir, you are welcome to stay until May-day in the morning, and make this your stopping-place while you are in this country." So he did afterwards. This man became the subject of saving grace. The writer had the pleasure of seeing him fifty-three years after that time, in the year 1843, when he travelled that same Circuit commenced by Mr. Graham. Such Gaiuses should not be forgotten. O, how wise and kind is God, who

"From seeming evil still educeth good!"

Thus cheered, and escaping from what he called "the remnant of a shattered town," he proceeded to Tralee, little knowing what awaited him there. He describes the town as "famous for folly and dissipation," and the country as "a barren land." He strove to get a house for hire in which to preach, but could not succeed. He asked a respectable man, but one whom he calls "a weak brother," to assist him, but all to no purpose. There was no room even in the *inn* for an entertainment on that fashion. So he had no alternative but to deliver his message—which he resolved to do somewhere—in the street. He tells us that he addressed "an unruly group of gapers," who turned out in a short time to sow something stronger than "gape seed,"—that of a volley of "Irish grape shot," or rather Irish bullets, which proved that he was about to receive what 'the hundred evangelical heroes" obtained a few years ago, who visited our native land—that of "a warm reception." I would say of that band, "all honour," even more so than that of

Spartan or Balaclava notoriety. Of the brave "six hundred" we justly and proudly say, in the nervous lines of Tennyson:

> "Honour the brave and bold,
> Long shall the tale be told,
> Yea, when our babes are old,
>   How they rode forward."

But still this was more the result of "stern military necessity," while the other was "voluntary." At the same time, we are free to say, that, perhaps, no body of men ever responded more cheerfully than did that lion-hearted band of British soldiery, when—

> "'Charge!' was the captain's cry;
> Theirs not to reason why,
> Theirs not to make reply,
> Theirs but to do and die,
> Into the valley of death
> Rode the six hundred."

But here was Graham, *alone*, in a strange land, with his motto like that of another Arthanasius, *Contra Mundum*—opposed to the world; or, like the nobler Paul, on Mars' Hill, proclaiming, "And the times of this ignorance God winked at, but now commandeth all men everywhere to repent." The uproar on Mr. Graham's first attempt at street-preaching in Tralee was so great, that he had for that time to desist, as he states,—

> "With holy indignation filled,
> Thus by the prince of hell withstood."

But it was only to try it again—which he resolved to do, to conquer or die—and it is said he did conquer most successfully, under the following circumstances:—Having taken his stand in the same place as before, a plan was immediately adopted by two accomplices to stone the preacher, and if possible to wound him mortally. One of the party was to stand close to the preacher to guide the other in his aim, while the latter took his post behind a dead wall opposite. The signal was given, the stone flew, missed Graham, but struck the stone-thrower's accomplice, and cut him desperately, some say mortally. He acknowledged his crime, and was taken off in his blood to the Infirmary, crying out aloud for mercy; thus literally fulfilling the Scripture, "He made a pit, and digged it, and is fallen into the ditch which he made. His mischief shall return upon his own head, and his violent dealing shall come upon his own pate." (Psalm vii. 15, 16.) From this forward, the servant of the Lord was allowed to preach unmolested. From Tralee he repaired to Milltown, on entering which he enquired of a lad, "Do you know any one in this town who reads the Bible?" "Oh, I do, Sir," responded the boy; "the Clerk of the Church." "Will you show me where he lives?" said Mr. Graham. "I will, Sir," said the guide, and brought him to the man's door. When he came out, Mr. Graham said, "I understand that you read the Bible?" "O, I do, Sir, on the Sabbath at church; but, Lord help me, I make a very bad use of it." "I am a preacher of the Gospel," said Mr. Graham, "and I would like to preach it here." "Will you come in, Sir?" said he. "I will," said Graham, "when I put up my horse at the inn." He did so and returned. That day salvation came to that man's house, and it became the constant resort of the missionary and of those who followed after. This man was addicted to drink, the prevalent sin of that day, and it is to be lamented of this day as well. Still, thank God, many have been redeemed from that "soul-destroying suicide where more than blood is spilt." It appears the town was filled that day with country people, as it was what is called a *holyday*, but which might be better designated an *unholy day*, from the evil practices which abound, and which have been long sanctioned by the "law of usage." Mr. Graham took his stand on a block opposite the market-house—which block lies there still, at least it was there about twenty-five years ago. He delivered his message faithfully both in English and Irish, the latter being well understood. The Word was "quick and powerful." The clerk was converted, and many deeply affected. The news reached Sir William G——, the lord of the soil, who immediately sent a message to the preacher not to preach there again; but Graham was after publishing that he would do so, and he was of sterner stuff than to be intimidated from his purpose by a threat of that kind. Accordingly, he preached, although he expected the bailiff every moment to interrupt him; but he was allowed to finish. He says, "I was willing to go to prison, and even to death, for Christ." The people flocked out from town and country; the power of God descended, and many received the message of salvation at that very service, and a foundation was laid in that town for a cause which lasted for years. It ultimately became the head of a circuit called "The Milltown Circuit." Thence Mr. Graham travelled round the country. Open doors presented themselves in all directions, and immediately Methodist Societies were formed, and several among Sir William G——'s tenantry, even some Roman Catholics, joined the Society. It was now reported all over the land that Mr. Graham was formerly a Roman Catholic priest—we suppose because he spoke so much in Irish. This only increased his popularity; for many came to hear him from mere curiosity. The Romish Bishop of Killarney took the alarm, and charged all his clergy to be aware of him, and to warn their flocks not to hear or go near him; that he was a "walking devil," and "a deceiver of the people." One of the priests who had abused him more fiercely than the rest, fell down stairs the same night in a drunken fit, and broke his neck. This alarmed the whole community, but not the clergy; for another priest met Mr. Graham shortly after, and said, "I will make you leave the country altogether," and raised his cane to strike him, calling him a "rascal," and stating that he would get Colonel Hassett to put him out of the country. Graham said, "I will not leave it for you or Colonel Hassett, for I came to remain, and will do so as long as I please." On this the priest raised his cane to strike him, but some person interposed. Then Mr. Graham said, "It is a bad qualification for any man bearing your profession to be 'a striker;' and, awful to relate, I saw his face no more, for he died shortly after, raving mad." "Vengeance is mine, and I will repay, saith the Lord." Peter Cartwright's physical-force system would not do in this country, however it may have done with the infidel settlers he had to deal with in his early days in America. We had, I understand, in this country a preacher somewhat of the same disposition as Mr. Cartwright. It is said of this Irish brother, that, during the time of the Irish rebellion, he was met by a band of rebels, and while the leader of the band took hold of the preacher's collar to pull him down from his horse, that the preacher took hold of his arm, and put spurs to his fine horse, and never let the rebel captain down until he landed him safe in the camp of the loyalists, a few miles distant. What became of the poor captain, the writer cannot tell—but we may imagine. It is said the Conference, for this heroic deed, forgave the preacher the next fault,—which leaned to virtue's side,—we mean some little physical-force interference, to prevent a greater evil. The record of his death is :—" As a preacher, his talents and usefulness were very considerable. And although it must be admitted that his natural temper was severe, and sometimes trying to his best friends, yet it is but justice to his memory to state that he has not been known to speak to the disadvantage of an absent person." But of another referred to on the same page of the Minutes it is more happily said,—

> "His preaching much, but more his practice wrought
> A living sermon on the truths he taught."

The latter is surely "the more excellent way." Still, is there not an allowable holy indignation against evil, which has been sometimes erroneously attributed to a bad natural temper? How can we account for Nehemiah's conduct on any other principle? (See Neh. xiii. 25, 28.) In another part of the country the priest called out the names of sixteen persons from the altar, for having heard Mr. Graham preach. He insisted that each of these should go by night to a distant graveyard, barefooted and bare-headed, and through bogs instead of the high road, and for each to bring back a human bone, and then appear on the following Sabbath in the congregation in a white sheet, and with his right hand lifted up, holding the bone in it. But all this did not do. "The common people still heard him gladly," for he made the way of salvation very plain, and that in their own loved Irish language. Thus Graham, like another Luther, persevered in his hallowed toil, indifferent to threats or maledictions. The Protestant ministers of the Established Church sometimes opposed him very strongly. It is likely his zeal had put there indifference to the blush. Well might

Cowper warn Episcopal authorities, as he does in the following lines, against ordaining such ministers,—

"From such apostles, O ye mitred heads,
Preserve the church, and lay not careless hands
On skulls that cannot teach and will not learn!"

It appears from the persecutions with which this servant of God had to contend, that neither the *Bonner* nor the *Laudean* school was dead, and it is to be feared their *spirit* is not altogether dead yet. Dr. Clarke remarks, in his commentary on the words "No striker," (1 Tim. iii. 3)—"Not quarrelsome, not ready to strike a person who may displease him, no persecutor of those who may differ from him, or prone

"To prove his doctrine orthodox,
By apostolic blows and knocks."

While opposed and maligned by the clergy, the Lord gave Graham the hearts of the people. Even the higher classes saw his worth, and hailed his visits with delight. But, best of all, He gave him many "souls for his hire." In every direction he had seals to his ministry. The following are specimens:—In the harbour of Dingle lay a man-of-war. The burser, as he was called for purser, was a rigid Roman Catholic, although married to a Protestant lady. This lady came to hear Mr. Graham. The word reached her heart. She penitently and believingly sought, and soon found, the priceless pearl. At once she joined the little Society just then formed in the town, and met by a Mr. James Leggett, also the fruit of Mr. Graham's ministry. But this so exasperated her bigoted husband, that he became her most determined enemy. He tolerated her being an Episcopalian; but to unite herself with the "sect everywhere spoken against," was outrageous. Still she persevered, although he often resorted to violence. He used to watch her coming home from "the conventicle," and rush on her with a bludgeon, inflicting very severe bodily wounds. No doubt, prayer was continually offered up for her by Mr. Graham and the little Society. On one occasion, while thus waiting close by for her to come out, he was attracted by Mr. Graham's melodious but powerful voice. He listened, and "at each sound the pleasing wonder grew," until he was induced at length to enter the house, which caused those present to feel as much surprised, if not alarmed, as if a roaring lion had appeared amongst them. But ere long the lion became a lamb. He was completely subdued. He earnestly sought and speedily found the mercy of God, and went home with his more than overjoyed wife, a pardoned and happy man. Indeed, all partook of the hallowed delight, but there was greater joy "through all the courts of paradise." At once he renounced the Church of Rome, joined the little Society, and for many years ornamented his profession, and then removed to England, where both himself and his good wife spent some years, and ultimately passed triumphant home. They could, after his conversion, well understand Cowper's beautiful lines—

> "Domestic happiness, thou only bliss,
> Of Paradise that has survived the fall !
> Thou art not known where *Pleasure* is adored."

Another remarkable case of conversion greatly cheered him. It was that of one of the most bigoted Roman Catholics in Kerry. His name was Roche. He was also an abandoned drunkard. He heard Graham preach, and "the entrance of the Word gave light." He, too, speedily became the happy participant of

> "The overwhelming power of saving grace."

He came at *first* to "mock, but remained to pray," and his conversion produced a thrill of wonder throughout the community. But, alas! in his case the wife became the tormentor. She remained a bigoted Romanist, and greatly persecuted him. He, however, continued faithful, and "finished his course with joy."

These instances are only specimens of hundreds of cases in that country, which shall be "the crown of his rejoicing in the day of the Lord Jesus;" and thus "mightily grew the word of the Lord." A thorough reformation of morals took place in every direction, and all this in one short year. It was almost literally "a nation born in a day!" Graham received about two hundred members into the Methodist Society, besides many on trial. He was regarded as "an angel of light," and was actually called, even then, "The Apostle of Kerry." How true to the life are the following lines,—

> "Blessed time, when every dwelling
>   Shall our joyful anthem raise;
> Every heart with rapture swelling,
>   Thrilling every tongue with praise;
> Firmament now glowing o'er us,
>   Mountains, rivers, isles, and sea,
> All combine to swell the chorus
>   Ringing in earth's jubilee!"

CHAPTER VI.

EVANGELISM IN CORK.

> "Work, ye ministers of flame,
>   Fill the world with Jesus' name;
>   Bold and fearless, clear and strong,
>   Tell it to the careless throng;
>   Work for Christ and in his might,
>   Turn earth's darkness into light."

AT the Conference of this year, Mr. Graham stands in the Minutes as the third preacher on the Limerick Circuit, in order that the other two, Messrs. David Gordon and Andrew Hamilton, jun., might visit the counties of Kerry and Cork alternately with him; but from the account which he gives, it appears that he had to take up those far off stations altogether himself. Very likely they imagined that he was the right man for the work; he knew the country better than they possibly could. He seemed to feel this a little, especially as his family had still to remain in Limerick during the second year. There was no alternative, and off he started again; and as he had now a large portion of the County Cork committed to his trust, as well as the County Kerry, he was fully convinced that

> "An arm of flesh must fail
>   In such a strife as this;
>   He only can prevail
>   Whose arm immortal is;
>   'Tis Heaven itself the strength must yield,
>   And weapons fit for such a field."

When he commenced his incursions from Kerry into the County Cork, but found few intermediate places. This involved very long journeys, but the Lord permitted, or rather overruled, the following circumstance to obviate this difficulty :—A lady who lived about half way between Killarney and Kanturk paid a visit to a family in Kerry who entertained Mr. Graham, who was there that very day. She told him that herself and husband were very much alarmed from what occurred a few days before she left. It appears that the servant-maid had just laid the cloth on the dining-room table for dinner, and returned for the plates, but when she came up the second time she found the cloth all saturated with blood : she was terrified, and called the family to witness the scene; they were equally alarmed, and concluded that it must be the forerunner of some awful judgment. She asked Mr. Graham's opinion. He said that it might be intended as a warning, and that they should humble themselves before the Lord, and pray that he might either avert or otherwise sanctify any trial which might arise. She said they would do so, and asked Mr. Graham to call at their place, passing and re-passing. This was just what he wanted—a stopping-place to break the long journey. Mr. Graham also said, "Too many in this country are like the children of Israel, who sat down to eat and drink, and rose up to play." Mr. Graham called at the house soon after, and his visit resulted in the conversion of that interesting family. We may surely, with the greatest propriety, adopt the oft-repeated lines as suitable here :—

> "God moves in a mysterious way,
>   His wonders to perform ;
> He plants His footsteps in the sea,
>   And rides upon the storm.

> "Deep in unfathomable mines
> Of never-failing skill
> He treasures up his bright designs,
> And works His sovereign will."

In his visits to the County Cork, his success and openings in spreading Gospel truth were, if anything, more remarkable than even in the County Kerry. The first place visited was *Newmarket*. Here the hotel-keeper received him most cordially, and would make no charge. This gentleman had been a Roman Catholic, but now went no where. He heard Mr. Graham preach, and expressed himself as greatly pleased. There was hope concerning him that he received the truth in the love thereof. This was a good beginning. Mr. Graham next proceeded to *Kanturk*. Here he found " a few well-disposed people," whom he joined into a class after preaching, and believed they would " hold fast whereunto they had attained." Thence to *Mallow*, of which he humorously observes, " From a child I heard of 'the Rakes of Mallow' as proverbial for drunkenness, cock-fighting, and all manner of dissipation." Several discouraged him in going to this place at all, but he answered,—"The deeper sunk, the greater danger, and the greater need of my message." He called at the inn, the proprietors of which were Protestants. When they found out his errand, the husband flung his hat into the fire, saying, " If you convert me, you may convert the devil." Mr. Graham was amazed, and yet had hope of this man before he left the town. The landlady said, " We have a religion of our own here, and as for your 'repentance,' and 'faith,' and 'pardon,' we do not want such things; we have our own clergy." Mr. Graham meekly replied, " Except a man be born again, he cannot see the kingdom of God." But, unlike Nicodemus, she did not even enquire, " How can these things be?" He

obtained a room for hire, and spent two nights among them.
He preached, and also visited from house to house, and succeeded in obtaining a good congregation, and even formed a
Society of twenty-five persons, who manifested a sincere desire " to flee from the wrath to come." Whether it was at
this or a subsequent visit the following remarkable conversion of a gentleman (and afterwards of his whole family)
took place, we will not assert, but we may as well introduce
it here. It was communicated to the writer several years ago
by the late Rev. James Olliffe, who was contemporary with
Mr. Graham for a considerable period of his life. Mr. Olliffe
says:—" In the year 1804 I met in class a gentleman who
was brought to God in Mallow many years before. I was entertained in his house as one of the regular stopping-places for
our ministers. His conversion occurred thus: Mr. Graham
preached in the street of Mallow, and took his stand directly
under the window of a Freemason's lodge. The members
were meeting at the time, inducting one of their order.
They heard the sound of the preacher's voice, always clear
and musical. They approached the window, listened attentively, and became much concerned. When the preacher
had done (and I suppose when they had done also), a messenger was despatched from the body to request his attendance at the room. He accordingly ascended the *ladder*, laid
justice to the *rule* and righteousness to the *plummet*, and
squared off at least one living *stone* for our spiritual building; and by so doing made a *sun-house* for our ministers
for many years, and the whole family became the partakers
also with him of the grace of eternal life." Mr. Graham
regularly visited Mallow during the year, and left 150
members in Society, which led to its becoming the head of a
Circuit immediately after. Of the Society he remarks,

"A more loving people, for a young Society, could hardly be found." How marvellous the change in such a short time! Even the innkeeper, who regarded his own conversion as hopeless as that of the devil, became Mr. Graham's best friend, and invited him to his house; and it is hoped that the good lady also was led to see the way of salvation more fully. The next place visited was Doneraile. This visit caused a great stir in the neighbourhood. The news reached Lord Doneraile immediately, that "a wonderful missionary had come to town." His lordship sent for his steward, and inquired all about this stranger. He told his lordship that he came to reform the town. His lordship replied, "It would be well if it could be done." Graham opened his commission, and not in vain, for before he left he joined in Society seventeen; and besides, there were many others who gave evidence that they did not hear in vain, and a great change was effected in the town; thus verifying the truthfulness of the apostolic song, "Now thanks be unto God, which always causeth us to triumph in Christ, and maketh manifest the savour of His knowledge by us in every place." Lord Mountcashel related the triumphs of truth in a neighbouring town through the instrumentality of a Wesleyan missionary, in a speech delivered in London, at the anniversary of the Wesleyan Missionary Society, in the year 1828. Our readers will judge for themselves.

LORD MOUNTCASHEL'S SPEECH,

At the Anniversary of the Wesleyan Missionary Society, held in London, May 5th, 1828.

"I would mention one anecdote respecting a Wesleyan missionary, for the truth of which I can vouch. He went to one of the villages on a Sunday, and taking his station near the Catholic chapel, he preached in the open air to a large multitude who surrounded him. The Catholic clergyman, feeling much annoyed at this, placed himself not far from the preacher, at the head of a crowd; and when the missionary came to an important point in his discourse, he (the priest) raised his arm as a signal to the people, who set up a loud shout, so as to drown the voice of the speaker. This, however, did not discourage him, but he proceeded to the end of his discourse. A few days afterwards the priest was passing near the place, when raising his arm and pointing to it, he said to a friend, 'That is the spot where that cursed heretic preached to the people.' At the very moment he raised his arm he was seized with paralysis, his arm dropped by his side, his mouth was distorted, he staggered backwards, and was taken to his own house in a state of insensibility, and until this moment he is not perfectly recovered."

Thus in labours more abundant did this veteran of the cross spend the second year of his ministry among those moral wilds and waters of Kerry and of Cork, at the conclusion of which he remarks:—" The Lord turned the barren wilderness into the fruitful field, and opened rivers in high places, and springs in the valleys;" and then asks, in all the confidence of faith and hope—

> "Is anything too hard for thee,
> Almighty Lord of all?"

Before he left he could pass through every part of the country without the slightest annoyance. Rich and poor both loved and respected him, and now bitterly mourned his departure from them; and he, in turn, might truly say of them, "For in Christ Jesus I have begotten you through the Gospel." But the time was come when he must bid this loving and hospitable people a final adieu—at least as their minister and pastor. But he did return in the capacity of a general missionary many years after. He felt very deeply at leaving them; for, whatever he was to others, he was truly an apostle to them. He writes—"I would have a deeper sorrow in leaving Kerry, but that I am fully convinced the Lord enabled me to do the work for which He sent me to this country, and of which I had so clear a revelation before I entered on it at all, even by remarkable dreams and visions." It would appear as if he had the whole scene laid before him, as Saint Paul had when he was told of a certain place—"I have much people in this city." I know there is a large amount of suspicion with many as to the reality of anything connected with dreams. I will not here enter on what some are pleased to call "the philosophy of dreams," but we have the clearest evidence that the Most High frequently employed such in giving intimation of His will, so that it would be utter folly to question their genuine character in numberless instances, especially in the absence of the clearer visions of revealed truth. In a recent life of the reputed Saint Patrick, which now lies before me, the following occurs:—" When I was about to return to Ireland, where I had been a slave for six years, I heard, in a dream, a voice which told me I was soon to return to my own country (Scotland,) and that a ship would be ready at the sea side. In compliance with this I repaired to the place, found the vessel unmoored and ready to sail. I reached home in safety, and was heartily received; and after four years I returned by a voice I heard in another dream. I saw a large quantity of letters brought to me, one of which I opened, containing these words—'The voice of the Irish.' I opened another, which said—'We entreat thee, holy youth, to come out and walk among us.'" **He** states this dream haunted him day and night for four years, during which he went to Gaul, and studied under Germanus and others, and then came back to Ireland, and it is said brought twenty assistants with him, landing on the coast of Wicklow in the year 432, at the mouth of the river Vartry, from which Dublin is now supplied with wholesome water. He met with much opposition, but ultimately succeeded in spreading Gospel light through the length and breadth of the land, which, no doubt, obtained for it the appellation of "Island of Saints." If Saint Patrick's history and doctrines could have been faithfully preserved from the *legend* which too often shrouds it, we would have had transmitted to us one of the most brilliant examples of missionary life and success which took place since the days of the apostles. He might well be called the Apostle of Ireland. Thus we might say of dreams with a certain writer—

"Many truths
Have been made known in visions and in dreams."

As we have introduced this marvellous man, of whose existence we can have no reasonable doubt, although Ledwich, a well known writer on Irish antiquities, questioned his existence, and Mr. Wesley had his misgivings on the subject also; yet others have written as strongly of the reality of his existence, of the genuine character of his piety, and the purity of his doctrines. We will make no apology for introducing a part of his reputed Creed, and also an extract from what is called his Hymn, when going to Tara to meet Laoghaire, the supreme monarch of Ireland, and of his interview with whom he had strong fears.

SAINT PATRICK'S CREED.

"There is no other God, nor ever was, nor will be after Him, except **God** the Father, without beginning, from whom is all beginning, who upholds all things; and his Son Jesus Christ, whom, together with the Father, we testify to have always existed, who, before the beginning of the world was spiritually present with the Father, begotten in an unspeakable manner before all beginning, by whom were made all things visible and invisible, who was made man, and having overcome death **was** received into heaven to the Father; who will render to every one according to his deeds; and has poured out abundantly on us the gift of the Holy Spirit, **even the earnest of immortality; who make** those that believe **and obey to be sons of God the** Father, and joint **heirs with Christ;** whom we confess and adore, one God in **the** Trinity of the sacred name."—See late Archdeacon Hamilton, P.P.'s, version of *the Conversion of Saint Patrick*, page 7 (O'Reilly, 139 Capel Street, Dublin.)

SAINT PATRICK'S ARMOUR OR HYMN (IN PART.)

"I bind to myself to-day,
The power of God to guide me,
The might of God to uphold me,
The wisdom of God to teach me,
The eye of God to watch me,
The ear of God to hear me,
The Word of God to give me spirit,
The hand of God to protect me,
The way of God to prevent me,
The shield of God to shelter me,
The host of God to defend me
Against the snares of demons,
Against the temptations of vices,
Against any man who injures me,

Whether far or near,
With few, or with many,
Christ with me to-day,
Christ before me, Christ behind me,
Christ within me, Christ beneath me,
Christ above me, Christ at my right hand,
Christ at my left hand, Christ in the fort,
Christ in the poop, Christ in the chariot seat,
Christ in the heart of every man who thinks of me,
Christ in the mouth of every man who speaks of me,
Christ in the eye of every man that sees me,
Christ in every ear that hears me.

"I bind to myself to-day the strong power of an invocation of the Trinity, the faith of the Trinity in unity, the Creator of the elements—

"Domini est Salus,
Domini est Salus,
Christi est Salus,
Salus tua Domine sit semper nobiscum.

Translation.

Salvation is of the Lord,
Salvation is of the Lord,
Salvation is of Christ
Thy salvation, O Lord, is always with us."*

In all the above, " Christ is all and in all," and not a word about the invocation of saints or angels, or of purgatory; which proves that Saint Patrick was a sound Protestant, in creed and worship, and not a Roman Catholic.

ST. PATRICK'S DEATH.

We now give from the most authentic sources we have an account of the happy death of this great and holy man. This event took place at Saul, his favourite resort in the

---

* See Dr. Todd's *Life of St. Patrick*, pp. 426, 429.

County Down, on the 17th of March, 465, now 1403 years ago, not noticing the difference of style. He laboured for thirty-three years as a general missionary in Ireland, and left behind him as the fruit of those labours, under God, 365 churches, 365 ordained ministers, and 3000 elders. His last words are recorded to be, "Now I commend my soul to God, who is faithful, whose mission I perform, lonely that I am. I pray God that He may grant me perseverance, and that He may vouchsafe to permit me to bear faithful witness to Him even unto death. I pray those who believe in and fear God, whoever may look into or receive this writing, which I, Patrick, a sinner and unlearned, wrote in Ireland, that no one may ever say that I, in my ignorance, am to have the merit of anything I may have done according to the purpose of God—but believe and take it for certain that it was God who did it, and this is my confession before I die."

His motto, and the secret of his power both in life and in death, was, "Christ with me;" and if this be ours all will be equally well for time and eternity.

CHAPTER VII.

MR. GRAHAM'S APPOINTMENT TO THE NORTH.

> "Do not tell me of to-morrow :
> Give me now the man who'll say—
> If the act is truly worthy,
> Let me do that act to-day.
> We can thus command the present,
> If we act and never wait;
> True repentance is the phantom
> Of the past, and comes too late."

Mr. Graham having now given up the Kerry mission, he came to Limerick, where his family resided, and called to see Mr. Gordon, the superintendent, in order to present him with the financial and numerical character of the mission, which was very satisfactory. He waited in Limerick until his appointment was confirmed. Before Mr. Gordon went to the Conference he said to Mr. Graham, "Where do you wish to go next year?" "Where the providence of God casts my lot," said Mr. Graham. If this spirit were more fully acted on by Churches and ministers, we would not have so many *calls* as we hear of now-a-days, and perhaps not so many cases of dissatisfaction. In apostolic times they were *sent*, and in the early days of John Wesley it was so also. "How shall they preach except *they be sent ?*" is an important inquiry ; but if we

> "Leave to His sovereign sway
>   To choose and to command,
> So shall we wondering own His way,
>   How wise, how strong His hand."

"He would then choose our inheritance for us," and if so, all would be mutually well for both minister and people. Mr. Graham received his appointment for the Enniskillen Circuit. He left work enough in Kerry and Cork to justify the Conference in appointing four preachers to travel the Limerick Circuit.

Of his own appointment thus he remarks:—"I received a letter from the Conference to say that I was appointed for the Enniskillen Circuit, with the Rev. Matthew Stuart as my colleague, and from the acquaintance I have of him, I rejoice at my lot." Mr. Stuart was a man greatly owned of God wherever he travelled, and possessed a kindred spirit with Mr. Graham in love for the salvation of souls and the revival of God's work. He finished his course very happy in God, in 1827. On leaving Limerick for Enniskillen, Mr. Graham remarks, "I shall never forget this precious people who 'bore the burden and the heat of the day:' they took care of my little family for the two years I was in Kerry." He was now much drawn out in prayer for his new Circuit, and when he arrived he found what he calls "a praying people, and many of them experienced Christians." It was mutually impressed on the minds of both these brethren, Stuart and Graham, unknown to each other, that God would grant them a glorious revival-year, and "according to their faith it was done unto them." Indeed, both of them would be miserable without conversions, and those with which they were favoured were always regarded as truly genuine. Mr. Graham attracted great crowds by his preaching, especially when he preached in the Irish language, as many in the County Fermanagh understood it at that time. There was a great movement among the Roman Catholics, as they understood the Irish well, and several left the Church of Rome. "The word was quick and powerful, and sharper than a two-edged sword." The priests took the alarm, and strove to prevent as many as they could from listening to words, "whereby they might be saved." Mr. Graham merely calls them "an unhappy class of men." The greatest enemies of truth were convinced and converted; and so subdued were former opposers that they dare not now move a tongue against the word which was being so divinely acknowledged. It would appear as if the whole land would "stretch out its hand unto God."

Thus these heralds of mercy spent their happy year, "the Lord working with them by signs following; so mightly grew the word of the Lord." They returned nearly a hundred of an increase.

At the Conference of 1793, Mr Graham was appointed to the charge of the Enniskillen Circuit, with Messrs. Michael Murphy and James Bell as his colleagues. Of Mr. Murphy we may remark, that he was converted to God in Dublin, through the instrumentality of the Rev. John Fletcher, during a visit he paid to the city. The record of him is: "He was a useful preacher. His manner was warm and affectionate; his piety sincere and uniform; his conversation was animated and devout; he loved the means of grace; and he joyfully finished his earthly course in the 80th year of his age." Of Mr. Bell we will require to speak hereafter as a missionary. The enemy of peace endeavoured to disturb the Circuit during the year, but, by the blessing of the Most High, and the forbearance and courage of Mr. Graham, it was soon restored to perfect tranquillity. He writes—" I think I never saw a greater growth in grace, or the work of God more prosperous, than on this Circuit." The increase during the two years was 372. He reviews the whole of his regular ministry thus—" Glory to God, who has in the course of the last four years added many seals to my ministry. It bears me up that I have not 'run in vain,' neither 'laboured in vain.' Although He has brought me through deep waters and fiery trials, I have also during that time witnessed the happy deaths of many who were converted to God by my humble ministry. Having therefore obtained help of the Lord, I continue to this day 'preaching to small and great repentance towards God, and faith towards our Lord Jesus Christ,' urging all to go forward to the attainment of that holiness 'without which, no man can see the Lord.' And being now in the 44th year of my age, it is with gratitude I can look back on the many dangers I have escaped, and the many deliverances wrought out for me, also the many favours which have followed me all the days of my life. The only return I can make is to give myself afresh and 'all that I have and am' to that God who 'loved me, and gave Himself for me,' and 'washed me in His own blood;' and had I a thousand lives, and a thousand worlds, I could count them all too little to be devoted to His service, for He alone is 'worthy to be praised, and to be had in everlasting remembrance' throughout all ages, world without end. Amen." Oh, how refreshing, even at this distant period of seventy-four years, are those hallowed aspirations, the grateful and overflowing emotions of a heart filled with love to God and man. How true to the life is the following description by the immortal Young—

"Thou my all,
My theme, my inspiration and my crown;
My strength in age, my rise in low estate;
My soul's ambition, pleasure, wealth, my world;
My light in darkness, and my life in death;
My boast through time, bliss through eternity;
Eternity, too short to speak Thy praise,
Or fathom Thy profound of love to man."

Mr. Graham's next Circuit, in 1794, was Birr, in the King's County, latterly called Parsonstown, from Parsons, the family name of Lord Ross. This town is now the second town on the Roscrea Circuit. On this Circuit he travelled two years, and we have no record but what is included in the address of the Irish Conference to the British Conference, which bears on the work in general, but no doubt on this Circuit in particular; for we find no less than 335 members of an increase during the two years. It states: "We rejoice and bless God that we have it in our power to inform you that He hath owned our labours during the year that is past, and that He is building up Jerusalem in troublous times. The Great Head of the Church has wonderfully preserved and prospered us." Mr. M'Quigg was his colleague, who was afterwards appointed as one of the general missionaries. There is a singular "N.B.," in connection with their appointment in the year 1794. "Birr—Charles Graham, James M'Quigg. N.B.—These shall be also considered as missionaries for the County Clare; and shall visit it alternately, as often as possible." This was surely sharp exercise, for to any one that knows the distance by which those parts of the country are separated, and the mode of travelling in those days, it will appear that the Word of the Lord was scarce indeed! 1796, 1797.—Mountrath, in the Queen's County, was his next appointment for two years.

The record in the Minutes is as follows:—"The past year has been very favourable to Zion in this land. In many places the Word of the Lord has been glorified. Numbers have been convinced, converted, and added to the Church." During those two years the Rev. Adam Averell stands on the Minutes as connected with the Mountrath Circuit as a supernumerary, perhaps because he had property close by at a place called Tentower, but he laboured most faithfully with Mr. Graham, who was the superintendent. On pages 207, 208, 209, 210, of Mr. Averell's Life, by Messrs. Stewart and Rivington, the following is recorded as having taken place about the spring of 1798:—"But," observes Mr. Averell, "amidst all the confusion occasioned by these dreadful scenes we had seasons of great refreshing. All glory to the Lord for His peculiar care over His servants in these eventful and trying times." He accompanied Mr. Graham to Ballyhuppahaun, and remarks: "We found the country almost deserted, and on arriving at our destination, our friends expected a visit from the rebels that night. We had, notwithstanding, a large congregation in the evening, and Brother Graham preached a deeply-affecting sermon; and afterwards in our prayer-meeting, our God inspired us with confidence that we would be preserved to see the return of another day, and we were not disappointed. At our quarterly meeting (Love Feast), next day, in Mountrath, the Lord made bare His arm, and manifested Himself in great blessing." On the 9th of June, Messrs. Smith, M'Farland, Graham, and Averell, set out for Conference. They reached Monasterevan the first evening, where they had a hallowed season. Next day the two former brethren took coach for Dublin, leaving their horses, no doubt alarmed by reason of the awful reports, while Graham and

Averell proceeded on horseback confiding in God. When they came to Naas, they heard that the two coaches were burned a little outside of that town. All was terror, but after feeding their horses they proceeded. They found one of the coaches burned—that on which the two good brethren had travelled for safety. Their lives were spared, but they lost all they possessed, and then the rebels allowed them to pass on. O, how delightful it is to hold life from God as the boon of the moment!" Shortly after this Mr. Averell was instrumental in the conversion of a gentleman in Athlone, a nephew of the poet Goldsmith, under very remarkable circumstances. A very singular case of the preservation of the life of Dr. Waddy and that of the death of Friar Burne, are recorded on page 225 of the same volume. In 1796, Mr. Averell accompanied Messrs. Joyce and Smith as representatives to the English Conference. On their return by Bristol they sailed for Dublin in a brig called the "Sturdy Beggar."

They had great stress of weather, and had to put into a coast-town called *Ilfracombe*, where they had to remain for a full fortnight. "On the second night after we landed I had a dream," says Mr. Averell, "in which I thought it was said to me, 'You must preach the Gospel here, for therefore have I sent you.'" And, accordingly, they were made very useful to the inhabitants. Several conversions took place. Neither the Episcopalian nor Independent ministers would give them any encouragement, but rather preached against them, although Mr. Averell had his regular letters of ordination as a Church of England clergyman. However, they sent the bellman about, who, unknown to himself, by a humorous mistake, succeeded in obtaining a tremendous crowd. He was told to publish that "*two Wesleyans*" had come to town, and would preach in the evening at a certain place. The bellman proclaimed—" Take notice that two *Welch Lions* have come to town, and will preach" at such an hour and in such a place; mistaking the word Wesleyans for *Welch Lions*. As may be imagined a motley group assembled, but marvellous results followed. How often has *curiosity* been overruled when other methods failed! "Come see a man that told me all that ever I did," led to the conversion of many of the Samaritans. Surely "He maketh a way in the sea and a path in the mighty waters." What was a great trial turned out to be a blessing. At the Conference of 1798, that memorable year of rebellion, Mr. Graham was appointed to the Longford Circuit. In the address of the Irish Conference of this year to the British Conference we read the following, and we may well imagine what was the state of the country :—" Never did we expect to see so awful a day as we now behold. The scenes of carnage and desolation are truly affecting. To attempt a description would be vain indeed. The loss of trade, breach of confidence, fear of assassination, burned towns, country waste, houses for miles without an inhabitant, the air tainted with the corrupted bodies of thousands, form some idea of the melancholy picture. Many of our Societies scattered, and many of our people without a place to lay their heads, constrain us to cry, ' O Lord, shorten the days of our calamity, or no flesh can be saved.'" Messrs. George and Andrew Taylor's escapes from death in Wexford, was most miraculous. The former was a local preacher, and afterwards wrote a history of the rebellion. The latter was a regular minister in our connexion, and laboured most successfully for many years after. This year, July, 1798, he was appointed, together with Mr. James Smith, to labour with Mr. Graham on the Longford Circuit. The Rev. William Reilly, Mr. Ouseley's biographer, speaks of Mr. A. Taylor thus :—" In the early part of Mr. Taylor's ministry he was in perils oft among his own countrymen, and was taken and sent a prisoner, as a heretic, to the garrison of Wexford, where hundreds of Protestants were already sacrificed at the shrine of intolerance. He was brought before the inquisitorial court. When asked, " What are you ?" Taylor said at once, " I am a *Methodist preacher*," not knowing but the next hour would have been his last ; and strange to say, one of the party said, " He is an honest fellow, and must not be injured." Thus, through faith, we may still well say, in this instance at least, that he " escaped if not the edge of the sword," he did the point of the pike.

> " O for a faith that will not shrink,
>   When pressed by every foe ;
> That will not tremble on the brink
>   Of any earthly woe ;
> That will not murmur or complain
>   Beneath the chastening rod ;
> But in the hour of grief or pain
>   Will lean upon its God."

The remainder of this year passed sweetly away in the mutual sympathy and happy toil of these good and martyr-spirited brethren. Thanking God that they were counted worthy to suffer so much as they did for Christ in the dreary winter of '97, and fearful spring of '98, they rejoiced now in their new sphere of labour on the Longford Circuit, comparatively free from those " cruel mockings," and even of death in its bitterest forms, which some of the excellent of the land had to submit to, but which only

> " Dragged them into fame,
> And chased them up to heaven."

About this time Mr. Graham apprenticed his only son and namesake in a respectable establishment in Dublin, and, from the first letter which he wrote to him afterwards, we consider the following extract is worthy of record, as it may serve other young lads. It appears Mr. Graham bought a nice dress-coat for Charles, to be worn on the Sabbath and on special occasions; but, after the father left the city, the young lad thought well of exchanging it for one more suitable to his taste, which the father told him not to do. However, the new coat was stolen from poor Charles, and a letter of lamentation reached the father, to which the following extract is the reply:—

"LONGFORD, *December*, 1798.

"DEAR CHARLES,—I sincerely think the loss of your coat is a kind of judgment for your disobedience and pride. The same cast the angels out of heaven. How few let well enough alone. But I hope you will learn obedience by the things you have suffered. 'A reproof sinks deeper into a wise man's heart than hundreds of stripes into a fool's back.' Tell your master to purchase the coat and send me the bill. You had need to be more watchful and prayerful, and secure an interest in the favour of the Almighty. The weather is very severe here. Mother and I have colds; your sister is well. My rides are long, but it is a mercy I am able to get through. All join in love to you and the family.

"I remain, your affectionate father,
"CHARLES GRAHAM."

The following is an extract from the answer of the British Conference to the Irish Address referred to already. It shows much brotherly kindness in those peculiarly trying times:—

"VERY DEAR BRETHREN,—Though the common means of intelligence have made us acquainted with your truly calamitous condition before we received your very moving address, yet, on its being read in the Conference, the tenderest compassion and most affectionate sympathy were excited in every breast. We *saw*, we *felt* the difference of our situation! You were in the midst of various perils, while we were comparatively resting in safety. We were in 'a land of peace,' while you were exposed to 'the swelling of Jordan.' Surely those words were eminently fulfilled among you—' Persecuted but not forsaken; cast down but not destroyed !' Not only had good angels 'charge concerning you,' but God Himself was with you, and kept you 'as the apple of His eye.' Your conduct, dear brethren, is worthy of the highest degree of approbation. You evidenced your attachment to 'the flock of Christ over which the Holy Ghost had made you overseers,' by continuing to watch over them and share their lot, when hirelings would have manifested themselves to be *such* by fleeing at the approach of the wolf! O brethren, rejoice that the Head of the Church hath thus honoured you to suffer for His name's sake! Go forward and fear nothing. 'As your days so shall your strength be.' And should any of you be called upon to lay down your lives in so righteous a cause, it will be dying like the Prince of life, and the crown of martyrdom will be your eternal reward."

We will conclude this chapter with the lines of Charles Wesley, so suitable to the trials and patience of the Lord's servants at this time in Ireland :—

> "Welcome alike the crown or cross ;
> Trouble I cannot ask, nor peace,
> Nor toil, nor rest, nor gain, nor loss,
> Nor joy, nor grief, nor pain, nor ease,
> Nor life, nor death, but ever groan,
> Father, Thy only will be done."

CHAPTER VIII.

THE IRISH GENERAL MISSION, JULY 1799 TO JULY 1800.

> "Rejoice, ye sons of Erin,
>   Your dawning is begun,
> In hymns of triumph welcome
>   The rising of the sun !
> The happy day is coming,
>   When thou will reach the goal,
> Thy great emancipation
>   Of heart, and mind, and soul."

THE Rev. William Smith, in his *Consecutive History of Irish Methodism*, alludes thus to the establishment of the general mission:—"Dr. Coke having successfully established missions in New Brunswick, Newfonndland, and the West Indies, resolved this year (1799) to adopt a plan by which to introduce the Gospel among the benighted peasantry of Ireland, and that by means of missionaries who understood the *Irish language*." He met with opposition from the Conference in consequence of the expenditure, but the Doctor, undertaking to become responsible, surmounted all the difficulties, and saw the plan crowned with success. The subject was also introduced into the Address to the English Conference, thus :—" Two respectable brethren, of considerable standing, Messrs. M'Quigg and Graham, have entered upon one of the most arduous undertakings that has been attempted since the primitive times—that of teaching the native Irish the way of salvation in their own language. They sacrifice every social comfort, that they may bring lost sinners to 'the Shepherd and Bishop of souls.'" This was the apostolic spirit. Dr. Coke may be truly called "The prince of missionaries, and the undying friend of Ireland." The subject of Ireland's evangelization had long occupied his most anxious solicitude. About fourteen years before this he wanted Mr. Graham to engage in some enterprize of this character, but some difficulty always presented itself. Mr. Graham, as we mentioned before, would not undertake it at the first interview.

Matters had now come to a crisis. The country had undergone a fearful scourge during the winter and spring before. The atrocities were fearful, and vengeance did not slumber. The minds of the people were subdued, and it was only acting the part of the good Samaritan, to pour the balm of Gospel truth into hearts and minds torn with anguish on the one side, and subdued into sullen silence and black despair on the other. Before the Conference closed there was another brother added to the two general missionaries already mentioned, namely, the *immortal Ouseley*, appointed also out of the *ordinary* mode of receiving candidates, being a married man. This note is affixed to his name in the Minutes:—"Gideon Ouseley is not hereby received into the regular travelling connexion, but is to have the allowance of a travelling preacher for himself and his wife while he is employed on this mission." Gideon did not care what restrictions were imposed on him, only let him preach as "a dying man to dying men," and to tell them of "the dire disease and the sovereign cure." He was to take Connaught and Ulster, with Mr. Graham as his senior and superintendent. Hence the phraseology always obtained, while they **travelled for** five or six years together, "Graham and Ouseley," but latterly many of our good brethren have changed the order, and style them "Ouseley and Graham," but from **the** beginning it was not so. Mr. Graham kept regular journals for many years, most of which are in the hands **of the author.** He is not sure that Mr. Ouseley kept **any journal.** Mr. Graham tells us that he had to wait —that is, wait in daily toil—for about a month, in and about Sligo, for Mr. Ouseley, after the Conference, until he regulated his temporal affairs, having filled a literary situation, **where** he had preached *locally* for two years previously **with great** acceptance and success. **The** Rev. Matthew **Lanktree** speaks of him at this time thus :—"It was here (Sligo) I first saw my friend and brother, **Mr.** Gideon Ouseley, **that** eminent Irish missionary. **He was** not then **in our** itinerant ministry, though exceedingly zealous in public and private, **by** ordinary and extraordinary labours, calling sinners to repentance, particularly in the Irish language. A remarkable influence attended his ministry, and I shall scarcely **ever** forget his power with God in prayer." Mr. Ouseley was the descendant of a highly respectable family in the County **of** Galway, and was born in Dunmore, near **Tuam, in the year 1762,** twelve years after Graham. His juvenile character discovered the **workings** of an ardent and generous mind; bold, noble, intrepid,

> "The first in danger as the first **in fame."**

He breathed the love of liberty as freely as he did his native mountains' air. In early life he was the subject of powerful religious emotions, especially in reference to Eternity, but had no one to guide him. He would often **exclaim,** "Lord, help me, what **shall I do?**" O, Eternity

"Eternity for ever future."

At length deliverance came. He visited Tuam, where the Wesleyan minister used to preach. Mr. Ouseley went to hear him. After preaching, the minister invited all serious people to remain for the class. Ouseley said to himself, "I'll wait until I see what they are about; but if I find any juggling, or black art, or Freemason's tricks among them, I'll have nothing to do with them." At this class-meeting the arrows of keen conviction entered deeply into his soul, and he cried, "I will submit." His distress continued until the following Sabbath, when, at home wrestling with God in mighty prayer, in secret, the Son spoke peace to his weary and burdened spirit, and his language no doubt was,—

"Thine eye diffused a quickening ray,
 I woke, the dungeon flamed with light."

He joined the Society at once, and used ever afterwards to call the class-meeting, "A little judgment-day." He began immediately to proclaim, as with a trumpet clang, "the dire disease and the sovereign cure;" or what has been quaintly called the three R.'s—" Ruin by the fall—Redemption by Christ—and Regeneration by the Holy Spirit;" and these constituted the life-long burden of his future ministry For a further account of Mr. Ouseley see the last chapter of this work.

Mr. Graham records his own entrance on the general mission work in the town of Longford, as follows:—"On the day after I returned from the Conference (20th July, 1799,) to Longford, I heard there was a man to be executed. It was on a Saturday. A little before the execution I went to the prison, where I found the priest engaged in saying prayers out of a book for the poor man. There were three prisoners besides in the place. I knelt down and said *Amen* to every good petition, but was silent when he prayed to saints and angels. When he had done I took the opportunity of pointing the dying man to 'the Lamb of God that taketh away the sin of the world.' The priest said, 'You should not have interfered.' I said, 'My dear sir, don't be displeased; every one should be willing to assist the dying.' The man fastened his eyes on me. I directed him again in *Irish*, to Christ, and he showed so much earnestness that I was constrained to kneel down with the poor man again, and pour out my soul in prayer, in the Irish language, for his conversion. The man cried aloud for mercy; I directed him again to Calvary, and he calmed down into peace of mind. The priest was confounded, but could not oppose." Mr. Graham states, "The man went to the drop with a firm step, and I trust he was in Abraham's bosom that very day." This was the first trophy of the general mission labour, and a befitting one it was, as a grand specimen of the power of Divine mercy, and to convince His servant that he was to despair of no case this side of the pit of perdition: and, oh! what a triumph of the abounding grace of God over superstition and sin, was this instance of the possibility of a sinner of the deepest dye finding mercy. It was almost literally

"Snatching the fire-brand from the flame
And quenching it in the Saviour's blood."

It was a marvellous victory of grace. Everything would seem to forbid his going at all to the prison; but, oh! the value of one human soul, and that on the brink of woe! It was "now or never."

> "What is the thing of highest price
> The whole creation round?
> That which was lost in Paradise,
> That which in Christ was found,
> The soul of man. Jehovah's breath,
> That keeps two worlds at strife;
> Hell moves beneath to work its death,
> Heaven stoops to give it life."

Let others speak of deeds of moral valour and of Christian heroism, but this will compare with any we ever heard of,* knowing as we do, the difficulties of dealing (in Ireland especially) with such a case, where the everlasting destiny of the spirit is infallibly bound up with the *last* rites of the Church of Rome; although, strange to say, a person is never anointed who is to be executed, because *not sick*, and when not *given up* by the doctor. This is still more passing strange, when one considers that *anointing* or extreme *unction* is one of the seven sacraments indispensably necessary for salvation in the Church of Rome! A case occurred in Sligo about that time, of a man who fell from the drop, the rope having broken, and he was greatly mangled. The priest then came and anointed him, because he was sick; and yet, alas! he was all safe if he had not fallen! This speaks for itself, but "the unjust knoweth no shame." Encouraged by this prison scene, Mr. Graham took the street next day in Longford after public worship, and preached to a vast multitude. He describes the scene thus:—"On Sabbath, the 21st of July, 1799, I resolved, in the strength of the Lord, to give my mission a full trial on the open street. I had a crowded

---

* The case of the Moravian Missionaries who entered the Lazaretto, or Leprous House, from whence they could never return, in order to preach Christ to the inmates, supplies a noble case.

congregation, a vast multitude. I took for my text, 'For Christ also hath once suffered for sins, the just for the **unjust, that he might bring us to God.**'" (1 Peter iii. 18.) **A more** suitable text he could **not take. He** spoke in Irish and English, as he had a mixed multitude of Romanists and Protestants. The power of God descended, and he observes, "I think I never saw a congregation in a public street more affected—some bathed in tears, others kissing the ground, others smiting their breasts, others keeling on the street. I hope it will be a day never to be forgotten." This was surely a hopeful beginning, as the *first* attempt in *this* department of his general mission labour, for he was a general missionary all through. Yet it was very cheering to him to have these pledges that the hand of the Lord was in this appointment. The Rev. Mr. Reilly observes:—"In the choice of the agents who were, in the first instance, selected for the undertaking, the Conference was evidently under Divine direction. And the *time* chosen for its commencement, while it evinced an ardent zeal and tender sympathy for those who were perishing, showed also 'the wisdom from above.' The land was weary of hostility, and sickened **by** the sight of surrounding desolation. Indeed, the Irish, at all times disposed to attend to the preaching of the Gospel, when not terrified by altar denunciations, were at this time more particularly willing to listen to the invitations of Divine mercy and peace." Mr. Wesley observes—"What a nation is this! Every man, woman, and child (except a few of the great vulgar), not only patiently but gladly suffer the word of exhortation." In fact, the *time*, the *agents*, and the *mode* of their operation, were all in keeping with Divine arrangement. As to the *time*, the land, weary with *projects*, just as it is now in 1868, and fruitless in everything but disappointment and misery! As it regarded the *agents* especially Graham and Ouseley, they seemed to be chiselled by the hand of the Divine Lapidary from rough blocks of granite, *mentally, morally,* and *physically.* As it regards their *mode* of labour, it was as wise as it was benevolent. They were not to be confined; they were to go everywhere, and fill Ireland with their doctrine. They had nothing to do but ceaselessly cry, "Behold, behold the Lamb." Their motto, in substance, may be well expressed in the following lines :—

> "Freely to all ourselves we give,
> Constrained by Jesu's love to live
> The servants of mankind."

With those sentiments, Mr. Graham immediately prepared for and set out on his arduous mission. He first visited Sligo, where he was to meet Mr. Ouseley. This was close to his native place, which he had not seen for nine years. On his way he spoke to the Romanists in Irish. One of these fell on his knees on the open road, and cried aloud for mercy, which led Mr. Graham to record, "that the Scriptures have a powerful effect when spoken in the Irish language;" and exclaims, "Oh, that the Lord may raise up and send forth more labourers into this harvest field!" He entered the town from his native place on the 28th of July (Sabbath), as an ambassador with a commission higher than ever fell to an ermined judge or a crowned head. He felt a little reluctance *at first* to take the street, as it was so close to his former residence; but this feeling was only temporary, and vanished as gossamer before the wind. "I set my face," says he, "as flint, and conquered in the strength of Christ." He took his stand at the corner of two streets, to command both Church and Mass people.

He was soon surrounded with what he calls "a gazing, unthinking multitude." He was interrupted for a few minutes, but order was soon restored, and he finished in peace. Many were well affected towards him, but on the following Sabbath an attempt was made by a rabble mob to annoy him. The presence of some gentlemen kept them in check. He says, "The opposition only roused my soul, and God enabled me, both in English and in Irish, to denounce the judgments of heaven against impenitent sinners." On the 29th, next day, he preached in a country place, where, twenty years before, he laboured as a local preacher, and where he had much fruit. On the 30th he preached in his native village, and had several Roman Catholics to hear him, whom he formerly knew. One woman cried aloud, and blest the day she ever heard a Methodist preacher. Next day he preached in his brother's house close by. He found this brother "striving to seek and serve the Lord." Here he went from house to house, praying everywhere in both languages. August 4th, he took the street again in Sligo, where he was annoyed at the commencement by the shrill noise of a pig, which some son of Belial held by the ear on purpose to annoy the preacher. When this was over, a soldier came forward, and began to bark like a dog. He was soon taken away, and confined to barracks, and allowed neither to bark or bite. Then an oyster-man came up, shouting at the pitch of his voice on behalf of his "shell-wares." Still Graham waited patiently, for he saw that earth and hell were resolved to baffle him; but there he stood,

> "Firm as an iron pillar strong,
> And steadfast as a wall of brass."

At last, when silence was restored, he appeared to be gifted and girted afresh for the conflict against sin, and earth, and hell; and, by one of the most awful and powerful appeals ever brought to bear on head, and heart, and conscience, in the street, he literally thundered as from Mount Sinai on the solemnities of death, judgment, hell, and eternity. He himself says, and he never was accused of inflated statements, "it bore down all before it." They would have listened to him until midnight, "although," says he, "earth and hell were stirred up at first against me." He also remarks that "many by this open air preaching will hear who otherwise would never hear at all." The same observation was made in a letter lately received by the author from one of the first noblemen in the land. It runs thus: "I thank you for your letter and annexed paper, and beg, in token of approval of missionary effort by out-door preaching, to enclose a donation in aid of the movement. The Gospel may thus be brought within the hearing of some who might otherwise never hear it." A dignitary of the Church of England writes within the last few weeks (and in reference to the vindication of this practice at the late trial in Longford, 1868,)—"I would be glad to see the outdoor triumphs of Wesley in England repeated in Ireland, when in every fair and public gathering the Gospel could be preached. Of course, Satan would howl, and his children rage, but the word of the Lord would not return void." It is pleasing to know that the *right* of public open-air preaching has been fully asserted. The parties were convicted who opposed the preacher, by a most outrageous and murderous attack on his person, for merely passing through the town of Granard, because he happened to preach there about two years before.

On the 5th and 6th of August, Mr. Graham went to the sea-side, and preached to the bathers who came there for healthful purposes affecting the body, but who now heard words whereby the soul, which is afflicted with a disease no human means can remedy, might be healed, and that by resorting to the river of the water of life, "without money and without price." He says, "Many Romanists heard the **word**, and wept under a deep concern for salvation." Next day they brought to him a deranged woman, to see if he could cure her. He prayed with and for her! She paid the greatest attention to what he said, and was remarkably quiet and friendly. Mr. Graham only remarks, "I hope the Lord will restore her to her reason." August 11th—This day may be regarded as a memorable one in the history of **the Irish** Mission, as it was the *first* on which both those kindred spirits (Messrs. Graham and Ouseley) united **in** public, and in hallowed and honourable toil! They may be called the giant missionaries, and princes in our Israel! We may apply the word used in reference to Jonathan and David, " they were lovely and pleasant in their lives, and in their death they were not divided" (in affection). "They were swifter than eagles (on ministerial wing); they were stronger than lions" (in strength divine). They repaired on Saturday evening, 10th, to Riverstown—an old Methodist station **ten** miles from Sligo, a place often visited **by** Mr. Graham during the years **of his early** career. He states: "This place is like the garden of the Lord, and well watered by Methodist husbandmen, a holy and a happy people." Mr. Graham preached on Saturday evening, and **met** the class on Sabbath morning, and had what he calls "a melting time." As soon as the Mass people came out, **Mr. Ouseley at once got into** their midst, and commenced to preach in Irish. It appears that the priest heard of their coming, and had his flock well warned. They resolved to give the black caps a *warm reception*, and the priest resolved to head them himself; but, Mr. Graham and some of the Methodists coming up at the moment, rather disconcerted the scheme. The priest then thought to get the people away altogether, but this also failed; and then and there these two worthies continued for about an hour and a half in alternate addresses, while many, from deep conviction of the truth, cried aloud, "*it is the truth.*" "I trust," says Mr. Graham, "they will never forget that day." The two brethren rejoiced greatly "according to the joy in harvest, and as men rejoice when they divide the spoil." Thus cheered, as having triumphed over a well-designed priestly plot, they thanked God and took courage, and laboured away round that country for several days, and with marked success. On one of these days they met a number of Romanists coming from "a pattern," or holy well station. The people stood still, while these singular men—like *Elijah* and *Elisha* in their own way, and no two men ever appeared more like them in that country—addressed the pilgrims on the great subject of salvation by faith alone, and not by the deeds of the law, or human performances, mortifications, or penances. They were moved with compassion toward them, and regarded them as "sheep having no shepherd." "The poor creatures," says Mr. Graham, "fell on their knees, smote their breasts, and with uplifted hands and streaming eyes called on God. We directed them to a crucified and willing Saviour, powerful and present to save. One cried out, 'What must I do?' Others rushed forward, and such a scene of penitential sorrow as took place on the open road! They would almost adore us, and we had hard work to prevent them from kissing our feet. After commending them to the grace of God, we moved closer to the well, and here the scenes of wonder rightly began." The first affected was a hoary-headed sinner, who ran after them to the well. He called on all to listen to the Gospel message; the people gathered round them, and one woman knelt behind until he had done. She cried piteously all the time, and so did the old man. They all listened as for life, and Mr Graham hoped that their salvation began that very day, and that many of them would be saved at the last day. Already they might sing in the language of holy triumph:—

> "Who the victory gave.
> The praise let Him have;
> For the work he had done,
> All honour and glory to Jesus alone."

Sabbath, 18th.—Mr. Graham writes, "Bro. Ouseley and I went to *Manorhamilton.* I preached in the morning, and met the class, which was like the opening of heaven." It was reported that the *wayfaring men* would preach in the street. The priests took the alarm and went to the magistrate, who was also the minister of the parish, and stated that these men had come to town to put them out of their chapels. "If that be so," said the weak magisterial clergyman, "they will put me out of my church; so I will order them to be taken up." Mr. Graham heard of the dodge, and sent two confidential friends to inform him that the statements of the priests were falsehoods. However, neither priest, magistrate, or minister dared to interfere, for "the common people heard them gladly" in the open street. "A good day," says Mr. Graham, "from morning until night." The Irish language was fully used in all that country, especially in the counties of Leitrim and Sligo. It was a powerful weapon in the hands of "these ministers of flame."

It was so with the Hebrew language in St. Paul's time—
"And when they heard that he spake in the *Hebrew* tongue
to them, they kept the more silence." (Acts xxii. 2.) And
still there are multitudes in those parts who would be glad
to hear the word of life in their own loved language. In
Thomas Walsh's time the people frequently rose *en masse*,
and said, after " hearing in their own language the wonderful works of God," " we will follow you all over the world."
It was equally so in the hands of those heaven-appointed
messengers, and the people uttered again and again the
same language to them. The following lines on preaching
in the Irish language are highly appropriate here :—

> " Fail not to scatter wide the holy word
>   In *native seed*, congenial to the soil,
> And fear not for the blessing of the Lord,
>   Who will not render void thy faithful toil ;
> And soon, oh, soon shall Erin's fertile field
> A rich return, a glorious harvest yield."

Never, perhaps, in the same space of time, or by any two
men, was a larger portion of this *native seed* of Divine truth
scattered in any country or in any language than by those
two men, especially by Graham, who had been at least sixteen years proclaiming it before Mr. Ouseley began at all.
On the 21st they attended a funeral, and taking advantage
of the churchyard, they preached to a multitude, who heard
with profound attention. " It was a great day." At the
evening service the power of the Highest overshadowed the
assembly. On the 21st " Mr. Ouseley was assailed," says
Mr. Graham, "by a *spouting* controversialist of some
Romish order—a poor, conceited sinner—but he soon was
foiled and disappointed ; then he strove to prevent the
people from attending, but all in vain. They, poor crea-

tures, flocked to hear us, and entreated us to return to them speedily; they were nearly all Romanists." On the 22nd they went to the country again. Graham preached from Hebrews vi. 12, "That ye be not slothful, but followers of them who through faith and patience inherit the promises." He had great power; but while Mr. Ouseley prayed, the heavens were opened, and "there was a noise and a shaking among the dry bones." It was a remarkable night, and they came home weary *in* body, but not *of* their hallowed work. Now, in incessant labour, day after day, and night after night, Mr. Graham uses **those** words, a truth unknown to worldly minds—

"Labour is rest, and pain is sweet,
If Thou, my God, art here."

On the 23rd they went to a village close to the town, spoke to the Romanists by the way, but they were again attacked by what Graham calls "a blaspheming Rabshekah. He cursed and damned, and offered all manner of insult, and would lay violent hands on us if he dare;" but they bore it in the spirit of David, when assailed by Shimei, saying, "It was the Lord permitted the tongue of slander to be let loose upon us for having so long refrained from *publicly* proclaiming Christ." He told Mr. Ouseley that **if he had** a book, he would swear that there was neither God or devil, heaven **or hell**. Graham exclaims, "O Lord, what is man!" On the 25th, however, they were well rewarded for all this reproach, which, perhaps, prepared them the better to bear it. On this day, Sunday, they took their stand at the old Market-house in Sligo, then situated in Market Street, where our excellent friend, T. **W**., has now a first-rate house of business. Here they spent a full hour and a half in proclaiming to a listening and deeply attentive multitude "the unsearchable riches of Christ." A gentleman who lived opposite was so deeply affected, that he came over and invited them to make his house their home. Many were enabled that day to distinguish the difference between the *form* and the *power* of godliness. Graham writes, under this date, "I was determined to hurl the artillery of heaven against the devil's kingdom. *Persecution*," says he, "never intimidates me, but *fear* sometimes does. Mr. Ouseley took his stand the day before, Saturday, among the fish-women in the open street, on which Mr. Graham remarks—" I came forward to assist him, and was now delivered from that cursed shame which has long pursued me." One would think that he was a perfect stranger to such sensibilities, but he had "like passions with us."

Monday, 26th.—Mr. Graham preached again at the Market-house from Heb. xiii. 9, "For it is a good thing for the heart to be established with grace." Here he says, he found many people tossed about by Calvinism and Antinomianism, but the Lord carried on his work in spite of all opposition from every quarter. With gratitude he exclaims, "Glory to God; wherever I turn in this country I find some of the fruits of my first labours twenty-six years ago!" Ouseley waxed stronger and stronger. His arguments in Irish with Romanists were irresistible. Graham observes here, "I had faith to believe that all the devils in hell, or all the powers on earth, would not be able to keep back the people from hearing us. This faith was tried powerfully in a day or two after. On the Sabbath, Mr. Ouseley stood at the market-place, and I accompanied him." It appears the priests anticipated their coming, and had a great scheme formed to frustrate the preaching of "the black caps," as the two missionaries were called. A vast crowd assembled, and were attentive while Graham spoke from Prov. xv. 29, but when Ouseley began it was the signal for a general shout. The mob tied old kettles to the tails of dogs, and hunted them through the streets, making a frightful noise. Ouseley had to desist, but this only roused Graham, and up he stood, and with stentorian voice shouted, "It is all in vain for the sons of Belial to endeavour by such means to uphold the devil's kingdom, for the Lord Jesus has resolved on its ruin, and down it must come." Silence immediately ensued; and although a few raged, the people listened attentively, and they were allowed to finish in peace, by prayer and the benediction. Surely we may well say after this, that "the righteous are as bold as a lion!" and with the poet we cheerfully and believingly sing—

> "Truth crushed to earth will rise again,
> The eternal years of God are hers;
> While error wounded, writhes in pain,
> And dies amidst her worshippers."

The week following this Sabbath's street-service was marked by signs of good. The chapel could not hold all that came each night to hear. Careless Protestants and backsliding Methodists were all roused. The missionaries attended the funeral of a Roman Catholic next day. Here they had a fine opportunity for preaching in Irish and English. Such a scene as that grave-yard presented

Several began to cry over their dead, and the women knelt at the graves and cried with a bitter lamentation. Ouseley fell on his knees with them, and began to pray in Irish. The people thought some wonderful thing was about to take place, perhaps that the end of the world was coming quickly; others thought it must be some token of good from God. "How long, O Lord!" After this, there was a conspiracy devised by the soldiers and the base Romanists to murder the preachers the next time they appeared in the street to preach. The plan was this: They were to meet on the outskirt of the crowd, and in one body make a desperate rush, and by force bear all before them, tumble the preachers, and tramp them to death. They met accordingly, but Graham observed their movements, and quickly took Ouseley by the hand and quietly walked off. One of the officers was in the secret of the plot, and was to attend and protect them, but he did not appear at all. It was likely to cost him the loss of his commission, and the soldiers were likely to be punished! Thus the two brethren laboured in and around Sligo for about six weeks, "warning every man, and teaching every man publicly, and from house to house," and glorious signs followed in the conversions of members of all churches. The Sligo Circuit return showed an increase of about 200 members after this. Mr. Ouseley was now fully free from all temporal concerns, and those two companions in labour, started off for Collooney, Ballymote, Boyle, and all the towns around. The Romanists flocked to hear them in all directions, and several renounced the Church of Rome altogether; in fact, it was one continued stream of divine influence following in every direction. Wherever they went the Lord worked with them. In Boyle they met with stern resistance. Even the army officers behaved most infamously; for they encouraged the mob to throw rotten eggs and other offensive missiles. Here also they encountered a great controversialist of the Church of Rome, a Scapularian; but when he became impertinent they refused to argue with him. The Romanist then called Graham "the old devil;" and Ouseley "the young devil," and "the son of the old fellow." Here also the Established Church minister opposed them. But these things moved them not. Opposition rather inspired them afresh with greater faith and fervency in prayer, and more signal triumphs and victories awaited them in other places. At this time, they wrote a joint-letter to Dr. Coke, dated **October 10, 1799.** In it they say—

"The enemy's kingdom is falling before us. The Roman Catholics are exceedingly affected in every place. We are preaching in the streets, in the markets, and by the highway. We preached lately in Jamestown, beyond Carrick-on-Shannon, to the largest congregation we ever beheld. They wept in numbers on every hand. Also at Mohill and Longford markets we spoke three times **in the open** air in one day. (I suppose in different parts of the **town.**) The Lord is **with us** of **a** truth.

"CHAS. GRAHAM.
"GIDEON OUSELEY.

"**To the** Rev. Dr. Coke."

As the Doctor took such an interest in this mission, and in everything Irish, perhaps we could not find a better place to introduce the first interview which the Rev. Matthew Lanktree had with him, than here. His record is—"Early this **summer I** commenced my acquaintance with that eminent **man** of God, Dr. Coke. He greatly edified me by his public ministry, and greatly delighted **me** by **his** amiable manners; **he** preached from Psalm **xlviii.** 31, "Ethiopia shall soon stretch forth her **hands unto the Lord.**" Ethiopia he described as representing the whole sable race of Africa. By "stretching out her hands unto **God,**" he understood to mean, her *lamenting* her moral and degraded condition, and *imploring* redress from God's righteous administration; but especially did it mean, her *seeking* with earnestness the blessings of Gospel salvation. He quoted Genesis ix.

25, 26, 27—"Cursed be Canaan; a servant of servants shall he be unto his brethren. And he said, Blessed be the Lord God of Shem; and Canaan shall be his servant. And God shall enlarge Japheth, and he shall dwell in the tents of Shem; and Canaan shall be his servant." "**Cursed be Canaan,**" the fourth son of Ham, this must be a prediction of the future wickedness of his descendants, the Canaanites, whom the curse overtook in the most awful manner. "**A servant of servants,**" this was his destiny for ages, and **was even such in what was called free-born America and the British colonies!** Poor Africa! "Blessed be **the Lord God of** *Shem;* and Canaan shall be his servant." He considered that America was peopled from Asia by the descendants of Shem, to whom the unfortunate blacks, the race of Ham, became slaves, and slavery which Mr. Wesley called "the sum of all villainy." "God shall *enlarge* Japheth," whom he persuaded to emigrate to *Europe* (and had a numerous family in Asia Minor). "And he shall dwell in the *tents of Shem;*" that is, God shall dwell as He did among the Jews, in tents, that is in the tabernacle and temple. And finally Canaan himself shall be His (that is, the Lord's) servant. Thus Japheth means Europe; Shem, Asia and America; and Ham and Canaan, denote Africa. Ingenious enough. The doctor and the noble band of missionaries did more to melt the chains of slavery than either a Clarkson, a Buxton, **or a** Wilberforce.

> "O, 'tis a god-like privilege to save,
> And he that scorns it is himself a slave;
> Inform the mind, one beam of heavenly day
> Would heal the heart, and melt the chains away."

Mr. Graham writes to his son in Dublin, from Tullamore, shortly after **he wrote** to Doctor Coke. In it he says—

"The devil's kingdom is falling before us. We preached yesterday to a crowd of hardened sinners, but they gave us a patient hearing. We are now become *fair* and *market* men. This is the most effectual way which has ever been devised to spread the Gospel. We do more in spreading truth in one fair or market day, than we could in weeks or months in private houses. In some markets the cries and tears of the people are enough to rend the heavens. Whatever I could say on this subject would fall far short of what it is in reality, and will appear more and more."

After this, Graham and Ouseley proceeded to Dublin to meet Dr. Coke, and came round by Balbriggan, Drogheda, Ardee, the Poles, Bailieborough, Kingscourt, Cavan, Killeshandra, Belturbet, and back to Sligo. An extract from another letter to Dr. Coke, just after they arrived in Sligo, will best describe this tour. It is dated Sligo, Nov. 1799:—

"We have come to Sligo (their families being there), and all glory to God, we have had a blessed time of it. The power of the Lord attended us wherever we came, which confirms us more and more that the Lord has called us this glorious work. At Balbriggan the Catholics attended night and day. One woman cried aloud for mercy, and found it. We preached on the street, and had a patient and a profitable hearing. A man cried out, 'Every parish in Ireland would want two such men.' We took the street in Drogheda, and were summoned to appear before the magistrate; but he ordered us to get the *Tholsel*, or Sessions Room (Town Hall), and he came himself, and brought the sheriff with him to hear us, and also a Church of England minister. We had a vast congregation of Catholics, who seemed to be greatly impressed. Both of us spoke at the meeting, and the Lord blessed the word very greatly to many. After the service the magistrate told one of our friends, that we 'might preach whenever and wherever we pleased.' We were men greatly wondered at by the people of Drogheda. In *Ardee* the Catholics wept aloud in the open street, and clapping their hands inquired, 'what they should do to be saved?' The Gospel was indeed 'the power of God to the salvation' of many that day. At *the Poles* near Kingscourt, the heavens were opened unto us. At Kingscourt the Catholics and all were powerfully affected. At Bailieborough we attacked the devil's kingdom at once. The poor Methodists were alarmed, having never seen mission work on that fashion; but they had their eyes opened very soon. One girl said, 'the day of jugdment was coming.' The word of the Lord like thunder awoke many, and one Catholic woman found peace with God. Next night, two more shed tears like the pouring out of water. We came to Cavan sounding the Gospel-trumpet all the way. It was a fair-day. We were as wet as could be, but neither of us dried or refreshed ourselves until we preached in the fair. A lady who saw us through her window wept all the time. The people remained uncovered all through in the rain, and were bathed in tears. They entreated us to preach that night again in the court-house, and they would come and hear, which we did. We also visited the prisoners in the jail. One was in for murder and robbery, a fine-looking young man, and a respectable Protestant. Our hearts clung to him, and both he and several others cried aloud for mercy. The servant-maid, where we lodged at Mr. Smith's, found salvation, and the whole town was moved. At Killeshandra the effects of the street preaching were amazing, and the cry of the vast multitude was raised in the publican's petition, 'God be merciful,' &c. It was a great day for the poor Catholics.

"C. GRAHAM."

From Graham's journal papers we have a continuation of this tour, and of the marvellous scenes which took place from day to day. From Killeshandra they went to Mr. Martin's, within a few miles of the town. Here the whole neighbourhood was moved, and even the preacher on the Circuit was overwhelmed with wonder, having never witnessed such power from on high. At Belturbet they met with a hard attack from the enemy. It appears they stood close to the door of a public-house. The wife of the publican, whom Mr. Graham calls "a Jezebel," fearing their "craft was in danger," went up to her window and cried, "False prophets—it was foretold they should come in the last days." When this did not lead them to desist, she sent for a constable to remove them, but he "feared the people," who were so numerous and so attentive. So the two missionaries had the **opportunity** of denouncing the sins both of drunkenness and of covetousness tremendously, **the latter** of which, they said, caused Judas to sell his Master. The foolish and wicked woman was confounded. How characteristically **does** Cowper describe such a case—

> "Ambition, avarice, and the lust of fame,
> And woman, lovely woman, does the same;
> The heart surrendered to the ruling power
> Of some ungoverned passion every hour!"

Thence they came to a place close by, where they were received as **"angels of** light," and where a Roman Catholic manifested the most astonishing concern about his **soul's** eternal interests, and entreated these men of God to bless him, and said if they did he **would** be blessed. Mr. Graham merely devoutly exclaims, " Blessed **God, open** the **eyes** of these poor creatures, and **let** them know the **truth as** it is in Jesus." From this place they went to Sligo, as we have **seen.** After resting a few days with their families, they **started again for** another tour northwards, to Ballyshannon, Enniskillen, Pettigo, Ballinamallard, &c. But **his own** words to Dr. Coke will explain it better than any language **of ours.** He says,—

"We spent the last month (December, 1799) **in the** North, and met with no opposition, although we preached on the streets. The poor, the rich, the learned, listened with astonishment. We denounced the judgments of heaven against the sins of the day. The Catholics attended from place to place in spite of all entreaty **by their** priests. The fame of the *Irish preaching* had spread through all the country. Numbers of cases of conviction and conversion took place. We were astonished. In Ballintra the place was too small, so we had to go from house to house. The people crying everywhere aloud for mercy. We went to Pettigo, not far from Lough Derg. [*We wonder they did not visit the Pilgrim's Island, where poor Bartley Campbell found the mercy of God.*] Here we took the street. This was a blessed day. The Catholics were greatly struck, and followed us night and morning. We came on to Ballinamallard and Enniskillen, where the power of the Lord attended us in both places, in public and private. The meetings lasted some nights for five and others for six hours, until we were literally worn out. We can give but an imperfect account of the work. Two Catholic girls found peace with God in Sydare; and on last Monday night, several souls were brought to God. As soon as we recover we shall go to the North again. 'O Lord our God, strengthen Thy poor servants for this great work.'

"Yours, &c.,
"CHARLES GRAHAM.
"G. OUSELEY."

Thus ends the first half-year of this wonderful missionary toil and success! For it we glorify God in His servants! The above letters and records are, however, but the merest outline of the papers which fully describe their herculean efforts. The rocks and glens which had reverberated the clangour of arms, and the cannon's roar, now echoed the joyful sound of an evangelical jubilee. The very streets which had been deluged with human blood, were now refreshed with streams from the life-giving fountain of water divine. "If ever," says the Rev. W. Reilly, "Ireland is to be regenerated, there must arise a succession of noble spirits, inspired with the zeal that glowed in the bosoms of Walsh, Graham, and Ouseley, to go forth to the streets and public places, to the fields and highways, to persuade sinners to be 'reconciled to God.'"

The labours of this half-year would supply one of the richest chapters of evangelism which, perhaps, ever blessed the world since the days of the apostles, and yet it only supplies a specimen of what is to follow for the next five years and a half, during which those "Boanerges" laboured together. We must not, however, confine our attention altogether to the labours of Graham and Ouseley, even during this period.

The *South* was visited as well. On the southern district, the Rev. James M'Quigg laboured with great success, which the following extract from his letter to Dr. Coke will fully establish:—

"In the beginning of August, 1799, I made my first trial as a missionary in Bandon. I stood under a tree, and a large number of people came around me. Some admired the Irish, and others were in tears, crying to the Lord for mercy. The next time I had many of the Caithness soldiers to hear me, who did not understand English well, but they were greatly affected when I spoke in the Erse dialect. Good was done. I afterwards went to Innishannon, and preached to a multitude in the street. With many of them I conversed afterwards, and they declared they would come to hear me whenever I came, especially if I preached in Irish. The name of Jesus was precious to them. In Macroom, fifteen miles west of Bandon, I preached to a large congregation in the Court-house. One young soldier wept incessantly, and while listening to the Word, felt it to be 'the power of God' to his salvation. He was a Carmelite. In Cork I preached four times in Irish, twice on Barrack Hill. I had thousands to hear me, who were not only attentive, but bathed in tears. When I was leaving them they cried aloud to God for blessings to rest on me. In Youghal I preached three days on the quay to thousands, who fell on their knees in the wet street, and some followed me through the street for advice, declaring that they had an awful sense of their sinfulness since they heard me preach. I conversed with a learned Catholic in Youghal very pleasingly. He seems anxious for truth. I feel much gratitude to the magistrates and inhabitants of Youghal. In Newtown-barry many of the Roman Catholics came to the preaching-house. Half of the congregation were of that persuasion, and when the Protestants left, they remained to shake hands with me and to bless me. Our friends besought me to come here again.

"JAMES M'QUIGG."

The following short extract is from a letter by Mr. Tydd, of Cloughjordan, to the Rev. Mr. Averell :—

"Mr. Macklin informs me that Messrs. Graham and Ouseley were at his house. The Catholics flock to hear them from place to place. They preach on horseback in the fairs and markets."

This reference is to the first half-year's labours, as it is dated "October 22nd, 1799," and alludes to their work when on their way to Dublin to meet Dr. Coke. In compliance with what he states, "I have made it a rule that the Irish missionaries shall spend some time with me when I visit Ireland. The last time they spent about a fortnight with me.—T.C."

I must reluctantly refrain from giving any further extracts here from Mr. Graham's journal, in reference to his work during the following three months, although there are passages which abound in singular displays of Divine power. These two "labourers in their Master's cause," travelled through nearly all the Circuits of the North, which took them about three months to accomplish, from January, 1800, until April following. In lieu of those extracts, I can only give the letter which they wrote to Dr. Coke after their return, dated—

"SLIGO, *April* 6, 1800.

"We have now returned to Sligo after travelling all the Circuits in the North of Ireland, and all glory to God, our labours have been crowned with great success. The fire of the Lord has attended us wherever we came, and His fear fell upon the people. We have preached to thousands in the open streets and in the fields, in the fairs and markets, and in the principal towns of the North. Numbers of Catholics have been awakened, and many of them converted, especially at Clones, Brookborough, Ballinamallard, and their respective neighbourhoods. We can give you but a very imperfect account of this great work ; but if you **are spared to come to this** kingdom, the preachers from their different Circuits will be able to satisfy you fully as to what we now relate. All glory to God, the harvest **is great.** It was not in our power **to** spend half as much time with the poor Catholics as they required, though we spent three months in our last tour. We are come home to rest a little, but I think our stay will be very short. Nor can we, with a good conscience, rest while **so** many thousands **are now** willing to hear, and are perishing for lack of knowledge. It is a wonder, indeed, **how we have** been sustained under such great labours and exertions. The preachers and people thought it impossible that we could hold out, having not only the labours of the streets and fields, but a revival almost in every part, which keeps us preaching, exhorting, **and** praying for hours. But still we are alive, and resolved to go on with our glorious work. At Newtownstewart we preached **a** little out of **the** town, and numbers out of the fair came to hear us. Many of the poor Catholics, bathed in tears, came forward to shake hands with us, entreating us, according to the custom of their priests, to lay our hands upon them and bless them.

"C. GRAHAM,
"G. OUSELEY."

We must glance at the journals **for the quarter** following this period, as I have no directer means **of** affording information of how it was spent. **They** resolved **on** removing **their** families from Sligo to Clones. They had spent a large amount of labour **in** the neighbourhood **of** Sligo, but a **wider** field had **now** opened **up to them in** the County Monaghan, and they thought Clones a better centre. Before they left Sligo, however, Mr. Ouseley resolved to make one grand charge on the Church of Rome, which all through life he regarded as "the dire apostacy," and he seemed to be raised up like another Luther to wage war with it, until the last gasp. Mr. Graham writes:—" We determined to make another trial in the street, although the priest commanded great power, in preventing the Catholics from hearing us; yet, on this occasion, contrary to our expectation, we were attended with a crowd of the Catholics, who stood quietly while Brother Ouseley proved to them that they were deceived, and had not the doctrines preached by Saint Paul in his Epistle to the Romans; and that their priests were blind guides, and false prophets, and knaves, and took their money, but did them no good. I exhorted after him, not minding sect or parties, but directed them at once to turn away their attention from creeds, and from church and chapel walls, and to look to Him who could alone grant them what they all wanted, '*real happiness*,' which could only be found by faith in Christ. They heard with attention, and the power of the Lord attended the word. The hearts of many were melted, which also proved a blessing to my own soul. I am now about to leave my native county again, and I have strong hopes that the devil's strongholds will be broken down even here."

This ends their labour for the present in the town and neighbourhood of Sligo, for which they prayed, and laboured, and hoped, and wept so much.

Mr. Graham states that he set out May 1, 1800, with his family from Sligo, on his way to Clones. He preached in Manorhamilton the first night. He states, God made the service a blessing to himself as well as to others; and on the next night he preached also, which was a time of breaking down. All the people were in tears. On the 3rd of May he arrived in Clones. It was Saturday, and he felt much fatigue with his journey; but on next day, the Sabbath, he went to the Market-house, and there proclaimed, as formerly, the unsearchable riches of Christ. He states, "some souls were set at liberty." The work begun here before had not declined, although the priest was hard at work to undo what was done among the Romanists. The good work was very deeply grounded among the Methodists, and likely to spread far and wide. Now we find him starting out afresh. He went next day to the fair of Roslea, and felt the need of Mr. Ouseley, who had not yet arrived from Sligo. But the Lord stood by him, and although the place had a bad name, the people gave him a very attentive hearing. Many hearts were melted, and a wonderful reformation took place, even in a change from cursing, swearing, drunkenness, and lying. This was a place where Satan had his seat, and many subjects—a place "where dragons lay," as Graham expresses it, "but now it begins to grow grass, with reeds and rushes." The Catholics followed him that evening to Mr Whitley's, where they had to stand outside for want of room. They came again next morning, and a revival commenced, in which the kind family participated largely, and many of the Catholics went home broken-hearted. He prays—"O Lord carry on this glorious work."

Next day he met Mr. Ouseley, who had arrived from Sligo, with Mrs. Ouseley. The following day they proceeded to Smithborough, scarcely allowing themselves a day to rest. Numbers flocked from different quarters. The heavens were opened, and showers of blessings descended in rich abundance. They met several Catholics coming from mass, whom they addressed, when many were convinced of all and judged of all on the spot. In the evening they preached at a Mr. Mitchell's. Here they had many Seceders, who, Graham states, "had been preached to death by long harangues." It was ploughing on the rocks for a considerable time, but before they concluded the Lord touched many hearts. He observes on this, "*two* were far better than one."

Graham mentions that he felt great loneliness during the few days Ouseley and himself were separated. Mr. Ouseley stood the street in Sligo on the Sabbath after Mr. Graham left; Mr. Banks, the Sligo superintendent, assisting, and preached to an attentive congregation. Graham expresses his gratitude to God for the success of his dear brother Ouseley thus, "Blessed be God that we have encouragement to go back to Sligo again, notwithstanding all the priest has done—namely, his very worst—to keep his people from hearing; but neither men nor devils can prevent them now." He also states, "Mr. Ouseley preached in Lisbellaw on his way from Sligo, and God set some souls at liberty; and at Maguiresbridge also he preached to a mixed multitude." "I never knew," says he again, "such a desire for hearing; we have now more invitations than we can attend to."

From Smithborough they went to the Monaghan market. The people ran with eagerness to hear them, as if there had been a famine of the Word in the land. Some appeared to be stunned, some bathed in tears, but some of the clergy strove to keep up their courage by laughing at the solemn scene, like the school-boy, when passing the church-yard by night, "whistling to keep their courage up." Their countenances, however, soon changed, for "the Word of the Lord was with power," and bore down all before it. "The Catholics," Graham writes, "ran after us, inquiring 'when would we come again?' All the priests' curses or threatenings are insufficient to prevent their attendance." The impressions of the former visit were not effaced. God gave them the hearts of this people, and they were willing to follow them anywhere. Again, next day, in Smithborough, we find them preaching to a mixed multitude of Episcopalians, Presbyterians, Seceders, and Roman Catholics. Before the meeting closed the rocks began to rend, and when they went into the house they could not be heard on account of the loud and bitter wail of distress and anguish of spirit. The Lord wounded and healed, broke down and built up. Many witnessed that day for Christ that He had " power on earth to forgive sins." Mr. Graham quaintly observes, " I doubt not but we have left enough for priests and ministers to do for awhile. These have been stumbling-blocks, for one of them challenged a Methodist preacher to dispute the subject of the *decrees*—they have other subjects to dispute about now—a great number have been truly converted to God." They next proceeded to Newbliss, where, in the market, many where cut to the heart, and found it to be the best market they ever attended. Next day they went to the market of Clones, where they had from a thousand to fifteen hundred to hear, and the Spirit's " two-edged sword" did great execution. They thundered the law from Mount Sinai ; the people trembled, and the devil's strongest snares were broken. The priests were losing their power. Then to Newbliss again, where the scene was on the most marvellous scale. Young and old, husbands and wives, rejoicing together as having " found peace with God." Not a word now about purgatory or unconditional election, things debated *hard* before in all this country ! A young man heard them, and conversed with them, who was preparing for the Roman Catholic priesthood. He now declared he believed the Methodist doctrines, "and I trust," says Mr. Graham, "he will never read a Latin mass." At Cootehill the sensations among the Romanists amounted to a complete moral revolution; anxious to get *liberty*, and yet afraid of the power of caste, and several of them, too, in "orders." They were convinced of their errors, and did not know what to do. Mr. Graham prays for them, and says, "from such bondage, good Lord deliver them." At Ballybay the priest got behind them in a window, and heard his system exposed, and his people warned against it. They followed the preachers out of the fair in order to get more light. They told the people that their religion was "a religion of money and not of mercy." Thence they both went to Rockcurry, where they had about fifteen hundred to hear. Such numbers made them tremble. Graham exclaims, "Lord, what am I? a helpless creature! O Lord, give me wisdom and power. The work is thine, and worthy of Thee." A young, half-drunken gentleman gave some annoyance, but soon withdrew. No marvel that when the devil's kingdom is in danger, he is always sure to send some of his servants to prop it up. It was then tottering all round that country. Next morning a woman who was "struck" the day before in the street, was set at liberty through believing in Jesus. Her husband also was struck down, as well as many others. The preachers then left for Cootehill. Here they obtained the Presbyterian Meeting-house, and had several Dissenting ministers to hear. They also preached the next morning, when many were alarmed. Thence they went to Cavan, where they had a crowd, and many of the Tipperary militia, who heard with astonishment, being mostly Roman Catholics. The Lord sent home His word with power to many hearts. It was a good time to all. In the evening they preached again when they had both to reprove and encourage. Some soldiers behaved badly, but the rest heard gladly. Writing of this, Mr. Graham says, "It is impossible for me to give a full account of this great work now going on; and here I must confess that anything to equal the conversions from Romanism I scarcely ever read of; and they were all of a most marvellous type."

We shall not proceed with any further details from the journal now, lest we might weary the reader. We will finish the record of this year's labours in the next chapter, and here give an extract from a letter written by Mr. Graham to Dr. Coke, dated—

"CLONES, June 28, 1800.

"Could we attend to all the invitations we have from different places in the country, I know not when we should leave it, for such a call for preaching I have never known, nor such crowds to attend it. The whole country is in a flame. The Lord is truly doing great things, and those who are eye and ear witnesses must conclude that some great event is likely to take place; such an outpouring of the Spirit of grace and supplication I have never witnessed before.

"CHARLES GRAHAM."

Thus they now arrive within a few weeks of the end of the first Conference year of this marvellous general mission enterprise, the success of which fully justified the appointment. It was one continued stream of labour, and of almost uninterrupted health, and of equal prosperity. Those two apostolic men, although in some things very dissimilar in their natural temperaments and gifts, yet never had they a word in the way of a misunderstanding. "Each esteemed the other better than themselves," and rejoiced in each other's success. They could truly sing with melody in their hearts to the Lord—

> "Still may we to our centre tend,
>   To spread Thy praise our common end—
>   To help each other on :
>   Companions through the wilderness,
>   To share a moment's pain, and seize
>   An everlasting crown."

CHAPTER IX.

JULY, 1800—GENERAL MISSION CONTINUED.

> "Rouse to some deed of pure and holy love,
>   And thou an angel's happiness shalt know;
> Shalt bless the earth, while in the world above
>   The good begun by thee shall onward flow
> In many a branching stream, and wider grow.
>   The seed that in these few and fleeting hours
> Thy hands unsparing and unwearied sow,
>   Shall deck thy grave with amaranthine flowers,
> And yield thee fruit divine in heaven's immortal bowers."

IN the last chapter we brought down the labours of the self-denying missionaries to the 28th of June, and here it may be interesting to record the mode of their journeyings to Conference, and their preparation for it, which was anything but rest for either body or mind. As one remarked—

> "They scorned their feeble flesh to spare,
> Regardless of their swift decline."

On the 8th of July we find them at Belturbet, preaching in the Market-house to a large congregation, among whom was a considerable sprinkling of ladies and gentlemen, many of whom felt the power of the Word. They were much astonished to hear the cries of the people for mercy, and said, these missionaries were good men, and a great blessing to the country. But how hard for the rich to be *fully* decided for God. A love-feast followed; many strangers remained at it for the first time in their lives. Many were converted that day. Next day they preached at Ballyhaise. Many Catholics were cut to the heart, and some justified. It was said to be the greatest day that town ever saw. They next proceeded to Clones, and took the market again, as they thought it might be their last day in that place, fearing they would be changed at the Conference. Many were constrained to cry out for mercy. These they brought to the preaching-house, where the Lord set many of them at liberty, and some Romanists among the number. They preached on July 12th to a vast multitude of Orangemen, who, instead of spending the evening as formerly in drinking parties, came now to hear the sound of the Gospel trumpet, and conducted themselves with the greatest propriety. "Love worketh no ill to his neighbour."

The last Sabbath before Conference (July 13th) they preached in the country in the morning, and had a time of rich refreshing, numbers professing to be saved. "Religion," says Mr. Graham, "bears down all before it in this country; the most prejudiced have been convinced and converted." As the sequel will show, there was great anxiety now among the people lest these remarkable messengers should be removed from their district of country at the Conference; but it was not so.

On the evening of the same Sabbath they preached to about four thousand people. Before the open air service was held, many who came from a distance went to the Established Church. It is mentioned that a young man fainted, or was "struck," in the church, when the minister cried out, "Take him away, I will have no irregularity in my church; and if these strangers are my parishioners, I wonder I did not see them here before; but if they are following those *cavalry* preachers (so called from their preaching on horseback,) I wish they had remained at home in their own churches. Let no one say that I invited them here." This same clergyman was heard to say on the previous Sabbath, that he wished the Irish missionaries to come there; his preaching appeared to do the people no good, and that he thought it better for him to give up altogether; but when they did actually come, he got alarmed. All parish ministers, however, were not of his mind; for we find the missionaries shortly after invited in another town by the minister of the parish to preach in his church.

We find them on their way to Conference on Monday, July 14th. They passed through Ballyhaise and Cavan, preaching in each place to multitudes inside and outside. They met the Rev. Joseph Armstrong and Rev. George Brown, who assisted them in Cavan. The word was with power to all classes. There were many soldiers in the town also, who inquired as of old, "And what shall we do?" Thence they journeyed to Oldcastle, which Graham calls "a hardened and corrupt town;" but a Mr. Henry, with whom they spent the night, declared that "it gave him the greatest happiness to see so many poor, ignorant Roman Catholics calling on God for mercy, and so broken down." The Romanists would willingly remain for hours on their knees without apparent weariness. The missionaries, leaving Oldcastle, proceeded to Dublin, where they were appointed by Conference to preach at "John's Well." They had a very large, well behaved, and very attentive congregation, especially Roman Catholics. Others passed and repassed carelessly. One poor Romanist was convinced, whose eyes poured out tears like water. Another in the street manifested great concern, and immediately a crowd gathered round, to whom Mr. Graham preached a short sermon. Before they left the city they called at a Doctor Stoke's; and while Mr. Ouseley was writing a card to leave his name, as the doctor was out, Graham spoke to the servant-maid on the subject of personal religion. She manifested the greatest concern, and wept bitterly. They commended her to God in prayer, and had good hope concerning her. Mr. Graham prays thus :—"O Father of mercies and God of the spirits of all flesh, how many of Thy creatures are perishing in darkness, and none to take them by the hand: send light into the world, O Lord, and disperse the gloom that has overspread the face of all nations." How well to be instant in season, and out of season, so pointedly expressed thus :—

> "We have no time to sport away the hours;
> All must be EARNEST in a world like ours.
> Not *many* lives, but only one have we—
> One, only one ;
> How sacred should that one life ever be,—
> That narrow span !
> Day after day filled up with blessed toil,
> *Hour* after *hour* still bringing in new spoil."

Having rehearsed to the Conference the wonderful dealings of God with them throughout this remarkable first year of their enterprise, they were again "commended to the grace of God," to continue their glorious toil ; and, in addition, the Conference expressed its great satisfaction by augmenting the number of general missionaries to six, who stand thus on the Minutes :—

"Galway, Tipperary, Queen's County, Kilkenny, Dublin, Westmeath, Longford, Leitrim, King's County, Sligo, Mayo, and Roscommon—JAMES M'QUIGG, JAMES BELL;

"The Province of Ulster, and the Counties of Louth and Meath—
    CHARLES GRAHAM, GIDEON OUSELEY.
"Cork, Limerick, Kerry, Waterford, Wexford, Wicklow, Carlow,
    Kilkenny, and Clare—LAURENCE KANE, HENRY WEBB.

Graham and Ouseley left Dublin on the 1st of August, and arrived in Drogheda, where they preached at the Tholsel (Town-house) without the slightest annoyance. Many Romanists heard with respectful attention, as Graham states, "The Lord gave both liberty and power, and the Word appeared to fall as seed in good ground." The difficulty now, as then, seems to arise more from the cowardice of Protestants than the antipathy of Roman Catholics. "Arise, O Lord, thou and the ark of thy strength!"

They reached Ardee on the 2nd of August, where Graham became ill; but Ouseley took the street, and preached to the Roman Catholics. Graham says,—"We thought to storm the place, but I was laid aside for a day." This is the first time we find him to complain of illness. They proceeded next to a place called Poles, near Kingscourt. The Roman Catholics heard with great avidity. It was a time of breaking down; and one intelligent young man, a Roman Catholic, "was cut to the heart." His distress was poignant, and he cried out, "I am full of fire." Prayer continued to be made for him until his soul was set at liberty. It was now the fire of heavenly love; and, oh, the expressions of gratitude for ever having heard those servants of the Lord!

Kingscourt was next visited on the market-day. The former visit—last November—gave intensity to the desire for hearing: great power attended the word. Tears flowed freely; or, to use Graham's expression, "*plentifully*," and many called most earnestly on God. The Irish language was freely spoken here : the people knelt in the open street. The Lord was very present, and the word reached every heart. Graham prays,—" O Lord, water the seed with the dew of Thy grace."

Thence they went to the market of Shercock, where a similar scene to that at Kingscourt took place. Most of those who heard were Roman Catholics, who, with uplifted hands and streaming eyes, cried aloud for mercy. The minister of the Established Church,—who was also the magistrate—heard attentively : a happy contrast to his unworthy brother at Clones. A Roman Catholic shopkeeper asked them to take some refreshment, and said,—" The man who would pin his faith to the sleeve of any individual deserved to be lost." His wife said,—" We heard of you, and we were afraid you would not come to us." Some of the Catholics said also,—" What shall we do? You have told us that the priest cannot forgive us our sins, and we are greatly alarmed." Mr. Graham prays again,—" O Lord, send light, nor suffer these any longer to remain in the shadow of death."

They soon after arrived in *Clones*, where their families resided, but which they could scarcely call their *home*, from the short time they allowed themselves to remain quiet. They scarcely ever gave themselves more than a day to rest after an absence of months! Indeed they generally preached on the evening of their arrival. Now a great trial awaited them. The curate, who was also a magistrate, vowed not to allow them to preach in the street. Mr. Graham waited on him, but the decree was passed. We shall see the result forthwith. After labouring round the country with great success for some days, multitudes from all directions flocked to hear, and some who " came to mock remained to pray ;"

and others, who thought to laugh at the cries of penitents, were "struck," and cut to the heart. Some of these were Seceders, or Reformed Presbyterians. One young woman cried aloud, saying, "I came here although afraid to be seen, but the Lord has found me out, and has blessed me." They continued in prayer for the mourners for a long time. They brought some of these into a barn. A Mr. Whitley came in and said, "Oh, come out and see a man stretched on the ground, who used to offer to swear oaths for a wager; he is roaring for mercy." Here the missionaries were joined by Mr. William Hamilton, who assisted them greatly. Several were justified, some of whom were Roman Catholics, who followed them from place to place, in opposition to the entreaties of their priests. The threats of the priests, it is but just to say, were mild in comparison with the persecution of the Established Church ministers and gentry, and more especially from the Episcopal ministerial magistrate of *Clones*, by whom they were prevented from preaching on the previous market-day, as already stated. Mr. Graham says, "We determined to go out to-day, cost us what it would. Accordingly we went to the middle of the street, and the people gathered round. The captain of the Tipperary militia, another persecutor, and in league with the clerical magistrate, came to us and said we must not preach there—that it was too near his lodging. We moved a little, and remained for about two hours, although it rained most of the time. Invitation upon invitation poured upon us; nor can we give this country either the time or labour they require." So far, so well. Wonders soon followed.

At Kilmore, in a day or two after, many were set at liberty; and, says Mr. Graham, "The Lord be praised, this country is all on fire—travelling preachers, local preachers, leaders, and hearers are flaming with zeal for the glory of God." Next day, at Castleblaney fair, a large concourse, mostly Roman Catholics, heard the word with joy. Soon there was a noise and a cry from every quarter; not "the confused noise" of the battle-field, but the result of the burning power of the Word, and the fire of heavenly love. The Gospel soon spread far and wide. In the evening, at Mr. M'Birney's, the scene was more surprising. The people followed the missionaries. Roman Catholics smote their breasts, kissed the ground, and, crying aloud for mercy, wept bitterly. O for such times again! It was the Lord's doings, and truly marvellous. The following Sabbath exceeded all the others. No house could hold the people. They got liberty to go into Lord Blaney's demesne, and the power of the Most High was so overwhelming, that, to use the words in Graham's journal, "The people could neither sit nor stand, but fell on their knees during the time of preaching, and then with one voice cried aloud to God for mercy. It was a day never to be forgotten."

At Keady, in the evening of that day, they preached again; and the Irish language had a wonderful effect upon the Roman Catholics. The exclamations of some of them were a little humorous. One of these was,—"The rest of the ministers may throw their caps at them,"—the missionaries,—meaning thereby that they should uncover their heads before their superiors. At Monaghan, multitudes heard them—mostly Roman Catholics—and were powerfully affected. Again they preached in the evening on the street, with similar effects. Here Graham records the happy death of a young woman, who found peace with God in this revival.

The next remarkable account is that of their preaching to a wedding party, while the priest, who was waiting for them, looked on from the chapel door. Ouseley alighted from his horse, and knelt down in the road to pray with the young people, who also knelt, and truly it was "a time of refreshing." "We," says Mr. Graham, "exhorted them to get themselves joined to the Lord Jesus Christ, and to prepare for the marriage supper of the Lamb. The word was blessed to them, and soon their tears began to flow." Mr. Armstrong, the Circuit preacher, who then accompanied Graham and Ouseley, was so overcome at seeing those poor Roman Catholics so broken down, that he declared, "I could lay down my life for them." All this time the priest did not seem desirous to appear. He looked as if thunderstruck, and could not tell what to make of it; but probably he soon found it out. It was altogether a strange scene on a wedding-day, and not likely to be readily forgotten. It would present a fine subject for the pencil of a Raphael to see three Methodist preachers kneeling on the open road, holding their horses' bridles, surrounded by a wedding party, calling on God for mercy, while tears flowed apace, the chapel in the distance, with the priest peeping out from behind the half-open door, and manifesting all the emotions, no doubt of amazement and fear, as if inquiring "What does all this mean?"

The servants of the Lord went on their way rejoicing, while the bewildered party repaired to the chapel to meet their still more bewildered clergyman. Here we may surely say they were "*instant* in season," and, as in this instance, "*out of season*."

After this Graham and Ousely visited the lower parts of the North for about six weeks, during which their labours were incessant and marvellously successful, although Satan, here and there, strove to throw obstacles in their way. The chief hindrances are stated to be "*ministers* of religion so-called." This was peculiarly the case at Clones in the month of October of this year (1800.) Before we describe that painful scene we must glance at the work in the South, as recorded in two letters to Dr. Coke—one dated "Cork, 9th September, 1800—from Messrs. Kane and Webb :—

"We preached on the bridge of Bandon, and had a large congregation who heard with great attention, and were much benefitted. In Kinsale, a Roman Catholic knelt on the open street bathed in tears. We had hundreds to hear. Preached again in Bandon to a thousand people. One of our hearers was a woman who has two brothers priests; and, although they opposed her, and warned her against us, she declared she must hear the truth. Other Catholics came next night, and were in tears. In Ballyneen the Catholics heard us attentively, and helped us to sing; and when at prayer fell on their knees in the middle of the street. At Lisnegat, the Catholics who could not get into the house, knelt outside all the time of the sermon. One of them refuses to obey the priest. At *Cape Clear* we preached and reasoned with the people out of the Scriptures. They were all Catholics. The Reformation under Elizabeth did not extend that far. At Dunmanway we had upwards of a thousand people to hear us, and the Protestant clergyman amongst the number. At Cork, on our return, we had about sixteen hundred to hear, and several of the congregation were military officers. The people heaped all manner of blessings upon us. We are now preparing to set out for another missionary excursion, and beg an interest in prayer."

Here, at Cork, the above missionaries obtained Bishop Bedell's old Irish Bible, and were putting it into the Roman character for the use of the country people, with the English and Irish in opposite columns—a thing necessary to be done even now, 1868. They only finished the book of Genesis. Archbishop M'Hale, of *Tuam*, did the same with the Pentateuch, in the Douay version, some time ago; and here we may state that the *Irish-speaking* people number, by the last census (1861), 155,000; and those speaking the Irish and English, 800,000—more than all the Episcopalians in Ireland.

The **next extract** is from a letter by Messrs. M'Quigg and Bell to Dr. Coke, dated **October 13th, 1800:**—

"Many gentlemen seem pleased with our mission; wherever we go we are received, except by the priests. We were invited to Urlingford by highly respectable gentlemen. After mass we took the street, and had a vast crowd. The priest came rushing past like a madman while we were at prayer, and swore I should not preach there. The gentlemen who invited us declared I should, and shouted to me to '*Go on.*' I spoke in Irish. We had about 1500 Roman Catholics, and only 20 Protestants. Brother Bell (says M'Quigg) stood firm as an oak, in all the confusion. He is a most pleasing companion to me, for zeal, humility, and love, and withal a good voice. The magistrate made a speech after I spoke, and then took us home, and invited us back. The priest then pretended that he only came to save us, and that we may now preach away. We preach to thousands who otherwise would never hear the Gospel. The Irish language has charms which amaze myself. Many of the gentlemen are ready to fight for us in the street. Brother Bell glories in his heavenly calling. A minister of the Establishment at Roscrea, who heard us, exclaimed, '*There never was so useful a scheme adopted for the good of Ireland.*' In Mountrath an old priest strove to take away the people, but when I thundered in the *Irish language* he fled, and the people came back. The Roman Catholic Bishop heard us and said, 'It was severe work.' In Mountmellick I preached under the window of a paralyzed gentleman, who was one of our greatest enemies in Dublin. He came here for his health's sake. His servant wheeled him in an arm-chair to the window. The word smote him. He wept aloud, and made signs to send for the preacher. 'I never,' says M'Quigg, 'saw a man in deeper distress for salvation.' A gentleman, some time ago, horsewhipped a ballad-singer who annoyed us in the street, after which he was right glad to fly."

We have now to fall back on Mr. Graham's journals for the account of the persecution in Clones—and which is recorded nowhere else, except in a parody which the Rev. R. Crozier wrote on the subject, but we consider it too serious for that style of treatment, although we have the document, which is more amusing and humorous than edifying. Mr. Graham's account is in substance as follows :—

" On our return from the Dublin Conference in the month of August, we found the *rulers* of Clones took council together, that we should no more preach in the street : but we resolved to go on as usual. Some of our friends thought it right that we should speak to the magistrate, and explain our position. We did so, but all in vain. He resolved to carry out his threats, and prevent us from street preaching. We had to tell him that we would 'obey God rather than man ;' and that it would be an awful thing for him if he were found 'fighting against God' by opposing the proclamation of His truth. He said, he did not think so. On our return from a short tour northward, where we saw the glory of the Lord so remarkably revealed, we resolved to go a-head. Accordingly, on the 11th of October, we arrived. Next day was the Sabbath, and a *memorable* day it was." Mr. Graham continues :—"We purposed to preach in the street, and went out as the people were coming from mass. I had been half-way through my sermon when the rector's servant came to me with a note, but apprehending its contents, I requested him to keep it until I was done ; but he returned with the note to his master ; and immediately the curate, who was the magistrate (as already stated), came forward and commanded me to desist. Some of the people interposed and reasoned with him, but in vain. He said, '*They* are not sent to preach the Gospel, and I will not suffer them to preach here again.' He ordered the people to disperse. A Mr. Cochraine, who was lieutenant of the yeomen, told this magistrate that they would not disperse, as they were not acting illegally.

The magistrate called a Captain G——, of the militia, who came forward *blaspheming* by the name of the Most High. I told him, says Mr. Graham, 'not to swear.' He told me not to attempt to preach to him, or if I did, he would punish me. I told him 'I did not fear his punishment.' Then the magistrate, fearing consequences, said, ' But you must not preach so near my church.' Mr. Ouseley then said, ' Let us move on,' and as we were about to leave, the magistrate said to Mr. Ouseley, ' Did you not state that you were free from sin?' Mr. Ouseley responded, 'Blessed be God, nine years ago, the Lord made me free from sin'—alluding, no doubt, to Romans vi. 18, which runs thus—' Being made free from sin, ye became servants of righteousness,' &c. The curate replied, ' You are a *blasphemer*, for it is written, If we say we have no sin, we deceive ourselves, and the truth is not in us.' Cochraine, the captain alluded to, said, ' Quote the whole of the passage,' repeating, ' If we confess our sins, he is faithful and just to forgive us our sins, and to cleanse us from all unrighteousness.' 'He then turned on me,' says Mr. Graham, 'and called me *an infamous liar.*' Mr. Ouseley immediately reproved him for '*reviling* the Lord's servant.' We then went to Mr. Ouseley's door, the people following us. Mr. Ouseley ascended a block, and began to preach. The rector cried out, ' Call out the army.' The captain appeared, the drums beat to arms, and the men were drawn up. Immediately some of the yeomen ran for their firearms. The magistrate, seeing that this might lead to blood, ordered the soldiers back, and ran up to Mr. Ouseley and pulled him down from the block, when I, says Mr. Graham, started up to finish my sermon ; then he thought to pull me down, but he found to his confusion, that I was a little too *heavy* and *stiff*, and not so easily moved. I finished, and pronounced the benediction, and dismissed the congregation." Some say that he then ordered them into a prison called "The Black Hole," but Graham does not mention it.

Thus ended one of the most singular and disgraceful scenes which had been witnessed since or before in that country, at least in connexion with street preaching, or magisterial folly. It resulted in the disgrace of both rector and curate, while it only tended greatly to the increased popularity of the missionaries—as, indeed, persecution always does. The magistrate never had a day's prosperity afterwards, and the rector as little. We could record tragic scenes, but we forbear. We cannot, however, but exclaim—" Verily, there is a God that judgeth in the earth." The lines of a great poet, although written to condemn the mistaken judgment of Kirke White, and quite different to the case just mentioned, yet, by accommodation, they may be applied with the greatest propriety as descriptive of self-destruction :—

> "'Twas thine own *genius* gave the fatal blow,
> And helped to plant the wound that laid thee low ;
> So the struck eagle, stretched upon the plain,
> No more through rolling clouds to soar again,
> Viewed his own feather on the fatal dart,
> And winged the shaft which quivered in his heart.
> Keen were the pangs, but keener far to feel,
> He nursed the pinion which impelled the steel,
> While the same plumage that had warmed his nest,
> Drank the last life-drop of his bleeding breast."

In reflecting on this whole affair, one is at a loss to know whether to wonder more at the folly, the madness, or the wickedness, not to say the impolicy of such conduct. The rudeness, the ungentlemanly bearing, the unchristian course pursued by those two clerical fanatics, surpass description; **and all this, just after the rebellion, when the Methodists were known, and proved to be** the most loyal and orderly people on the face of the globe, and especially in Ireland ; but the truth was, their preaching bore down like thunder on the sins of the day, both of lay and cleric, and " galled them to revenge." Indeed, we are almost led to believe **that,** like as of old, the Lord *permitted* those " thorns in the flesh," **lest** by the "abundance of the revelations" (of grace), those highly honoured men of God "should be exalted **above measure."**

Immediately before this, **Mr.** Graham wrote—"At *Caledon* the bones were very dry. We preached in the fair, and brought weighty artillery to bear on the wicked ; we found it very difficult to get to their hearts. In the evening the Lord came to our help, and broke down some flinty rocks, and healed some backsliders ; but next morning, at seven o'clock, the power of the Lord descended so remarkably, that old and young were moved. A young woman screamed out in an uncommon manner, and seemed as one possessed of an evil spirit. Her whole frame trembled. She strove to tear something out of her breast. However, she soon began to praise God. A Roman Catholic woman fell down *stricken* likewise, under the power of conviction, and immediately her mother became similarly affected ; but all were restored. This ' thirsty land ' has now become ' springs of water.' It was never so seen on this fashion in *Caledon* before."

In *Charlemont* a number of officers thought to amuse themselves at the expense of the "black caps;" but soon "their folly was turned into amazement," although one of them, bolder than the rest, came forward and said—

"I charge you to preach no more in the street; your doctrine is very good, but you make such a d—— *noise* that the town is annoyed."

Mr. Ouseley answered, "Yes, we do make a noise; but ours is *hallowed* noise." I suppose alluding to the unhallowed character of those blasphemers' foul-mouthed oaths, "the drunkard's song, and the loud and vacant laugh," to which these same military gentlemen appeared to be no strangers."

At *Loughgall*, "the great men of authority" declared that if the "black caps" came there, they would "send them to h—ll." They did come, but neither the Established Church clergy nor Colonel C——, could stand before the artillery of heaven—the thunders of the law.

"At *Armagh*," says Mr. Graham, "all come to hear us except the rich. Alas! shall these go to hell because God is good to them?" They have too often "their good things" in this life, but not always, thank God.

At *Portadown* they had the most patient hearing, both outside and inside, except that a mad woman strove to annoy them. Mr. Graham remarks, "If such are at all close by, they are sure to join the crowd, as if the devil took them by the hand to the very spot." Many were converted at Portadown.

At *Bluestone* a Roman Catholic woman was alarmed, and said she was in company with twelve priests, and never heard anything like this way of salvation before, but quite the contrary.

At *Lisburn, Lurgan, Tandragee, Killalea, Hillsboro'*, and *Markethill*, "the power of the Lord was present to heal in all, and in great numbers." They then came to an old gentlemen's place of the name of Halliday, who had previously entertained Mr. Wesley. This man was 82 years of age, but not yet converted. They prayed earnestly for him.

It would fail the writer, as well as, perhaps, tire the patience of the reader, to record all the journal accounts from October until the end of December, 1800, but we will give a few extracts of letters, which will throw some light on this last quarter of the year. The first is from Mr. Graham to his son in Dublin, dated—

"ENNISKILLEN, *December* 25, 1800.

"MY DEAR CHARLES,—The fire of the Lord attends us wherever we go. It is astonishing the numbers who have been convinced and converted during the last week. I never saw the prejudices of Enniskillen conquered in the street until this day. We did not leave it until we left it in triumph. I think this was one of the best days it has ever seen. The Lord is riding in triumph through all this land, all glory to His eternal name. Mr. Stuart, the circuit preacher, mounted his horse, and took the street with us, and did valiantly. "Many hands make light work." Mr. Kerr also goes on courageously. The Lord is owning the labours of these men. Here many Catholics have been convinced and converted since we left Clones. Superstition and formal religion are flying like the chaff of the summer threshing-floor. The little stone cut out of the mountain without hands is becoming so powerful that it appears to me, at least, that it will shortly fill this nation. Whatever I can say comes far short of what the Lord is doing. To Him be the power and the glory for ever. Amen and amen.

"I remain your loving father,

"CHARLES GRAHAM."

This letter speaks for itself. It is a rich gem of missionary triumph. We may here remark that, from that time, street preaching was never regarded as a very formidable task in the street of Enniskillen. A few months ago, March, 1868, the superintendent minister of that Circuit, the Rev. R. Huston, joined the writer in a street service at the fair of that town, and we had the most profound attention from a vast concourse of Catholics and Protestants, many of whom knelt during the time of prayer, and this, too, just after the trial and conviction of the Granard rioters at the Longford Assizes, for their attack on the author for having preached on the street of that town some time ago.

The next extract is from the pen of Mr. Ouseley to Mr. Joyce :—

"NEAR ENNISKILLEN, *December* 23, 1800.

" MY DEAR BROTHER,—Mercy, peace, and love be multiplied unto thee and all our dear brethren, through our Lord Jesus Christ. When we arrived in Clones, Mr. Graham fell sick, but I preached abroad to vast congregations, and in the houses the voice of heaven-born children was heard rejoicing. God wrought a great work in the country where I had to go alone. Many souls were brought to God. Several Romans were awakened during the five days 1 was with Mr. Brown, and four of them were made happy in God. A father who had not spoken to his daughter for months because she quitted the priest, fell on the floor weeping. I prayed over him in Irish ; he got up, took his daughter in his arms, they kissed each other, and wept aloud. O, how people love when the love of God is shed abroad in their hearts. Some were converted this week who were like devils before. How mighty is the power of God ! On the Sabbath I preached in a *ball-room*, where gaiety and vanity reigned before ; but now there was another kind of noise and work there. The number was vast, and the crying of the penitents filled the house. The gentleman of the house and his whole family are turned to God. I came home hoarse and weary, but my God soon revived me. Now Mr. Graham set out with me, and we had another great week. Every day souls are converted ; we cannot ascertain how many, the number is so great, and the multitudes who throng around us are so immense. We found it impossible to find out all the mourners, or those who are made happy—we did not attempt to count. We conversed with a priest on Tuesday, and the result was pleasing. Many appear *literally* to *devour* the Word. On Monday another Roman Catholic was converted. At *Belturbet* the cry never ceased till nine o'clock at night. At *Ballyconnel* several wept, and some were made happy in God. These were mostly Romans. But, oh! at *Swanlinbar*, the vastness of the congregation, the eager attention, the loud lamentation, together with the sound of prayer which went up to heaven (when we were telling them that Christ ascended to heaven to send down the gift of the Holy Ghost), *all, all* was overwhelming. One of our friends met a Romanist that evening going home, weeping along the road, and lamenting how he had been blinded. These Roman Catholics love us, and are anxious to get pamphlets from us. Near Enniskillen we had a blessed meeting; scarcely a dry face. Glory, glory, glory to our God. I can say no more now. I am your happy and affectionate brother in the Gospel,

"GIDEON OUSELEY."

Doctor Coke remarks here, "It gives me peculiar pleasure that the missionaries are now putting the converted Catholics under the care of the most pious and sensible members of our Society, in their respective neighbourhoods. Without this or some similiar plan, these missions could never be permanently, or at least extensively useful."

Mr. Graham writes from Clones to Dr. Coke, dated—

"*January* 22, 1801.

"REVEREND AND DEAR SIR,—Since I wrote last we have had great success. The Catholics heard in the street of *Rathmolyon*, and seemed alarmed. At Mr. Fox's, of *Galtrim*, the greater part of the congregation were Catholics. The power of the Lord fell on all. Such a time I had not known in this place, and some Catholics professed 'to feel the pardoning love of God.' In the benighted town of *Athboy*, Mr. Ouseley sounded the alarm in the street, and then called them in to prayer. Many who could not get in knelt outside the window, bathed in tears. Oh! what a pity to see these poor sheep perishing for lack of knowledge. At Oldcastle, the Catholics flocked to hear us as they did before, and the Lord blessed His word to them; and at the market, next day they seemed as much athirst for the Word as the gaping land for the falling rain. It was truly affecting to see them falling on their knees, and looking up to heaven for mercy. At our last visit, one of them left the mass and never returned. The whole town seemed alarmed that night, for the market people waited to hear us at Mr. Henry's. At *Ballyjamesduff* we preached in the Presbyterian Meeting-house, and the presence of the Lord filled the place. Catholics attended, and all yielded as melting wax before the fire. Next day, at the market, many were cut to the heart. On these two market-days and the Sabbath you would imagine the whole country was alarmed. The family that invited us were truly converted to God, and their neighbours were all awakened out of their long sleep of sin. Within the last six weeks I may safely say hundreds of souls have been convinced and converted. Many Catholics were converted at the Quarterly Meeting (Love Feast). In Enniskillen, one Sally M'H—— appeared to be possessed. She screamed in the wildest manner. Five men could not hold her or keep her down. The more we prayed, the more she raged. She could not bear to hear the Saviour's name mentioned; but, at last, the Lord heard prayer for her, and had mercy on her, and on us also. After she had lain as if dead for some moments, she started to her feet and praised the Lord, and still continues to praise Him. 'All glory be to God, whose mercy endureth for ever.' Another Catholic woman was converted a few nights ago, when she cried out in the Irish language, *Meelia molla lath mo Launihore*—the author gives it in its English pronunciation form for those who could not pronounce it in Irish— that is, 'A thousand praises to thee, my Saviour.' Another woman, who had passed through different Roman Catholic orders, such as the *Scapular*,* &c., and was looked upon as '*a saint indeed*,' to the

---

* The word Scapular is taken from the Latin *Scapual*, which signifies *shoulders*, from the circumstance of those in this order wearing two bits of brown woollen stuff attached together by a pair of strings, and generally initialled with B.V.M., which stand for Blessed Virgin Mary; so that one part hangs on the breast and the other on the back. These are to be duly blessed by a priest. They

great surprise of the priest and all his people, gave them the slip. The priest sent her word, that if she feared to perish in her own old religion, he would stand in her place at the last day; but Mary would not be cheated.

"I remain, &c.,

"C. GRAHAM."

The foregoing extracts may be regarded as terminating the first half-year of their second year's appointment, namely, from July, 1800, to the end of December. But, before we close this important half-year's labours, we must introduce a copy of the "license," as a Protestant dissenting minister, which Mr. Graham obtained from the Quarter Sessions in Dublin, very likely through the influence and advice of Doctor Coke. It runs thus:—

"We certify that at an adjournment of the General Quarter Sessions of the Peace and General Gaol Delivery, held for the County of the City of Dublin, at the Sessions House of said city, on the twelfth day of November, one thousand eight hundred, Charles Graham, Protestant preacher of the Gospel, belonging to, and in connexion with, the Society of the people called Methodists, came into open court, and did then and there take, repeat, and subscribe the oaths of allegiance and abjuration; and make, repeat, and subscribe the declaration, as set forth and enjoined to be taken, made, and repeated by an Act of Parliament, made in the sixth year of the reign of the late King George the First, entitled 'An Act for the Relief of Protestants dissenting from the Church of Ireland,' in order to entitle him to preach and expound the Gospel, pursuant to the provisions contained in said Act, and which we certify at the office of the said court, this twelfth day of November, in the year of our Lord, one thousand eight hundred.

"ALLEN & GREENE, C.P.C.C.D."

---

are emblems of "the Lady of Mount Carmel," the Mother of Christ. It is said to be a charm against all misfortune, and *secures a passport to heaven*, as well as preserves from everlasting punishment.

It is likely the *initials* stand for *Clerk* of the *Peace* for the *County* of the *City* of *Dublin*. This document settled the clerical rulers of Clones, although "still *willing*, but afraid to strike." Many of the early Methodist preachers, both in England and Ireland, had to take out this "license" as dissenting preachers, in order to avail themselves of the benefit of the "Toleration Act," and to prevent clerical opponents from taking advantage of the law against "Conventicles." Yet the Methodist preachers did not wish to own dissent from the State Church; but clerical persecutors drove them into taking out dissenting "licenses," as in the case of Graham. The swearing of Graham to "bear true allegiance" was one of the necessary forms required to be submitted to before he could obtain the "license." But the true loyalty of the Methodists could not be doubted. "A more loyal man than John Wesley," says the venerable Thomas Jackson, in his *Centenary of Wesleyan Methodism*, "never existed. His loyalty was not a sentiment or a prejudice, but a principle. He succeeded in impressing the same character upon the Societies that acknowledge him as their founder. Amidst disaffection, the pinchings of the protracted war, and the rampant radicalism of a later period, the loyalty of the Methodists was steadily maintained, as their official documents fully testify."

Near Enniskillen, on the 26th December, no house could hold the people, and they had to go to the field, although they had to sit on the cold ground, and this in winter. About one hundred of them were Catholics. Those who entered an adjoining barn subsequently "were all broken down."

The following statement of Mr. Graham's own experience is to me most precious. Under date, the same day, December 26th, he writes:—

"All glory to God, He met me here (at the house of Mr. George M'Donald, near Enniskillen) in a manner that I can hardly describe. So much of His love and power did the Lord let down into my soul, that nature could hardly sustain. I thought for some moments I should have fainted; nor was I sure but that the Lord was about to call my spirit away from the body. O Lord, my God, give me grace and wisdom to guard this sacred treasure. Such a visit as this my soul had long waited for. This is the third time the Lord gave me to feel His 'fulness of love.' O, may I never grieve Him more. Where might I have been now had I been faithful to his grace?"

At Derrygonnelly the crowd was so great that the priest's brother and the Roman Catholics wanted the people to go into the Catholic chapel; but as the priest was not there, they would not do so. On the last day of this year, December 31st, 1800, about thirty were converted, and several obtained the blessing of "a clean heart." Among the latter were several young persons, whose countenances seemed to beam as if in a beatified state.

CHAPTER X.

JANUARY TO JULY, 1801—GENERAL MISSION CONTINUED.

> "Work in the wild, waste places,
> Though none thy love may own;
> God guides the down of the thistle,
> The wandering wind hath sown.
> Will Jesus chide thy meekness,
> Or call thy labour vain?
> The word for Him thou bearest,
> Shall return to Him again."

THIS year began with still more remarkable instances of conversion. One of these is recorded thus:—"A man of the name of Crawford, who heard us last year, and then one of the vilest characters in all the country, came and heard us again this time. He is now a burning and a shining light, truly 'a brand plucked from the burning.' A short time before this took place, he went to a wake, and got drunk, and then went and kissed the corpse of the dead woman, saying, 'Why did you go to hell until I would be with you?' using also many other awful expressions. Oh, the goodness and mercy of God!"

At Lowtherstown, now Irvinestown, the siege was heavy. Military officers raged, and threatened to *duck* or *bayonet* the missionaries if they did not desist; but the truth prevailed, and many received the engrafted Word.

At *Makenny,* in Brother Somerville's, about *fifteen* were converted that night, and among them, *two of the soldiers,* who followed from town. In the course of this month some *hundreds* were brought to God.

In allusion to this period, the venerable biographer of Ouseley writes:—

"The unwearied exertions and zeal of these two men were equalled only by the unprecedented results which attended their preaching, and which became a matter of surprise, even to those who had themselves been long accustomed to witness the power of the Gospel in the salvation of sinners. Men who had for many years preached the Gospel themselves, stood amazed at the ceaseless and exhausting toil of Graham and Ouseley, as well as at the glorious results which followed in the conviction and conversion of multitudes."

One of Dr. Coke's correspondents writes in reference to this period also, thus:—

"Permit me, my dear sir, to say something of the Irish missionaries, Messrs. Graham and Ouseley. The mighty power of God accompanied their word with such demonstrative evidence as I have never known, or indeed rarely heard of. I have been present in fairs and markets, while these two blessed men of God, with burning zeal and apostolic order, pointed hundreds and thousands to 'the Lamb of God, which taketh away the sin of the world.' I have seen the immediate fruit of their labour—the aged and the young falling prostrate in the most public places of concourse, cut to the heart, and refusing to be comforted until they knew Jesus, and the power of His resurrection. I have known scores of these poor penitents to stand up, and witness a good confession; and, blessed be God, hundreds of them now adorn the Gospel of Christ. I am wanting in language to set forth the wonders I have seen wrought by the mighty power of the Holy Ghost, and I am humbled to the dust when I see the usefulness of these dear men of God."

While we might multiply testimonies of this character, relative to the unprecedented labours and success of these marvellous men, yet nothing appears to us so satisfactory as the personal record from the *living* and *loving* hearts, expressed by the willing hand and the *ready* pen. And how Mr. Graham found time to keep those journals so regularly for each day, we are utterly at a loss to know, considering his constant and wasting labours.

The following few extracts will bring us to the close of this half year, and up to July, 1801, and will well repay an attentive perusal. But we must pass over nearly four months' journalism of the raciest and richest character:—

"On the 8th of May, 1801," writes Graham, "we came to the fair of Roslea, and stormed the devil's kingdom in the street. Surely the Lord was King this day, and the devil's bulwarks were going to pieces; nor had he one of his servants who dare stand up for him. No wonder he rages about his work, for never did anything appear so well calculated to sap the foundation of his kingdom. Here we have 'the able men of Belial,' the Atheists, the Deists, the Arians, the Predestinarians, the Socinians, the covert Pharisees, and the backsliders. These sinners are asleep in the arms of the devil; and when they hear the judgment of God denounced against them, they tremble even in the open street, and many of them have lately turned to God."

They came to *Wattsbridge* on the 10th, where they had about a *thousand* people. Both Protestants and Romanists were brought under the most powerful emotion and penitential distress, and several found peace. One man felt the power coming on him, and he fled, exclaiming, "O, I'm afraid I'll be struck." He did fly, but had to fall, crying for mercy, which he obtained, and came back rejoicing.

After taking one day's rest in Clones they went to *Clonkirk*, where they preached in a field to hundreds, and had "seals to their ministry" on that day. Thence they went to *Redhill*, to a Mr. Little's, which had been a *home* for the preachers, since his conversion through the missionaries. He first invited them himself to the house. It was a highly respectable place. Both Mr. Little and all his family were now devoted to God. He was truly generous. When Mr. Ouseley's horse died, while in that locality, he made him a present of a very good one in its place. Here Mr. Graham mentions a very powerful temptation under which Mrs. Little had laboured for some weeks, namely, "that there was no God, no heaven, no hell," &c.; in fact, no invisible world at all, and no accountability. This brought her into deep distress of mind; but one day, when alone, the most awful sensation came over her: eternity opened to her vision with the most fearful view of hell and its torments. She trembled all over; she "cried mightily to God," who again "lifted up the light of his countenance upon her," and from that day she never doubted those solemn realities. The whole family had been very careless and fashionable previous to their conversion. Others in that neighbourhood, who were formerly devils, now were lambs. Such were John E—— and Thomas B——, but now "burning and shining lights." One exclaimed, before he found peace, that "he would not wonder if the ground should take fire under him, because he was such a sinner;" and that "no priest or bishop ever got to his heart before." So exclaimed others also. That very man, and another young person found peace that night.

Thence the preachers went to *Ballyhaise*, where they met many of the poor "sheep without a shepherd," who felt that these men had more love in their hearts for them than all the clergy in the country. After this they found the Protestants in *Cavan* rather unyielding, but the Roman Catholics were alarmed, especially while they declared that neither *salt*, nor *water*, nor *oil*, nor *beads*, would ever save them; nothing but the Gospel of Christ, which is the power of God unto salvation to every one that believeth, and which was preached to the *old Romans*. (See Romans i. 16.) One cried out, "It cost me half-a-guinea for wine and spirits at the last *confession*." "Being called," says Graham, '*Father*' and '*Reverend*' will not do."

They next went to *Killeshandra*, where the crowd was immense. "The Word bore all before it." The clergy of all parties were alarmed. In those days many of them appeared to be very corrupt. The missionaries preached on May 20th, mid-day sermons at *Carrigallen* with great effect, and that evening at *Sunnagh*, where "*eight* or *ten* were set at liberty." On the 22nd the Spirit wrought by the Word on every heart at the market of Arvagh, and in the evening at Mr. *Johnston's*, near the town: no house could hold the people. Ten or twelve found liberty. On the 23rd they came to Mr. Harpur's, of Drumlarney. They had to take to the field. Graham states, "The heavens were opened, and the skies poured down blessings on all; about twenty found peace." We may here mention a circumstance relative to this family, which is worthy of record. Mr. Harpur, and the head of another respectable family in the neighbourhood, had a conversation about taking the preachers to lodge.

The neighbour said to Mr. Harpur—"I have resolved not to invite them; for," said he, "I see few but plain people joining them, and I have a large family of daughters, and my lodging the preachers might prevent them from being respectably married."

"Well," said Mr. Harpur, "I have a large family also, but I'll trust God and take them in."

He did so, and in the course of a few years it was found that all Mr. Harpur's family were comfortably and respectably, and better still, *religiously* settled in life; while those of the other friend were sadly disappointed, and afterwards some of the most tragic scenes followed, scenes over which we must cast the veil of oblivion. Drumlarney became the home of the preachers, and the centre of spiritual light, and power, and influence to the whole of that neighbourhood for years. One of Mr. Harpur's daughters, Mrs. Allen Nixon, a highly respectable Christian matron, still lives to this day, 21st July, 1868, near the town of Manorhamilton, with her worthy and zealous son-in-law, Christopher Armstrong, Esq., of Blackpark; and we may add, she lives to see, or at least to hear, of another glorious revival of religion on that Circuit, almost similar to the one described by Mr. Graham, when she was first brought to God sixty-eight years ago. She is now between eighty and ninety years of age. Surely godliness is worth a world; yea, two. It has "the promise of the life which now is, and of that which is to come."

On the Sabbath morning, May 24th, in Mr. Harpur's field, the missionaries preached to not less than a *thousand* people. The conversions were very numerous. All seemed affected, and the people were filled as with the "new wine of the kingdom." "So that one might," says Mr. Graham, "imagine they were, as on the day of Pentecost, drunk with new wine." The Catholics were not forgotten. In the evening of the same day, Graham and Ouseley preached on the hill of Drumbullion, near the far-famed Corlispratten.

The congregation exceeded a thousand persons, many of whom appeared to gasp for the Word of the Lord

"As a thirsty land for showers."

"The power of the Holy Spirit descended, while one preached from—'These men are the servants of the Most High God, which show unto us the way of salvation' (Acts xvi. 17). Conversions began on every hand, and both 'the slain and healed of the Lord' were many."

"This," says Mr. Graham, "was a high day, and I trust it shall be had in everlasting remembrance. All glory to God; His kingdom is coming."

They returned on the 25th to Carrigallen, and preached to a mixed multitude, some of whom never heard a Gospel sermon before. The whole market was moved, and "the place shaken." Such a day was never seen in Carrigallen previously. "A plentiful rain descended to confirm the inheritance, for it was truly weary." It was a time both of weeping and rejoicing. In the evening of the same day, at Mrs. Love's, of Corduff, they had to preach in the open field, and the heavenly fire spread all round. Many were set at liberty. The meeting continued until late at night.

"I trust," says Mr. Graham, "the fire will burn until it purges all the country."

These were surely days of the Son of Man. The writer has a particular interest in that part of the kingdom, inasmuch as, thirty years after, in 1831, he witnessed a similar outpouring of the Spirit. It is recorded in the *October Magazine* for 1832, thus:—

"The next place visited in an extraordinary manner was Carrigallen. Here, on the morning previously, the town was filled with blood-thirsty men, who beat each other most unmercifully. They were all Romanists, and one of them since died of the wounds he received. In a few days we had the gratification of seeing a house filled with mourners crying for mercy, ten of whom stood up and praised God for pardoning mercy.—W. G. C."

From Carrigallen the missionaries repaired to Cloone, still further into the County Leitrim. This, Mr. Graham calls, "Satan's seat," and where many of his "blood-men" resided, whom he employed "at fairs and markets for bloody work." They thought to begin their bloody work this day also, but the hook was in the jaw. The Lord made their wrath to praise Him. The country is mostly Roman Catholic, but the missionaries failed not to show how they were duped, and kept in the dark by the priests and the Pope, in withholding the Scriptures from them. The magistrates, Messrs. West and Crofton, attended the preaching, and testified their full approbation. This was surely bearding the lion in his own den.

> "How mean the triumphs shown by haughty Rome,
> When marched her heroes to the trophied dome,
> Compared with *those* celestial spirits yield
> To men who vanquished in a nobler field."

From *Cloone* they went to Mohill, where the Word was blessed to many. Thence they proceeded to Leitrim town, where their preaching produced similar results. They returned back to the market of Mohill again, where the Catholics cried out, "We never heard such things before!" but in the evening many were enabled to rejoice in a sin-pardoning Saviour. After this they arrived in Longford. Here they took the street, and most of the Methodists stood about them, which many are now, in 1868, very reluctant to do in several places. The priests were enraged, and warned their flocks not to listen. Numbers, however, did hear, and heard to purpose. The missionaries told them that neither their Church, nor their *priests*, nor *masses*, nor *purgatory* could save them. Nothing but faith in the atoning blood of Christ (Heb. ix. 22) could justify them. Of the following Sabbath Mr. Graham states, "I have seen good days in Longford when I travelled the Circuit, but I never saw a better day than this."

They then visited *Killashee*, where the minister of the Established Church, on the Sunday before, denied the "witness of the Spirit," and said—" We cannot discern the ordinary operations of the Spirit from our own feelings ;" "But," says Mr. Graham, " I preached from 1 Cor. ii. 12, 'Now we have received, not the spirit of the world, but the Spirit which is of God, that we might know the things that are freely given to us of God.'" At Kenagh, another place they visited, the cries of the people were alarming, but the Lord was present to heal. Thirteen joined the Methodist Society. At Barry, a village proverbial for blasphemy, the Lord sent His blessing with the street addresses, and added *ten* to the little Society. At Ballymahon, "which," Mr. Graham states, "lies in the 'region and shadow of death,' the devil raised a tumult by sending a mad woman to annoy us. She made a horrible noise by loud blasphemy. The mob began to throw stones, encouraged by the Bishop's brother. One of the stones cut one of our friends in the head."

This appears to have been an old practice in the County Longford, and a recent one as well, as was witnessed lately in Granard. The missionaries besought the Most High to overturn the devil's kingdom in this ungodly town.

At Ballyhownas they ploughed on hard rocks, but some of them gave way at length. In Mullingar, on the market-day, they preached with their " black caps on." Nearly all the market people followed them, and among the number the *priest*, but not to hear ; rather

" To *scatter, tear,* and *slay.*"

He ran through the people like a mad dog, and strove to hunt them away. Mr. Graham spoke softly to him, on which he walked off, and they then preached. The people heard attentively. Graham and Ouseley continued here for a few days, and the Lord gave them *ten* souls "for their hire." But they had to suffer a little more in the way of persecution, for a mob shouted them out of what they call " a wicked town of ignorance and error."

From this they repaired to *Goshen*, and it was so in *reality* as well as in *name*. Here they stopped with the M'Cutcheon family, and spent " a very happy Sabbath." A rich shower of blessing descended on the little inheritance, and some were "added to the Lord and to His Holy Church by His will." At Lisduff they had to preach outside, and had "a glorious awakening." Roman Catholics as well as Protestants were alarmed, and cried for mercy. The priests here were very active to keep the people away, but they could not. Still their curse was dreaded, especially by those whose minds were only half-opened. On the 8th of June the Missionaries came to *Granard*, now a place of greater notoriety than ever. They preached in the market.

" The priest," says Mr. Graham, "spoke in his chapel against us, yet hundreds followed us as we rode through the market. The people stopped to hear, and did so with the greatest patience. We denounced purgatory, and told them of a simple cure to get rid of all this superstitious nonsense, namely, to keep a good, hard hold of their money."

The people commended them for their honest dealing and plainness, and it would appear as if *truth* so far prevailed with double sway. While at prayer there was a great sensation of deep concern through the whole street. The following portion of the prayer is recorded :—" O Lord, water the seed with the dew of Thy grace, and cause it to bring forth fruit a hundred-fold." Hundreds also followed the Missionaries to the market-house, and there they had cause to believe " their labour was not in vain in the Lord."

They returned, on the 10th of June, to Mr. Harpur's, of Drumlarney, after this very arduous tour. Mr. Graham remarks—" This country (Killeshandra Circuit) is all on fire. The work of the Lord goes on rapidly. The meeting to-night (June 10) lasted until eleven o'clock. Vast numbers saved from guilt, and others sought and obtained ' sanctifying grace.' Several Roman Catholics have been converted since we left, and have left the mass altogether. Nothing," adds Mr. Graham, " will do now but hurling the artillery of heaven against the strongholds of Babylon. Nothing else will shake her foundations, and destroy her hell-born errors." Two of the Roman Catholics were saved at this meeting. Next day Graham and Ouseley preached in the open air; and such was the deep distress of many, that they had to retire, when the shades of night came on, to a large barn, and did not leave it until twelve o'clock that night. About *forty* found peace. Four of them had been Roman Catholics. This was surely " the Lord's doings, and marvellous in *their* eyes," at that time, and marvellous in *our* eyes still. At *Ballyconnel* the ingathering was great, and many Roman Catholics heard for eternity.

At *Swanlinbar*, on the 13th June, it was still more so. The *rich* heard as well as the *poor*. The Catholics were greatly affected. At some of the meetings, many swooned away, and lay motionless for some time; but they invariably came out of it unspeakably happy; and not one injured in body or mind. Here they dealt heavy blows against the practice of the priests *quenching candles* and *ringing bells*, to excommunicate those who heard " the black caps ;" but the people said, " *The preachers tell the honest truth.*" " Yes," says Graham, "and the cause of truth, like Aaron's serpent, is swallowing up error." At *Violet Hill* the prospect was that of *millenial glory*. At *Lisbellaw* the cry of the Catholics for mercy was most affecting. It was literally a *wail*. At the next service it was still more surprising—fear and shame had fled. The Catholics cried aloud, " Have we," said they, " believed the doctrine of devils, and renounced the Gospel of God for the commandments of men?" It was the same in *Brookborough*.

We come now to the last extract of Mr. Graham's journal for this half-year, and which brings their labours up to the time of Conference, July, 1801 :—

"We accompanied Mr. Alcorn," says Graham, " to the Quarterly Meeting (or Love Feast) near Fivemiletown, on the Brookborough Circuit. Here we had a great company, which no house could hold. We took possession of a large garden; it was nearly full, and there we held the Love Feast. Oh, such an ingathering of souls! The Spirit of the Lord descended in an abundant manner. The shout of a king was heard in our camp, and the voice of new-born souls was sweet. It was a day of the Son of Man."

On their return to Brookborough, they met a man who appears, from Mr. Graham's description, to bear all the marks of Terence M'Gowan—familiarly called Terry M'Gowan—the famous cock-fighter, who lived near Maguiresbridge. His conversion was on this wise: He came to the town with a game-cock to enter that day in "the ring." On his turning the corner of the street, with the cock under his long swallow-tailed coat, two men on horseback, with "black caps," presented themselves to him. He was astonished, but more so when he heard them describe, in his own sweet-toned *Irish* language, the solemnities of the "day for which all other days were made;" together with the fearful doom of the wicked for ever, as also the joy of the righteous at God's right hand, and then urging all to an immediate surrender to Christ. Poor Terry was indeed terrified, and actually thought the day of judgment was just at hand. He also thought it was high time for him to begin to pray, and involuntarily put both hands together, and lifted them up towards heaven, and no doubt with streaming eyes. Of course the *game-cock* fled, perhaps to fall into better hands; but this was a matter of perfect indifference with Terence. He prayed, and wept, and cried aloud again and again to God for mercy, and for Christ's sake; and while pleading thus, the Lord, in compassion, spoke peace to his bewildered and alarmed conscience. Then and there he could now sing, as with buoyant heart and step he bounded home to tell his wife and children the strange *victory* he obtained, not at the cock-pit, but the one described, in the language of Charles Wesley:—

> "My God is reconciled,
>   His pardoning voice I hear,
> He owns me for His child,
>   I can no longer fear;
> With confidence I now draw nigh;
> And Father, Abba, Father, cry."

Of course his terrified wife and children did not know what to make of it, and thought he was deranged. He had all of them on their knees at once, to return thanks to God for the deliverance obtained. His wife, supposing him insane, sent one of her children to a neighbour's house, to beseech them to send immediately for the priest, for that "Terry had come home from the market out of his mind."

The priest was not long coming, and inquired of Terry "What was the matter?"

"Never better in my life," said Terry.

"Nonsense," said the priest. "Did you hear the black caps?"

"I did," said Terry, "thank God."

"So I thought," said the priest; "those fellows would set the world mad. Will you now mind your business, Terry, and go to your duty on next Sabbath?"

"I will," said Terry, "if your reverence does one thing for me."

"What is that, Terry?" said the priest.

"It is to come with me to Maguiresbridge, in order to get the Lord to undo what He did there for me to-day."

"What did He do for you there?" said the priest.

"He said to me there—'Terry M'Gowan, your sins, which are many, are all forgiven you.'"

"I give you up as a lost case," said the priest.

From that time forth Terry was allowed to go on his way rejoicing—"waxing stronger and stronger." He began to hold prayer-meetings round the country, and became a "burning and a shining light"—at least in his own plain way. He was made exceedingly useful for many years, and has long since passed away "triumphant to the skies." The writer went out of his way to see his daughter some years ago, in the County Fermanagh, and found her aged and afflicted, but very happy in God. It is most likely that all the family have landed safely ere this in "the palace of angels and God." It is said that his Roman Catholic neighbours made a hard struggle to secure a visit from the priest before he died, and when he was very feeble; but they were baffled, and when the Church of England clergyman came, he would not even allow him to use a *form* of prayer in the celebration of the Lord's Supper at his dying bed, lest it might have the slightest semblance of changing the elements; he required him to pray twice extempore, and then prayed himself, as he said he "wanted a clearer manifestation of God's countenance!" The power of God descended, and His glory filled the place. It is said that the Episcopal minister had cause to bless God for that day. Thus the Lord put honour on His servant in death as well as in life, proving that "precious in the sight of the Lord is the death of his saints." We are here reminded of the motto on Latimer's crown, "Win and wear;" and of Terry M'Gowan we would record one, in his own beloved tongue, "*Thrid she agus boohee*," that is, "He fought and conquered."

We find a condensation of the labours of Graham and Ouseley during the few closing weeks of this Methodistic year, 1801, namely, those in the end of May and the beginning of June, written by one of the Wesleyan ministers, who was an eye-witness in several places. Writing to Dr. Coke, he says:—

"The two Irish missionaries—Brothers Graham and Ouseley—met me in Carrigallen, in the County Leitrim, where we had the greatest outpouring of the Holy Spirit. Brother Ouseley preached in a field, and towards the conclusion the cry of mourners broke out. There they continued until the clouds of heaven drove us all into a large barn, where we remained a long time. Many were converted; but next day surpassed all. Brother Graham preached on a hill near Corlispratten to many hundreds. It was the Sabbath. The cry of mourners broke out again. Ah, dear sir, how *awful* to hear persons crying aloud for mercy in the open air; and how encouraging to witness many finding 'the pearl of great price!'"

We would here record what Mr. Simeon used to say—"Of all men in the world, the Christian pastor should be a man of an affectionate heart; for as well might you have a marble statue to supply the place of a real father, as a marble preacher to supply the place of a real or an affectionate pastor."

"A sermon cold and poor," says Claude, "will do more mischief in an hour than a hundred rich ones will replace."

The affectionate, glowing, sanctified heart, after all, is the true source of genuine pulpit eloquence.

Jerome used to say, "It is not the clamour of praise, but the groans of conviction, that should be heard whilst the minister preaches." And again, "The tears of the congregation form the highest praises of the pulpit orator."

Summerfield said on his death bed,—"Oh, if I might be raised again, how I could preach as I never preached before! I have had a look into eternity."

No wonder that such glorious triumphs should lead these men of God to imagine that the whole land would soon bow to the sway of truth, and sin and error speedily flee from the earth. The increase for this year in *bona fide* members of the Methodist Society was 3,065, besides many on trial and vast multitudes of congregational members! They might well labour on while thus cheered, and sing and pray—

> "Jesus, the word bestow,
>   The true, immortal seed;
> Thy Gospel then shall greatly grow,
>   And all our land o'erspread."

CHAPTER XI.

JULY, 1801, TO JULY, 1802—GENERAL MISSION.

> "Lives of great men all remind us
>   We can make our lives sublime,
> And departing leave behind us
>   Footprints on the sands of time.
>
> "Let us, then, be up and doing ;
>   Let our armour be complete ;
> Still advancing—still pursuing—
>   Learn to labour and to wait."

THE General Mission appointments of the Conference of 1801, were limited to three men, as follows :—Graham and Ouseley, Province of Ulster, with south and west; and Laurence Kane, south of Ireland. Two brethren retired to Circuit work, from ill health. The other was appointed to Circuit work also. The great and unprecedented success of the General Mission in 1800, justified the Conference in inserting in the Minutes of this year (1801) the following, in the way of question and answer. It would do credit to apostolic times, and is worthy of the brightest days of the Church of Christ. It is truly a gem of missionary intelligence :—

Ques. 1. What success has attended the Irish Missions in the last year?

Ans. 1. The success of the *Northern Mission* (on which Messrs. Graham and Ouseley laboured) has been very considerable among the Roman Catholics; and secondly, its influence has been almost unbounded in stirring up the Protestants, and has been the means of the conversion of vast numbers in connexion with the labours of the regular preachers!

2. In respect to the *Western Mission*—first, in various places in the West many hundreds, and frequently thousands, of the Roman Catholics have attended the preaching of the missionaries; and if *weeping, trembling,* and *falling down* in the streets, be marks of being awakened, or at least being deeply affected, great good has been done in this quarter. Secondly, many Protestants have been stirred up, and a considerable number converted to God.

3. In respect to the *South*—first, very large congregations of Roman Catholics attended the missionaries in general in the streets, and many followed the missionaries to the preaching-houses deeply affected. Secondly, in the city of Limerick and the neighbouring country, multitudes of Roman Catholics heard with attention: many appeared to be truly awakened, and there was every appearance of a good work.

Dr. Coke, in reviewing the labours of the two first years of this Irish General Mission, writes:—

"In my humble judgment, the whole empire is, in a political point of view, concerned in the success of this mission. I believe there is not a nobler or a more important charity than the object which it contemplates, namely, the conversion and regeneration of all Ireland. If the warm affections of the Irish can be engaged on the side of truth, they will become one of the most virtuous and religious nations on the globe."

"What a nation is this," says Mr. Wesley, in his journals, in allusion to their willingness to hear; "for every man, woman, and child, not only patiently, but gladly, suffer the word of exhortation, except a few of the great vulgar."

In another place, in allusion to one of his visits to Athlone, he says, "Rich and poor, Protestants and Papists, gathered together from every side, and deep attention sat upon all." And again he calls them "the most immeasurably loving people in the world."

In the English Address of this year to the Irish Conference, the great revival is thus recognized in the form of prayer:—"May this great revival continue to increase until Ireland flame with the love and glory of God." The increase in Ireland this year was 4,941.

A modern writer, the Rev. W. Crook, D.D., and the impassioned friend of the General Mission, asserts—"The *General Mission* should receive a generous support from our people, both in England and America. Indeed, there should be a General Missionary for each of our Provinces, and it would well repay its costs a hundred-fold. We might double or treble our membership in Ireland in a few years; and who can tell what the result would be upon the cause of Protestant Christianity in this and other lands; and especially in America!

Immediately after this Conference of 1801, Mr. Graham, accompanied by Mr. Ouseley, set out for the South, and his letter to Doctor Coke will suffice, in lieu of his journal, to show the marvellous success which attended their united labours in that part of the country:—

"MONAGHAN, *March* 17, 1802.

"REVEREND AND DEAR SIR,—We had a prosperous journey on our way to Limerick. We took the streets as we passed along. The people everywhere heard, and wept, and prayed. The Romish clergy cannot keep the people from hearing us now. A great fire broke out on the country part of the Limerick Circuit, and continues burning. Catholics have left all to follow Christ. We passed on to the County Kerry, where rich outpourings of the Holy Spirit were vouchsafed. In *Tralee* hell appeared to be let loose. (Eleven years after his first attempt there, but which appears to be forgotten.) We took the street. My voice, which is pretty strong, was drowned, the uproar was so great; and *five magistrates, officers, yoemen,* and *many Protestants* availed nothing. We had to get a guard of soldiers that evening (Sabbath) while we preached to hundreds in the Courthouse; and many of the Catholics came in spite of their clergy. One of them charged the priest "for keeping him in the dark so long." Another charged three of them, saying, "Your people are in the dark, and so would you have it." From thence we went to Skibbereen and that neighbourhood, where the work, outside and inside, was most amazing. The whole country appeared alarmed. The Catholics flocked in multitudes to hear, but on the Sabbath the priest rode furiously through the people. The crowd was great, and great numbers tumbled over each other, while he lashed them with his whip; but we kept our ground. When the hurry was over, many of them came to hear us again, and declared "they would follow us all over the world." The power of the Lord fell mightily on the people at Bantry; no opposition there but from an old woman. Satan was far gone for friends. One Catholic young woman cried aloud for mercy; and many fell, powerfully convinced, and then believed to the saving of the soul

"'Deep wounded by the Spirit's sword,
And then by Gilead's balm restored.'"

After this they spent seven hard days' labour in and about Bandon, and were abundantly repaid by numerous tokens of "power from on high," both inside and outside of doors. These were days of the Son of Man. Mr. Graham heard of the illness of his wife, and resolved to return to Monaghan, Mr. Ouseley accompanying. They sounded the alarm in every place—an alarm well calculated to awaken " the dead in trespasses and in sins." In Kinsale and Cork the Word was with great power. They travelled on horseback, in all, two hundred and thirty statute miles, in five and a half days, more than forty miles a day, and preached *morning, noon*, and *night*, thus performing a journey on horseback, perhaps unparalleled even in Irish horsemanship, considering the amount of labour included. When they arrived in Monaghan, Mr. Graham says, "I found my dear wife just recovering from the jaws of death." Mr. Graham had had no previous intimation of Mrs. Graham being so unwell, until he received the letter in Bandon; but the Lord had mercy on her, and on him also, in thus having spared to him "one of the best of wives." After spending a little time at home, they prepared for another visit to the South, as they said they did not finish their work there, which they accomplished before the Conference of 1802. In this last journey they spent twelve weeks, in the former eighteen; making *thirty* weeks in the South and East alone during the year.

Mr. Lanktree, then stationed on the Waterford Circuit, writes concerning this last visit, thus:—

"We had a visit from the Irish missionaries, Messrs. Graham and Ouseley. I took my stand with them on horseback in the street of Clonmel. They were violently opposed by the mob, but they preached, notwithstanding, with fearless fidelity. The champions of Satan put up a madman to preach in derision, but he did them no harm."

Here they laboured in the midst of great opposition for some three or four days. "Their visit," says Mr. Lanktree, "through the goodness of God, tended very much to serve the cause of truth in Clonmel and in Waterford. Their word was with power."

Just at this time several letters were flying through the kingdom relative to the extraordinary work which was spreading and prevailing east, west, north, and south. One writes from Bandon:—

"Blessed be God, I have something worthy to communicate. The Society here numbers two hundred of an increase. The flame has spread through all the Western Circuits, so that it is little less than 'a nation born in a day.'"

Another writes from Cork:—"*Poor* and *rich, profane* and *moral, scoffer* and *inquirer, Papist* and *Protestant,* all indiscriminately fall beneath the mighty power of God. In ten days no less than one hundred and seventy souls were brought to God."

Another writes from the South:—" O brother! never did any one now living see such a day as this. At Ballydehob, it seemed in one sense as the day of judgment when penitents were crying for mercy; but it was the day of salvation, for no less than sixty found peace with God. In Dunmanway thirty, and thirty added to the Society. In other places twenty-nine found the mercy of God."

Another writes from the North about the same time:— " I cannot relate the sixth part of the good work. It broke out at Newry with us. In these places, including Newry, ninety-eight found peace; on the side of the mountain seventy-two were set at liberty; and at Dungannon, in one day, sixty were converted. The Irish Missionaries," writes the last correspondent, "Graham and Ouseley, travelled this country, but two such men for an apostolic, fearless spirit, I never saw. Great success attends their ministry. At Fivemiletown, a hundred and fifty have joined the Society since they left. Prisons and death seem no more to them than liberty and life. There is a revival in all the neighbouring Circuits, namely, *Brookborough, Clones, Ballyconnell, Sligo, Enniskillen, Ballinamallard, Newtownstewart, Belfast,*" &c.

This last communication is from the pen of the Rev. M. Ridgeway.

Another preacher writes from the North, to Dr. Coke:—
"I cannot but attribute the late extraordinary revivals in the North to general missionaries. They have 'provoked us to jealousy,' and made us ashamed to stand still whilst they are labouring with all their might, both day and night. We have added two hundred and twenty-six in *Downpatrick*, and a hundred and one on trial, and about two hundred were justified."

"It was," says the Rev. W. Reilly, "at this critical period, just after the land was saturated and sickened with hostility and blood, that these heralds of grace unfurled the banner of the cross to their perishing countrymen. The very rocks and glens which reverberated with the clangour of arms and the roar of cannon, now echoed the joyful sound of the Gospel trumpet of jubilee. The very streets, which had been deluged with human gore, were now refreshed with the streams of 'the water of life.' The towns and districts which had been the theatres of sanguinary conflict, were now cheered by the proclamation of a free and full salvation, 'without money and without price;' while the rolling tide of Divine power seemed to bear down all opposition before it, wherever they came."

Oh, that the Most High would now, in 1868, baptize and send forth another band of such wayfaring men, after the feverish excitement into which this country has been plunged for the last few years. And of this there is hope, thank God. A late writer states, that "With the man of the world religion is regarded merely as a *battle*, but no *hymn;* according to the *monk* it is a mere *hymn* and not a *battle;* but according to the practical Christian, it is both a *battle* and a *hymn together.*" It was so with these men of

God; constant *conflict* and constant *triumph* marked their daily and onward career.

> "Strong in our God, and in His might,
> The Spirit's sword we wield;
> And in His name abide the fight
> On our own battle field."

CHAPTER XII.

GENERAL MISSION—MEANS ADOPTED FOR A MORE EXTENSIVE REVIVAL.

> " And whilst Thou dost smile upon me,
>   God of wisdom, love, and might,
> Foes may hate and friends deceive me—
>   Show Thy love, and all is right.
>
> " Go, then, earthly fame and treasure,
>   Come disaster, scorn, and pain ;
> In Thy service pain is pleasure,
>   With Thy favour love is gain."

THE General Mission appointments for this year were as follows :—

"Connaught and the County Clare—LAURENCE KANE, THOMAS ALLEN.
"The rest of Munster, Leinster, and Connaught—CHARLES GRAHAM, GIDEON OUSELY."

The increase for this last year in the Irish connexion amounted to 2,467, which, added to the two former years, make exactly the amazing number of 10,473!—and that in three years!! Well may we exclaim, "What hath God wrought!" We can now see the kind hand of our God in all this, if it were nothing else but to cheer the hearts of His servants, who bore so patiently the burden and the heat of the day." It was at the risk of life they travelled through the kingdom during the past three or four years, and especially in travelling to and from Conference.

In the Irish Address to the English Conference for this year (1802) the following is recorded:—"Two thousand souls and upwards were added to our numbers this last year, among whom were several poor Catholics, now worshipping God in spirit and in truth. Thus has a gracious Providence favoured us hitherto, and especially so during the last year."

These two missionaries, now *chiefs* in the mission field, and giant champions for truth, having been appointed principally to the eastern part of the kingdom, immediately set out for *Wicklow*, *Wexford*, *Kildare*, *Carlow*, and *Kilkenny*. In *Enniscorthy*, near to which stands the famous Vinegar Hill, and where so much blood was wantonly shed, they took their stand in the principal street, mounted on their horses, with their black caps on. They first sung a hymn, which had a wonderful effect. Then they "preached the Word," which fell with great power on all who heard it; and some of the fruit remains to this very year, as the writer lately found out in a visit to that town. And no wonder. They went fresh from their knees in private, where they pleaded for the baptism of fire, and inflamed with a Saviour's dying love, they hastened to the rescue of the slaves of sin and hell, and then preached with "the Holy Ghost sent down from heaven." Yea,

"With cries, entreaties, tears, to save,
To snatch them from the gaping grave."

They had not, however, the same success or tranquillity in Wexford, for while Mr. Ouseley was preaching, a mason on a scaffold pelted him with stones, which was near costing

7*

the stone-thrower his life, for another desperado, in *his* way, rushed forward to pull down the ladder. Had this been done, the mason would soon have had little power to throw stones again. But Mr. Ouseley observed the act, and cried out, "*Let him alone.*" During this tour they preached *nineteen* times in the streets of *sixteen* towns, besides the sermons inside! Many Roman Catholics heard, and when any one disturbed the preachers, others came forward and quelled the rioters. Several were in each place awakened. In *Hacketstown* the priest passed by quietly, and all remained; the whole street was filled; tracts were taken eagerly. At *Fethard* two Catholic girls were cut to the heart. One of these was bribed for a while. The priest gave her three guineas,—"But she has since," says Mr. Graham, "given them the slip, and followed us four miles in deep distress of mind. I hope many more have received the seed of the kingdom. Our way was opened everywhere, until we came to *Kilkenny*; but here they were bent on murdering us. I got several bruises. The whole city was in an uproar. It was fearful to witness the flinging of stones, and to hear the *shouting*. We found shelter in the barrack, but it required all the power of the mayor and the commanding officer to escort us on safely out of the city. Some of the mob went before us to stone us again! I greatly pitied them," says Graham; "for how will they ever see the light unless it is thus brought publicly before them?"

"I wrote," says Mr. Ouseley, "to the Catholic bishop, and expostulated with him on the barbarity of his people. After this we took the street of Athy, and had a blessed time. We are greatly worn down, and Brother Graham had to keep his bed for some days."

We may surely appy these lines of Charles Wesley—

> "The tokens of thy love
> On every side we see,
> And crowds begotten from above
> Stretch out their hands to Thee."

FROM JULY, 1803, TO JULY, 1804.

The appointments for this year are as follows :—

"IRISH MISSIONARIES.

"The Counties of Limerick, Tipperary, Mayo, Galway, and Clare— CHARLES GRAHAM, GIDEON OUSELEY."

We see from the number of the missionaries being thus reduced, that Dr. Coke's resources must have failed. The demands on him from the foreign stations were very numerous, but he more than made up for this declension, as we will find during the following eight or ten years.

Mr. Reilly states, that "during this year they were acknowledged in every place, and some of the Circuits were remarkably visited by the power and presence of God."

Mr. Lanktree also states of this year—" In *Carlow*, during this second visit, they preached both in the street and in the chapel. The word of life was blessedly triumphant. Their preaching in the *colliery* was attended with the power of God. Prejudice and opposition were borne down by the influence of truth and love. *Twenty* persons have joined the Society."

In *Kilkenny* their reception was now of a different character to the former. Both clergy and laity, to their credit, hailed their visit with delight. The ringleaders in the previous disturbance had been imprisoned. Thus might they confidently trust and sweetly sing—

> "Through waves, and clouds, and storms,
>   He gently clears thy way;
> Wait thou His time, so shall this night
>   Soon end in joyous day."

Thus did they spend this laborious, but happy and successful year of hallowed toil.

During this year the venerable **John Johnston**, of Lisburn, passed triumphantly home, in the seventy-ninth year of his age. He was employed by **Mr. Wesley** for some time as general superintendent of our connexion in Ireland. Some of his last words were—"I can look back with joy on the day when Mr. Whitfield preached from the text, 'Christ our passover is sacrificed for us.' Whether I was in the body or out of the body, I could not tell; but when I appear before my Saviour, I will cast my crown at His feet." He soon beheld the God he loved so long. (See Minutes, 1803, vol. i., page 168.)

In the Minutes for the year 1804, vol. i., page 175, we have a most important question proposed, to which there are nine important directions by way of answers given; and it is hoped we may be excused for introducing them here, at least in part:—

Ques. 23. What can be done for the revival of the work of God in Ireland?

Ans. 1. **Let** us humble ourselves before God. The revival must begin with ourselves. Let us use self-denial.

2. Let us be more careful **in** giving to God, through Jesus Christ, **the entire** glory **of** all **the** good wrought **in** and **by us.** He must be our "all in all."

3. Let us, as preachers, be more simple, **evangelical,** practical, and zealous in our preaching.

4. Let us not aim at what sermon-hunters call "*fine preaching*," in order to be popular.

5. Let us frequently insist on the doctrine of original sin. It is not stale or worn out; it is fundamental.

6. Let us, above all things, be zealous to bring our **hearers to the** fountain opened for sin and uncleanness.

7. Let us **press** upon believers the necessity of increasing in holiness, and of dying daily and walking with God.

8. Let us faithfully preach practical holiness, and **tear the mask** from the face of the hypocrite.

9. Let us never omit a pointed, faithful, yet loving application at the close of our sermons.

JULY, 1804, TO JULY, 1805.

"The appointments for the General Mission this year are:—
"Province of Connaught and Leinster—CHARLES GRAHAM, GIDEON OUSELEY.
"Province of Ulster—WILLIAM HAMILTON, JAMES BELL."

This was the sixth appointment of Graham and Ouseley to be companions in honour and dishonour, and never did two yoke-fellows work so freely or so lovingly. Mr. Graham became unwell after the Conference.

Mr. Ouseley writes to Dr. Coke thus:—"Brother Graham is blessedly recovered, and we mean to set out to-morrow for our destination, namely, Counties Wicklow and Wexford first. I hope we shall have a good year. I dreamed last night that I was preaching and weeping over poor sinners. I have often found it so these five years past. I hope our dear friends and brethren will, as I believe they do, continue to help us in their constant prayers.".

Thus prepared, they started, and prosecuted the year's labour with unabated ardour. Prejudices were giving way in every direction, and Gospel truth bearing glorious sway even where the greatest obstacles opposed. In Carlow, whilst they preached in the street and in the chapel, the word of life was again triumphant—twenty persons gave in their names to meet in Society. In Kilkenny, where the missionaries were formerly ill-treated, they are now honoured. Indeed, they were greatly honoured and abundantly successful everywhere this year—as if the Lord would specially and signally mark the last year of their united toil with His richest blessings. In one place *ten* or *twelve* joined Society, six of whom were Romanists. In another place *thirty* joined class, of whom two were Catholics. In this place there was a great revival. In another town twenty-one joined the Methodist Society. During the latter end of this year they paid a third visit to Kilkenny, and the record of it is—"Several members were added to the Society;" and on the Carlow Circuit "there were one hundred and fifty added, and many of them savingly converted to God."

During this year, 1805, Mr. Graham received a letter from a highly respectable lady, who lived in Coleraine, but was now at Dungannon on a visit. She was brought to God through his instrumentality. The following is an extract:—

"Many thanks to my dear Brother Graham for his kind and very acceptable letter of the 13th inst. Blessed be God, who has done much for me, and kept my face Zionward. I think I take delight in everything whatsoever that has a tendency to promote His glory and honour. The more I know of my Lord and Saviour the more I delight in Him and in all His ways. I do determine, with the assistance of His Holy Spirit, to take up my cross daily and follow Him.

"I was truly thankful to hear from you that the work of the Lord was in so prosperous a way, and I sincerely pray that the

Lord may abundantly reward you both—(including Mr. Ouseley)—for your work of labour in His vineyard. On last Sunday we were favoured with two of the missionaries—Messrs. Hamilton and Bell. They preached at four o'clock, p.m., in the street, and in the house at seven. They read over their 'Journals,' of what had passed since they set out. Next day was the Quarterly Meeting (Love Feast.) I think that the power of the Lord was much there. It reminded me of the first Sunday you preached in Coleraine. There were numbers of penitents, both men and women, crying aloud for mercy. Such a sight I never saw before! Some found pardon before I left, about three o'clock. Others remained until near the evening service.

"Remember me, with much regard and good wishes, to your son and daughter; also to Brother and Sister Ouseley, who, I hope, are as well as I wish them to be.

"I remain, my dear Brother Graham, wishing you every happiness, spiritual and temporal, your truly affectionate friend and sister in the Lord Jesus,

"ELIZA OULD."

The period is now fast approaching when those two kindred spirits—Graham and Ouseley—must part; the very anticipation of which must have affected each other very keenly. They had travelled thousands of miles together—slept hundreds of times together—endured the rigours of winter and the heat of summer together—shared each other's trials and triumphs—preached thousands of sermons in each other's hearing—and, best of all, witnessed thousands of conversions together: and yet we never hear a word of jealousy, or even the breath of suspicion, to cause either a moment's pain. For this, we "glorify the grace of God in them." Their love was that of David and Jonathan; but still there may have been great wisdom in the act of separation,—each taking a young man, and thereby more effectually perpetuating and extending the missionary spirit.

Accordingly, at the approaching Conference, they were to be told off to different parts of the country, each with his new colleague, and the missionary staff to be greatly augmented. Very likely the state of the missionary exchequer was in a more healthy condition than it was previously, for we find no less than eight men paired off, as if to take the kingdom by storm.

They stand thus in the Minutes for July, 1805, to 1806 :—

"IRISH MISSIONARIES.

"Dublin and Cork Districts, and their vicinity—WILLIAM HAMILTON, GIDEON OUSELEY.

"Limerick and Athlone Districts, and vicinities—CHARLES GRAHAM, ANDREW TAYLOR.

"Belfast and Newry Districts, and vicinities—SAMUEL ALCORN, JAMES BELL.

"Londonderry District, and adjoining country—JOHN HAMILTON, WILLIAM PEACOCK."

Of William Hamilton,—Mr. Ouseley's colleague, as recorded above,—it is stated : " In his sermons there were frequent strokes of wit and keen invention, which fixed the attention ; and then, by terrifying appeals to the conscience, he would make the sinner tremble, as if he stood near the awful mount while the thunder rolled and the lightning flashed around him, constraining him to cry aloud,—' What must I do to be saved ?' With others, his mode of elucidating Scripture and its application would be considered eccentric ; with him they were ' apples of gold in pictures of silver,'—for instance, he once said, ' The devil played with the card of God's *foreknowledge* with our mother Eve, and won the game.' Again, ' I have a letter here from a Saint for any one who knows his sins forgiven.' "— (1 John ii. 12.)

CHAPTER XIII.

GRAHAM AND OUSELEY ARE APPOINTED TO DIFFERENT DISTRICTS—1806.

> "Toil on, toil on; and thou shalt find
> For labour, rest—for exile, home;
> Soon shalt thou hear the Bridegroom's voice,
> The midnight peal, 'Behold, I come.'"

Now as these venerable men, Graham and Ouseley, had to part, they, no doubt, could realize the lines which they often sung before—

> "And let our bodies part,
> To different climes repair;
> Inseparably joined in heart
> The friends of Jesus are.
> O let us still proceed
> In Jesu's work below;
> And following our triumphant Head,
> To further conquests go."

Messrs. Graham and Taylor started for the Midland Counties, while Messrs Ouseley and Hamilton repaired to the South. It appears to have been a year of great affliction to Mr. Graham, by reason of the death of his beloved wife. This mournful event must have taken place in the spring of the year 1806. Although we have no record on which to rely—many of Mr. Graham's papers having been lost—but from a letter which Mrs. Ousely writes to young Mr. Graham, in which she alludes to his mother "being now happy," we must conclude that she passed away some time previously. The letter is too valuable to be omitted. It does credit to the head and heart of the good lady who wrote it.

"SLIGO, *August 30th*, 1806.

"MY VERY DEAR FRIEND AND BROTHER,—I fear by this time you are beginning to say, that I am an ungrateful creature; do not say so, for I am not, I assure you. I remember with gratitude your kind attention to me. I find the people here are very affectionate. Some of your friends wept a good deal when they saw me, as your dear mother and I used to be together formerly; but she is happy, and you and I are still spared. O let us, my dear Charles, examine, are we living to please ourselves, or our God? It would be an awful thing to be separated in the great day from our good God, and our dear friends who are in glory. There is surely a revival of the work of God here. On Sunday week we had a field-meeting, and much good was done. Old and young backsliders were restored to the favour of God. I love long letters, and I love to have something said in praise of the heavenly country we are journeying to—mind this. I hope to hear you have attended class, and that your soul is prospering. Oh, do, my dear child, suffer one that loves you to urge you to attend to that comfortable means of grace. My dear Ouseley is about Ballina and Killala at present. The Lord is doing wonders. I expect him soon. We are to have another field-meeting in a week. I wish I had you here, and I am sure you would be the better of seeing the poor simple folk coming with all their sins to their offended Father. It has done me good. Be sure you come to us at Christmas. May every purchased blessing be yours, my dear child, for time and eternity. So prays your affectionate friend and sister,

"HT. OUSELEY."

This painful bereavement must have greatly affected both father and son; for they were all three greatly bound up in each other's fondest love. Mrs. Graham, no doubt, died as she lived, "looking for the mercy of our Lord Jesus Christ unto eternal life."

> "Happy soul, thy days are ended,
> All thy mourning days below :
> Go, by angel guards attended,
> To the sight of Jesus, go !"

We have little or no record of this year, except what is stated in the Address of the Irish to the English Conference. It is this :—" In many parts of the country much good has been done during the past year, by the preaching of the Word. A spirit of hearing has been excited in the minds of the people of almost all descriptions, insomuch that inconvenience of time (season) or place could not prevent hundreds from assembling in the streets. These encouraging openings will, we doubt not, be productive of the greatest benefit to mankind."

Miss Ould, of Coleraine, writes to Mr. Graham again. The following is an extract :—

"Your letter revived my soul very much ; it was a reviving balm. May the Lord bless and reward you with His best of blessings. Brother J. Stewart is a good young man, and a good preacher; he will have to exert himself very much here. The world is getting a great hold of some of our members. I am rejoiced to hear of all the good the Lord is making you the instrument of doing. It is a blessed employment to be an ambassador for the Lord Jesus. May you be crowned with success this year also. I am sure I have reason to bless and praise the Lord for ever having sent you to Coleraine, as you and dear Brother Ouseley were the instruments of bringing me, a poor, proud, vain sinner, out of darkness ; and, blessed be His holy name, I have never had the least desire to return to the world again. I only regret that I have it not in my power to do more for my Father's kingdom. I am just thinking what a happiness it will be when we and all the dear followers of the Lord shall meet, never more to part. May God of his infinite mercy grant this to be our case. Continue to pray for me as I shall do for you.

"ELIZA OULD."

JULY 1806.

At the Conference of this year there were ten men appointed to the General Mission work. It would appear that its popularity was increasing year by year. They were stationed thus:—

1. The Dublin District—ALCORN and BELL.
2. The Cork District—GRAHAM and TAYLOR.
3. The Limerick and Athlone Districts—W. HAMILTON and OUSELEY.
4. The Belfast and Newry Districts—KERR and M'CORD.
5. The Londonderry District—J. HAMILTON and W. PEACOCK."

Immediately after the Conference, Mr. Graham wrote to his son in Dublin, from Bandon, thus:—

"There is a *stir* in Bandon; but in Kerry, where we were lately, there are both convictions and conversions. Thank God, who did not suffer us to labour in vain, or spend our strength for nought. Oh, may we be grateful and humble. If *Lorenzo* is in Dublin, give him my love. I am glad to hear that he can labour there now. Remember me to the preachers. They are friends of mine. May they prosper abundantly."

The preachers were Lanktree, M'Mullen, William Stewart, Kerr, and A. Hamilton.

Of Lorenzo Dow, Mr. Lanktree remarks:—"I knew he had been made a blessing to many, and that God was with him; but with his eccentricities or infirmities I have nothing to do. But I know that he sent twenty-seven persons to me in one body to join our Society; perhaps most of these were converted to God. Among them are Mrs. C—— and her amiable daughter H——, now the well-known and esteemed wife of one of our most efficient preachers."

Mr. Lanktree, no doubt, here alludes to the late Mrs. Waugh, of Bandon, who was the first fruit of Lorenzo's labours. Mr. Ouseley writes of him thus, from Sligo, to Mr. Lanktree:—"I do, indeed, enjoy the tidings of the appearance of a revival in Dublin, and that the Lord is so manifestly blessing Lorenzo's labours."

In another place Mr. Lanktree says:—"Lorenzo was with us three days. How many were born of God I cannot tell. Not less than two hundred persons came forward to join our Society within this fortnight. We had a glorious Quarterly Meeting (Love Feast) in Carlow. Many hearts were rent, and some made happy." Lorenzo Dow was an American preacher.

"This year (1806) was one of great persecution," says Mr. Hamilton, Mr. Ouseley's companion. "At Eyrecourt, County Galway, and near the Shannon, we preached in the street, and had a battle with both priest and people, who beat my horse greatly, and threw him down on the street, and I on his back. Ouseley was hurt, and lost his hat in the fray. I thought we should never leave the spot alive. The soldiers were called out with loaded guns and fixed bayonets. They formed a square, until we preached again to the market people, and then they conducted us out of town; but some of the persecutors got before us, and shouted as if *Scullabogue barn* was on fire. We were robbed of our books, and only escaped with our lives." And then he apostrophizes thus—"Cruel mockings are nothing, and showers of stones are but child's play; but *bloodshed* and *battery* are no joke."

But in the midst of all this they were cheered by remarkable instances of conversion among both rich and poor, even in that very neighbourhood, and in other places also. The conversion of the Rev. Mr. Caldwell, the Presbyterian minister of Sligo, and his joining the Society, cheered them greatly. Mr. Caldwell did not leave his own body, but he attended the Class-meetings and Love-feasts of the Methodists; and his "experience" was of the richest type.

At this time also, Mr. Ouseley had to contend with great difficulties, in consequence of what were called "The Thrashers." They rose to a great head, and marauded the whole country at night. He says, "The Thrashers have come upon my poor mare, but they have only taken off her fore shoes, and the hair off her tail. Thanks be to God for His care of us in this troubled county, Sligo." In another place he says, "The people were afraid to receive me. My grieved soul complained to the Lord against Satan, and next day a respectable Romanist cried aloud, and prayed most vehemently; and when I was arranging for some stopping-places, he spoke out and said, 'Come, sir, to my house two days in the week, and welcome indeed. I don't care a straw for the priest! Not I, indeed!' I preached in a day or two after, in a fair in the mountains, among the Thrashers, and now they gave me thousands of blessings, and warned the priest to let *Ouseley* alone any more."

The Conference record, in its Address to the British Conference at the close of this year (1806), in reference to the results of this General Mission work, is as follows:—

"The joy you feel at the success of our missionaries, greatly encourages us to persevere in this very arduous undertaking; and we have the pleasure of informing you, that three additional missionaries have been engaged in the blessed work this year. To your kind exertions, and the generosity of the good people of England (under God), thousands of souls in this country are indebted for the light of the Gospel. May God reward you all a thousand-fold. The Lord greatly owns the missionaries. May Almighty God still uphold them, and prosper their way more and more."

In the answer of the British Conference, we have the following :—" In the success of the missionaries, we greatly rejoice, and congratulate you on the pleasing prospect which opens before you. Our prayers shall not be wanting in your behalf, that your labours in this blessed undertaking may abundantly prosper. Even so, Lord Jesus. Amen."

We must here refer to one or two circumstances of an interesting character, which took place in connection with Mr. Ouseley about this time. They are recorded in his *Memorial*, by Mr. Reilly. It appears that a Methodist class-meeting was established by Mr. Ouseley in a dark part of the County Clare, and that a leader was appointed to meet it who had to come from a distance. Some of the Romanists hearing that "a new religion" was to be thus imported to the country, resolved to destroy the house where the class was met. Accordingly, having watched the leader's movements, this party followed him on a Sabbath morning, resolving to make short work of this "new sect." They besieged the house, and sent in the ringleader to watch the movements, and to give the signal for their entrance at the proper time; but, to the great surprise of the gang outside, Pat did not reappear as soon as they expected. They were utterly confused and disappointed. The hymn was first given out and sung. "This is very *purty*"—pretty— said Pat; "I'll not disturb them yet." Prayer was offered up. "I'll let them alone until they have done with their prayers," said he to himself. The class began, and he said to himself, "I'll hear what they have to say." The leader at length accosted the rude stranger thus:—"My good man, did you ever know yourself a sinner before God, and that you deserved to be for ever excluded from His presence?"

Pat wept exceedingly, and cried out,—"Lord have mercy upon me! What shall I do? I'm a wicked sinner."

The whole meeting joined in earnest prayer for him, and very soon Pat was "sitting at the feet of Jesus," quiet, and in his right mind. What wonders grace can do!

"I knew him afterwards," says Mr. Reilly, "as noble an advocate for truth as he had been before a daring opposer."

The *banditti* decamped with all speed, when they heard Pat's cries, all of them exclaiming, "The devil is among the Methodists." It was surely "the Lord's doing, and marvellous in our eyes." This was quite in character with the account of the man in the County Wexford (of whom Dr. Stephens writes), who concealed himself in a sack at a Methodist meeting, that he might give a signal at a certain time to some outside to enter, and scatter, if not injure, the congregation. But the poor fellow in the sack found the preaching too powerful to lie quiet any longer, and at length he cried aloud for mercy. Some thought the devil was in the sack, and were afraid to go near it; but at length he was extricated, and came forth, to the astonishment of all, a partaker of Gospel freedom. The house was pointed out to the writer last June, where this occurred. How wonderful are the ways of the Lord, in thus "making the wrath of man to praise Him!"

The other circumstance in reference to Mr. Ouseley, about this time, occurred in *Granard*. It appears that Mr. Ouseley preached in the street, and that a person of the name of Caulfield threw missiles at him—an exploit not forgotten there yet—for which some persons gave Caulfield a severe chastisement at the time. He summoned those parties, and Mr. Ouseley summoned him. The cases were sent for trial. His bill was thrown out, but Mr. Ouseley's was found. Caulfield was found guilty, and sent to jail; while Mr. Ouseley came off victorious, and was found preaching at five o'clock in the morning, in the street, to a considerable number of labourers, waiting to be employed, and then went into the chapel to preach at six.

Mr. Lanktree remarks, "Often has my soul been roused by the unquenchable zeal and abundant labours of these men of God, the missionaries."

Mr. Ouseley writes again to Mr. Lanktree from the County Sligo. We give an extract :—

"I know it will be gratifying to you and my friends to mention the most striking occurrences. First, we are getting all the single people we can, with the children, to commit the holy Scriptures. Secondly, the Lord favours me in witnessing many conversions and lively meetings everywhere; many weeping, and many shouting the praises of God, and this in the midst of troublesome times. Hallelujah. In one place ten or twelve Romanists joined the Society, in spite of the curses of the priest, which he (the priest) said, 'Will make the hair of your head to fall off, and no ointment when dying.' While I was preaching on 'False prophets,' the Lord greatly blessed it to two souls who found peace. One exclaimed, 'O, the priest, the priest! why is he hindering us from all this comfort and sweetness ' Next day a large barn was filled, and it was 'heaven on earth.'"

CHAPTER XIV.

MR. GRAHAM RETURNS TO CIRCUIT WORK.
1807 TO 1812.

> "Sow ye beside all waters,
>   Where the dew of heaven may fall;
>   Ye shall reap, if ye be not weary,
>   For the Spirit breathes on all."

AT the Conference of this year Mr. Graham was appointed to the Athlone Circuit, having now finished seventeen years of hard labour; and eight of these on the General Mission, which he loved so much. In all, including from the time he became a local preacher, thirty-six years. The Athlone Circuit, or, as it was formerly called, "The Athlone Round," contained a tract of country now divided into several Circuits and Missions. There is no record left of his labours during this year. It is is said he was requested by Conference to place his papers in the hands of a Mr. Roger Lamb, of Dublin, for revision, and that many of them were thereby mislaid. The writer knew Mr. Lamb. He wrote a history of the American war, having passed through it himself. He was very quaint but talented, and truly pious, somewhat like the late James Field, of Cork. The writer heard Mr. Lamb say to a brother who had declined in religion, "Come again, brother; a cracked bell can never be mended; it must be run over again." To another he said, " Brother, we must be pitched within and without, like Noah's Ark."

Mr. Graham's next appointment was Mallow (1808), with Mr. John Wilson, who died in 1813. The record of his death (in part) is, " A man of piety and genuine simplicity." This was the very Circuit (Mallow) which was first formed by Graham himself, in the year 1791, seventeen years before. There can be no doubt but he must have had many pleasing recollections of his first labours in that country. The Circuit had now 246 members in it. During the previous year the increase in Ireland was nearly one thousand members. While Mr. Graham was thus labouring in the South, Mr. Ouseley was working hard in the West. He writes to Mr. Lanktree thus :—

"You inform me of three thousand souls being brought to God in one American meeting.* Hallelujah! If my brethren would send me to the East—where I hear there have been thousands of professing Christians discovered, and uncorrupted by Popery—I would be willing to go and die there. I saw a letter last week from brother Peacock, of the Milltown Circuit, saying that the Quarterly Meeting (Love Feast) in that town lasted from Friday until the Tuesday following. The Lord's power was great. Brother Tobias is all on fire in Coleraine. Good news from the missionaries. J. Hamilton and Bell are in those quarters. The North is giving up, and the South is not keeping back. About one hundred have been added in the Giant's Causeway."

The increase this year was 1,300. The record of Conference is, " Our missionaries are still much owned of the Lord."

* See Appendix B.

1809.

Mr. Graham remains in Mallow this year also. Of his labours I have no record. But during the year the missionaries seem to have been greatly acknowledged of God, although labouring in some of the most destitute parts of the kingdom. **Mr. Ouseley** writes, after a very severe illness, to Mr. **Lanktree**, then stationed in Armagh :—

"I must contrast my Circuit with yours. Yours is to range through meadows fair, and fields productive of crops, to make the tiller's heart to dance, while meandering crystal streams and sweet fruits cluster all around—such **is yours!** But to have the huge rocks, hard as adamant, wild deserts, where savage beasts seek their prey, and scarcely a green herb, or sprig, or fruit is found—how **dreary** is the sight, when the **poor** traveller does not know where to **rest his** weary head! How dismal the contrast; and such **is ours.** And yet, glory to God, **the** solitary **places** are become **glad, and the** desert is beginning to sing and **blossom as** the rose—friendship **and** good-will are beginning to appear. **We** have now twenty-four stopping places and about sixty members. Still I was greatly humbled lately, in beholding a sight such as I had never witnessed, near Gort, in the County Galway, and that under the name of religion—men and women promiscuously, in the most indecent and unbecoming manner, walking on their bare knees over rough gravel and stones, and their hands clasped over their heads, lest they should in their progress **derive** any assistance from them. You could have traced their track **by the blood** that streamed, **yea,** that flowed **from their** mangled knees. **In** another stage of the penance, some were running round the **extensive** ruins (old buildings). Others descending into a **narrow cell** called '**Purgatory,**' not unlike **that described** in Lough Derg. At a distance on the plain stood the stump **of a large** tree, which I had been told, for the most part, was cut away **piecemeal,** as affording a charm against every evil."

Such are the frightful superstitions by which thousands in our unhappy country are deluded. When Mr. Ouseley asked **the** guide of the whole scene why was the tree so much cut away, he said that the saint of the place, Macduagh, travelled round the world on his knees until he came to that spot, where there was a tree, and that there his girdle fell of—that the tree received such virtue that a bit of it would preserve him from sickness, from fire, and all accidents.

"Do, Sir," said he, to Mr. Ouseley, "take a bit of it yourself; it will keep you from harm of every kind."

"Thank you," said Mr. Ouseley, "I shall not mind it now; but where is the original tree?"

"It is all cut away, Sir, but the one that is there now is as good. Do, Sir, take a piece." But when Mr. Ouseley appeared unyielding, he added, "Ah, Sir, you are not Irish, but English."

Mr. Ouseley said he never was in England.

"If not," said the man, "you surely belong to them; so you do."

Mr. Ouseley departed with deep regret and indignation at such a soul-destroying system, and with his sympathies of compassion more roused than ever. Let no one ever blame him for having his hatred to it intensified to the extent it was when he called it "*the dire apostacy.*"

At the Conference of this year, 1810, the missionaries were increased to twelve, thus showing that the mission was becoming more and more popular every year. Mr. Graham who was the *first* who, in a *special* sense, assumed the position of general missionary in the county of Kerry twenty years before, is still content to fill the narrower sphere of a Circuit preacher. We find him now in *Longford* again, with the Rev. George Stevenson as his colleague—a man of deep piety, as gentle as a child, and a sound divine. Mr. Graham travelled here in 1798.

The Rev. Mr. Harrison, a clergyman of the Church of England, at Naas, in the County Kildare, died this year, **1810.** His conversion was the fruit of the General Mission in the year 1806, through the instrumentality of the Rev. Messrs. Alcorn and Bell. It is well recorded in the *Irish Wesleyan Magazine* for that year, and still more minutely by the Rev. W. Reilly, in his brief but admirable *Memorial* of Mr. Ouseley, thus—"In the autumn of 1806, Messrs. Alcorn and Bell, as at other times, preached in the streets **of Naas.** The Rev. Isaac Harrison was among the hearers. Mr. Harrison was a gentleman of accomplished mind, and ranked amongst the most celebrated advocates of the **charitable** institutions of the day. Mr. Alcorn preached from Matt. ix. 37, 38, 'The harvest truly is plenteous,' &c. The Word was accompanied by Divine power to the heart of Mr. Harrison, and after the sermon he came forward and addressed the preacher thus :—' I am a clergyman of the Church of England, but, alas! although a minister for twenty years, I have been one of those idlers you have described in your sermon.' Mr. Bell then preached also, after which Mr. Harrison invited both of them to his house, **where they** found a large party of ladies and gentlemen engaged at the card-table. The missionaries were introduced. The cards were soon removed, and the Bible **was laid on the** table. Mr. Harrison requested Mr. **Alcorn to** sing **the** hymn by which he had been so much affected on the street. While doing so, every heart heaved with emotion; every cheek was suffused with tears. He was requested to sing it again. He did so with equal, if not, with greater effect. Mr. Alcorn then engaged in prayer, and on that occasion Mr. Harrison received the indubitable witness of his acceptance with God—which he never afterwards lost. The whole family became 'heirs with him of the grace of eternal life.' The scene can be better imagined than described. From that day his house became 'the house of prayer,' and his motto was that of Joshua—'But as for me and my house, we will serve the Lord.'—(Joshua xxiv. 15.) His whole parish soon felt the benefit of this delightful change; but his career was short. He caught a fever in visiting one of his parishioners, and died in the full triumph of faith."

Shortly after his conversion he wrote to Mr. Alcorn. The following is an extract from this letter:—

"I reckon that a blessed day in which I met with you. It is a day that always returns with additional pleasure and internal comfort to my soul. Eternal thanks to God. O may I be the humble means of saving, if but one soul, from the pains of eternal death. We should unremittingly 'pray the Lord of the harvest that he would send forth labourers into his harvest.'"

A few days after his death his son and successor, the Rev. John Harrison, wrote to Mr. Alcorn, in which communication he says:—

"The public papers must have announced to you the decease of one who was your son in the Gospel, my dear father. He was brought from death to spiritual life, so that God was his Father by the Spirit, and Jesus his full Saviour. The love of Christ which was shed abroad in his heart made him happy in death, and it did cast out fear. The Sabbath meetings shall not be forgotten."

He here refers to those meetings established by his father from the time of his conversion, and conducted in a room belonging to the diocesan school, to the great edification and delight of many. The present writer may here remark that he called on the Rev. Mr. Harrison, jun., in Naas, about thirty years after the death of his father, and found him a well-disposed, and much respected clergyman. He conversed freely about his venerated parent, and inquired for many of the missionaries whom he knew in early life. He also died soon after. The writer may state that at that time (1838) he took the street in Naas, and preached, and the Lord soon raised up a considerable cause, which flourished for a season, until the famine came, and drove our principal friends to America and elsewhere. We trust it will soon revive again. The following is the hymn which was sung by Mr. Alcorn, and which first attracted Mr. Harrison, when walking carelessly along the street with some other gentlemen—

"From Salem's gate, advancing slow,
   What object meets my eyes?
What means this majesty of woe?
   What mean those mingled cries?

Who can it be? Who groans beneath
   That ponderous cross of wood?
Whose soul's o'erwhelm'd in fears of death;
   Whose body's bathed in blood.

Is this the Man? Can this be He
   The prophets have foretold?—
Should with transgressors numbered be,
   And for my crimes be sold?

O lovely sight! O heavenly form,
   For sinful souls to see!
I'll creep beside Him as a worm,
   And see Him die for me.

I'll view his wounds and hear His groans,
   Until, with happy John,
I on his breast a place may find
   To lean my head upon."

We find Mr. Graham stationed in the year 1811 on the Cavan Circuit, with Mr. Gustavus Armstrong, of whom honourable mention is made by the Conference thus:—" A man of great integrity and truth; a sincere and unalterable friend; and it was rarely known that, in the long space of more than forty years as an itinerant preacher, he ever quitted a Circuit without leaving it better than he found it. When asked, 'Are you afraid to die?' he answered, 'No, blessed be God, I am not.'" During this year we have three or four letters from Mr. Graham to his son, extracts from which will show that the fire of heavenly love and zeal still continued to burn in his breast with unabated ardour. The first is dated—

"BELTURBET, *July* 28, 1811 (*Cavan Circuit*).

"MY DEAR CHARLES,—I trust I shall spend my time to some profit among this people. Many rejoice to see me again, as I laboured a good deal among them when a missionary, and the fruits of our labours still remain. I had a blessed Sabbath morning in this town yesterday. Here we have a very respectable society. The judgments of the Lord are a great deep. [He refers to family affliction.] We may strive to fathom them, but strive in vain. It is only eternity which will fully reveal them to His children; but at the worst of times they are mingled with mercy; and who more favoured than I have been through all the changing scenes of life! I have clearly seen His hand conducting and preserving me.—Your ever affectionate father, "CHARLES GRAHAM."

The next letter of those to which we referred is dated—

"BROOKBORO', *October* 4, 1811.

"MY DEAR CHARLES,—I am on the Brookboro' Circuit, begging money for a preaching-house in Belturbet,* and I have to travel through the Clones and Monaghan Circuits; and you will think that by this time my face will be pretty well hardened at the work. Oh, that God may help me to do every work to His own glory.—I am, as ever, your affectionate father, "CHARLES GRAHAM."

---

* The Conference note is—"Brothers G. Armstrong and Graham are to raise subscriptions on the Clones, Monaghan, Brookboro', and Cavan Circuits, for the Belturbet preaching-house."—(Minutes, vol. i., 1811, page 264.)

8*

Another reads thus:—

"Thank God, we have nothing to complain of with respect to health and peace; and as to the other blessings of this life, we know no want. The Lord has hitherto helped us, and He will help; 'for He his good, and His mercy endureth for ever.' I hope you feel it your duty and interest to give yourself unreservedly to Him. Till then there can be do real peace or happiness in this world. I pray the Lord of His great mercy not to leave one belonging to me behind. Blessed be the Most High, this Circuit promises well this year. I trust we shall have some fruit of our labour. Oh, that He may **bless us,** and all that labour in the Word. **Although I** write but seldom, I pray often for you.—I am your affectionate father,

"CHARLES GRAHAM."

The next communication is more important, from the same Circuit:—

"The Lord has blessed our labours in some degree since **we came** to this Circuit; not a few convinced and converted. Blessed **be** the Lord, this will more than recompense for all our toil. It is a pleasure to labour among a people who receive the Word, and bring forth the fruits of it.

'"Tis worth living for this,
To administer bliss
And salvation in Jesu's name.'

May **He grant unto me that my life** and latest breath may be spent in His **service. I see more and more the necessity of** being a Christian, 'not **in word** only, **but in** deed and in truth;' and if **I** had my life to live **over** again, I think I should live more to purpose than **I have done. But I** can only now lament my failings and shortcomings before the Lord, and be deeply humbled as in the dust before Him. I daily see what need a Christian has of watchfulness and prayer, who acts under the inspection of that God who knoweth all the thoughts and weigheth the intentions; but I can only say, 'God be merciful to me, a sinner,' and grant that as I am drawing nearer to my final end, I may have clearer views of the 'inheritance of the saints in light.' I am, as ever, your affectionate father,

"CHARLES GRAHAM."

What little boasting is here! What humbling views had this great, and holy, and useful man of himself, even to the end! A short time previous to the above he wrote:—"The Lord gave me a long trial. May He grant that my last days may be my best, and keep me from sin, and all will end well."

At the Conference of the year 1812, Mr. Graham was appointed the superintendent of the Mountrath Circuit, with Messrs. Averell and Lougheed as his colleagues. Mr. Averell was generally supposed to have liberty to visit various parts of the kingdom, and his appointment to Mountrath was, no doubt, likewise in consideration of his having property close by, and its being his native place. During this year Mr. Graham's eldest brother, and maternal grandfather to the writer, who lived near Sligo, died very unexpectedly, to which event he very appropriately refers in the following letter to his son in Dublin :—

"MY DEAR CHARLES,—I had a letter from my nephew, James Graham, letting me know that his father departed this life on the 16th of February. He came home quite well from the market of Sligo, and in a moment after he dined, he got a stroke, which left him half dead. He lingered a few days, and then finished his course, but left a testimony behind him of his acceptance with God. Glory to God, it is no vain thing to serve Him. My dear, honest brother strove to serve the Lord for forty years. He supported His cause and His messengers; and now his work is with the Lord, and his reward with his God.

" 'Oh, what are all my sufferings here,
    If, Lord, thou count me meet
With that enraptur'd host to appear,
    And worship at Thy feet?

Give life or death, give ease or pain,
    Take life or friends away,
I come to find them all again,
    In that eternal day.'

"'Who next shall be summoned away? My merciful God, is it I?'

"This is truly a loud call to me to be ready. Oh God, make me faithful unto death, that I may attain the crown of life.

"C. GRAHAM."

Mr. Lanktree states that this was a most important year (1812) to the Methodist Connexion, as in it Lord Sidmouth's Bill was overthrown. It appears it would have operated most injuriously in relation to the whole economy of Methodism, especially towards its itinerancy. Mr. Butterworth, a member of our Society in London, and a member of Parliament that year, laboured most indefatigably to upset it. The united prayers of the Methodists of the United Kingdom went up to heaven, and the victory was gloriously triumphant.* Mr. Butterworth accompanied Dr. Clarke to the Irish Conference, and greatly cheered our brethren, who were suffering from an accumulating debt on the Connexion, and frequently had to tax themselves. In reference to the above Bill, Mr. Lanktree observes further: "How little God's people are aware how many enemies may be privately contriving their ruin, and as little as to the instruments He employs to effect their deliverance. But while we abide in Jehovah's counsel, and rely on His promise, 'no weapon formed against them shall prosper,

---

* The author remembers to have heard the following, in reference to this subject :—"On the night previous to the third reading of the Bill, Mr. B. wrote to the Prime Minister, saying, 'I have to inform your Lordship that if the Bill pass, there is a machinery in operation which will not only shake the earth but the heavens also,—I mean the prayers of God's people.' Next day he presented himself in the House with his arms full of petitions, and saying, 'If these will not do I will bring them in sackfulls to-morrow.' The Bill was accordingly thrown out, and Sidmouth upset in confusion and shame. How true the sentiment, 'Praying breath is never spent in vain!'"

and every tongue that rises against them in judgment shall be condemned.'" These observations are very suitable to the present times in 1868.

At the close of this year it appears Mr. Lanktree exchanged with Mr. Finley, in order to visit Innishowen, and on his return remarks—"This is one of the farthest places in Ireland from real religion. First, it abounds with Popery; second, the Church (Episcopalians) and Meeting people (Presbyterians) are also ignorant and bigotted; third, the people are generally drunken and slothful; fourth, they have short leases and rack-rents, to be paid by illicit distillation; and lastly, they have no regard for preachers, less desire for heaven, unless it could be procured by smuggling. And yet even here there are witnesses for Jesus. One young woman's deep experience surprised me. She spoke with a glow of sacred eloquence which could not easily be equalled."

CHAPTER XV.

DR. COKE AND INDIA—DIVISION ANTICIPATED.

"Shall we, whose souls are lighted
With wisdom from on high—
Shall we, to men benighted,
The lamp of life deny?"

"Our Annual Conferences," says Mr. Lanktree, "have been advancing in interest for many years past; but that of 1813 was distinguished by extraordinary evidences of the presence and blessing of our living Head. Dr. Coke was our President. This was his twenty-fifth visit to Ireland! He has been long our *attached, faithful,* and *indefatigable* friend and servant, for Christ's sake. His heart was set on a mission to the East, and to begin in Ceylon. He asked, in the Conference, 'Which of the brethren would come forward and engage in the mighty enterprise?' Two of our excellent and beloved brethren,—Messrs. Lynch and Erskine,—offered themselves at once to accompany the doctor. The doctor wrote to a friend thus :—'I am now dead to Europe, and alive for India. God has said to me, ' Go to Ceylon,' and so fully convinced am I it is the will of God, that methinks I would rather be set naked on the island of Ceylon, without clothes and without a friend, than not go there.' The last words he said to me were, 'Brother Lanktree, farewell. Remember **the Missions. Form missionary societies.'"**

The self-sacrificing spirit of this great-souled man of God reminds one of what Mr. Cox, an American missionary, who was appointed to Africa, said to a fellow-student—" If I die in Africa, you must come after me and write my epitaph." "I will," said the student; "but what shall I write." "Let a thousand missionaries die before Africa is given up," **was** the reply; and in this spirit he died. Elliott, "the Apostle of the Indians," said, "Prayers **and** pains through faith in Christ Jesus will do anything;" and **on** the day of his death, and in his eightieth year, he was found teaching the alphabet to an Indian child at his bedside, and said to a friend, "As I can no longer preach, the Lord **gives me** strength enough to teach this poor child his alphabet."

The following lines, **written on Dr. Coke's death, may be very** appropriately **introduced here :—**

"Immortal Coke has reached the highest heaven;
The radiant robe, the starry crown is given
By his approving Lord, while heaven resounds
With silver lyres and sweet seraphic sounds.
Those toils, those trials, which he patient bore,
By angel voice are now recounted o'er,
While souls, which crown'd his labours, quick **advance,**
And cast on Coke the fond, **endearing glance."**

He died **on his** way to India, **and** like another Moses, called to ascend, not an earthly Pisgah, but the mount of vision and of faith, to view the Indian landscape **o'er,** and **then,** like him, his happy spirit was kissed away beyond the **swelling** flood. An ocean **grave well became** him—a fit *emblem* of his world-wide purposes that every shore might be visited by the blessings of his high commission, and that every wave should be regarded as sounding his requiem until "the sea shall deliver up its dead."

On the results of the Irish Missionary operations this year, the Conference remarks—"Viewing the Irish Missions as bearing on the *navy* and the *military*, we consider them as objects of primary importance, and we are confident that if they be not supported by the usual means, a most serious evil must befal this country." The reply of the British Conference is of equal importance. "The Irish Missions, since their first commencement, have lain very near to our hearts. The introduction and spread of vital religion among the Catholics of Ireland is of the first importance to the British Empire, and we shall be happy at all times to promote it as far as our finances will admit."

There were eleven men appointed last year, but this year only nine. The increase in the Methodist Society in Ireland was about 1,000. Mr. Graham was appointed for the second year 1813—to the Mountrath Circuit, and had Mr. Gustavus Armstrong, with whom he travelled the Cavan Circuit a few years before, as his colleague. An extract of a letter from Mr. Graham to his son will show how the good work of God still prospered in his hand. It is dated from Mountmellick, being part of this Circuit :—

"MOUNTMELLICK, *May*, 24, 1813.

"MY DEAR CHARLES,—This has been a good year on this Circuit; the Lord has blessed the work abundantly. There are many brought in and convinced, and converted to God. He works, and none can hinder; and He is a friend that sticketh closer than a brother.—Your affectionate father,

"CHARLES GRAHAM."

About this time Mr. Ouseley preached a most solemn and instructive sermon in Limerick barracks, and had a large portion of the Sligo militia to hear him, then stationed there. The Rev. Wm. Ferguson, who was present, gave the following outline of it to Mr. Reilly, who records it :—" The text was Prov. xxii. 3, 'A prudent man forseeth the evil, and hideth himself; but the simple pass on, and are punished." The place and circumstances were peculiarly striking to the subject. The Shannon flowed under the window of the room in which he was preaching. He first described the *prudent* man; seecondly, where he hideth himself; and, thirdly, the character of the *simple*, and their punishment. The latter—the *simple*—he described as a man without the knowledge of God, and a stranger to the wisdom from above. " He may," said he, " be very acute in transacting the business of life; an able statesman, a profound philosopher, an eminent artist, or a distinguished scholar ;—but he lives according to the course of this world, and dies unconverted." Then his punishment ; the place—the company—the duration. In reference to the last particular,—*the duration*,—he observed, taking advantage of the Shannon flowing underneath, " If you were to count a thousand years for every drop of water that ever flowed in that Shannon, from Drumshambo (a small town in the County Leitrim, near the mouth of that river, more than 100 miles off), to the sea, it would be but a point, when compared with that eternity through which the simple will have to endure the wrath of God." Mr. Ferguson added, " It made an impression on my mind that can never be effaced—the mighty river flowing on in a continuous current, and had flowed on for near six thousand years, and flowing still ! What an emblem of eternity ! " exclaimed Mr. F. to himself.

Mr. Graham was appointed this year (1814) to Newtownbarry as superintendent, and Mr. John Hadden for his colleague; of whom the following record is found in the death-roll for the year 1843:—" As a Christian his piety was uniform; as a colleague and superintendent, his worth **was only** known to those with whom he travelled; and as a preacher he was instructive and persuasive." His children have arisen to call him and their faithful mother **blessed.**

Mr. Graham writes in the September of this year to his **son.** The following extract from it will instruct us as to the state of the Circuit, and his prospects for the year :—

"Newtownbarry, *Sept.* 26, 1814.

"My dear Charles,—We are well, blessed be God **for all** His mercies. I have been twice round my Circuit. I like it **well.** We are likely to have some good done this year. Our congregations are increased, and our meetings lively. I am after holding three Quarterly Meetings (Love Feasts), where we had much of the presence and power of God, and I trust much good was done. If the Lord spare me to finish this year, I shall be grateful. He has done great things for me, for which I feel thankful. May the little time I have be unreservedly given up to Him. It is short and uncertain. May the Father of mercies bless and keep you. So prays your **affectionate father,**

"Charles Graham."

The Hibernian Methodist **Missionary Society was** formed this year (1814), **and an** interesting **report of the** speeches delivered on that occasion was recently published under the **direction of** the Rev. Wm. Crook, D.D. It deserves general circulation. The Address of the Irish Methodist Conference **to the** British Conference **of** this year is one from which **we** cannot resist **the desire** to introduce the following extract:—

"The *unity* of the members of Christ's Church is its glory and its strength—the fellowship of one common system of uncorrupted doctrine, and of a discipline which is according to godliness. We do unfeignedly congratulate you on the success of the glorious Gospel of God our Saviour amongst you. We deplore with deep humility that our enlargement is not proportionate to yours. We appointed a committee to trace the causes and the directions suggested, respecting the necessary ministerial qualifications, the more faithful application of discipline, and above all, the habitual sense of the presence of an indwelling God, so necessary to render our preaching effectual, were accompanied with such overwhelming manifestations of Divine light, consolation, and power, as we never before experienced in our Conference. We contemplate with joy the future glory of the East, where 'the Sun of Righteousness first arose with healings in his wings' (alluding to the mission under Dr. Coke); and we rejoice to contribute to the means of its establishment. These are momentous and eventful times."

At this Conference—1814—we find no less than thirteen missionaries told off for the Irish Mission,—all men of note. Before Dr. Coke left the Conference last year, Mr. Ouseley offered himself for the East Indies, and entreated the Conference, with tears, to let him go with the doctor; but the Conference interposed, one brother stating, "Mr. Ouseley cannot be spared; he has not yet fulfilled his mission in his native country." The doctor pleaded hard, and assigned many reasons; but the Conference was inflexible, and, as the future proved, it was wisely directed in its decision. His place on the Irish Mission could not be supplied. He was appointed that year to the Counties of Antrim and Derry, where he continued for six years, and his labours there will only be fully known in "the day of the Lord Jesus."

His memory is still as balm to many a grateful, loving heart. Many young men were raised up, who became useful preachers of the Gospel, and several of them men of great power. Mr. Arthur Noble was among the fruits of the early labours of Graham and Ouseley. Mr. Reilly remarks—"Messrs. Graham and Ouseley, with their Bibles in their hands, and with their black caps on, rode into the town of Fintona, and opened their great commission to surrounding multitudes. Mr. Ouseley's text was Rev. vi. 17,—"For the great day of His wrath is come; and who shall be able to stand?" At the conclusion he vehemently cried out, 'O Fintona, Fintona! remember that a man sitting on his horse in the street warned you to prepare to meet your God. You will recall this day to mind, in the great day which I have been describing to you.' Young Noble was convinced, and soon after savingly converted to God, and became the travelling companion of Mr. Ouseley on the Irish Mission for some years."

Their united labours were crowned with marvellous results. Mr. Reilly mentions, in a letter to Mr. Ouseley, written from Wicklow, after one of his visits, accompanied by Mr. Noble, just referred to, that—"The most extraordinary conversions, which I have ever seen or heard of, have taken place. Some very respectable, some abandoned, one atheist, some most singular persecutors, have all been converted to God; and some of our own old members have been sanctified. Jehovah smiles on all the land, and the wilderness and solitary places are glad, and the deserts rejoice and blossom as the rose. One would almost imagine that the day of Ireland's moral and spiritual regeneration had arrived, and that the brightest anticipations of prophecy were about to be fulfilled."

Oh! the power of simply preaching Christ and Him crucified!

> "Yes, this my constant theme shall be,
>   Through time and through eternity,
> That Jesus tasted death for me
>   On the cross, on the cross."

Mr. Graham was appointed in 1815 to superintend the Newtownbarry Circuit again, with Mr. Hadden for his colleague. The following is an extract of a letter from a local preacher, who had been a member of the Church of Rome, when he first heard Mr. Graham:—

"DEAR SIR,—I hope you will bear me on your mind before a throne of grace. I am a weak vessel to be called in any wise to proclaim the unsearchable riches of Christ. The little Society feel much for your separation from them. They still continue faithful. I have great hope that much good will be done this year, and that Satan's kingdom shall meet a mighty overthrow, and that the enemies of the Lord will be much scattered. Adieu, till the archangel's trump shall summon our sleeping dust to the solemn day of decision!—

> "'Oh, that each in the day of His coming may say,
>   I have fought my way through;
> I have finished the work Thou didst give me to do.'

So prays your affectionate son in the Gospel."

The Rev. Thomas Blanshard, of London, wrote to Mr. Graham on the subject of superintending the great mission work just commenced in *Ceylon*. We give an extract:—

"14 CITY ROAD, LONDON, *June* 15*th*, 1815.

"DEAR BROTHER,—The Missionary Committee have directed me to state to you the following particulars, to which we earnestly beg your serious attention. We want, first, a brother of years and respectability in the work, to go to Ceylon, as Superintendent of that wide and important Circuit. Secondly, we want four or five young men, who, if they have travelled a year or two, will be the more acceptable, as helpers in the great work.

"We beg that you will take this into your serious consideration, and if you feel inclined to offer your services for that work yourself, please let us know as soon as you can.

"May the merciful God have mercy upon all pagans and idolators, and that they may be saved among the remnant of the true Methodists, and be made one fold under one Shepherd, Jesus Christ our Lord.

"Yours, &c.,

"THOMAS BLANSHARD."

Mr. Graham declined the offer, for, besides a consciousness of unfitness for the position, he was then in the sixty-fifth year of his age. The Rev. John M'Kenny, from Ireland, was shortly afterwards appointed to Ceylon, as a young man. He returned to Ireland after many years, and was received into "full connexion," as our ordination was then called, with the writer, at the Belfast Conference, in the year 1835; he had previously no opportunity of being publicly set apart to our ministry.

In the Address of the Irish to the English Conference, this year (1815), reference to the Irish Mission is thus made:—"The Irish Mission still continues to bless our land. Several Roman Catholics have, during the year turned to the Lord; and of the careless Protestants, not a few."

The answer supplies us with the following, and with many other cheering expressions:—"Heaven has cast a smile on all our missionary labour."

Many petitions were presented at this year's Conference in favour of the administration of the ordinances in our own chapels. The subject was discussed at large, and the votes taken. These were in favour of the measure. It afterwards was considered best to postpone their administration for another year, which was adopted. The Rev.

Adam Averell, an ordained minister of the Established Church, labouring as a Methodist preacher, was, however, appointed to administer them, whenever invited to do so, *during* the year.

We feel pleasure in recording, at least in part, what Dr. Stevens, of America, states in his *History of Methodism*, relative to the death of Mr. Averell:—" His piety beatified his last days, as with sun-set hues. 'Looking unto Jesus' was his favourite text. 'I can tell,' said he on his death-bed, 'from experience that the Lord is gracious,' and then took wing, exclaiming, 'Holy, Holy, Holy, Lord God of Hosts.'"

> "I can now with joy behold him:
> Face to face my Father see;
> Fall with rapture and adore him,
> For his love to me."

CHAPTER XVI.

FAMILY AFFLICTION—CONVERSION OF HIS SON—DIVISION.

"Let that sweet word our spirits cheer
 Which quell'd the **toss'd disciples' fear**—
  'Be not afraid.'
 He who could bid the tempest cease,
 Can keep our souls in perfect peace,
  If on Him stay'd."

Mr. Graham returned, in 1816, for the third year, to superintend the Newtownbarry Circuit. In the spring of this year **he** received an account of the death of his other brother. **He was greatly** affected by this event also, as **he** was **before** by the sudden removal of his eldest brother **four years previously.** An extract from a letter to his son will best **describe** this sanctified affliction :—

"Gorey, *May* 6, 1816.

"My dear Charles.—Your uncle James **is dead. This**, with the former news, has brought me low. I am left alone. **O Lord, be my** helper, and help me to be ready for the next call. I feel my spirits much depressed. My brothers loved me dearly. I shall see them no **more** until I arrive in that eternal world to which they are fled. I hope they made their escape from the evils of this world, and are gone to rest. Time is short; we shall soon meet again. Oh! that it may be with yonder throng who have washed their robes, and made them white in the blood of the Lamb. What is life, and what is the world and all it contains, when compared to an assurance of that rest that remains for the people of God? My dear Charles, lose no time in closing in with your Maker. You seem as if bowed down with a spirit of infirmity. Oh! may the Lord loose you, and let you go, as you ought to go, and serve Him.

"I am, your affectionate father,
"CHARLES GRAHAM."

At the end of this year he met with a very serious accident. He fell off his horse, or rather his horse fell and rolled over him, cutting and bruising his leg most seriously. He was brought home with difficulty, and lay under it for ten days. He says, in describing the scene to his son:—

"Blessed be the Lord, it happened near home. No bone was broken. Perhaps by this I escaped some greater evil. I am safely housed, and happy in my mind. Glory to the Lord, I had not one unhappy moment since it happened to the present. I can say 'It is good to be *here*,' and to be in His hands. He has said, 'All things shall work together for good to them that love God.' I have long proved His faithfulness, and I trust I shall prove it more and more in my old age. Oh, what an awful thing to live one moment without His favour, for 'in the midst of life we are in death." The Saviour's mandate is, 'Be ye also ready.' Lord, make me holy in heart and life, and in all manner of conversation. Here we have no abiding city: this earth is not my place. May I cast my whole care, living and dying, upon Him who careth for me.

"I am, as ever, your affectionate father,
"CHARLES GRAHAM."

This was the great controversial year in the Methodist Societies in Ireland, on the subject of sacramental administration in our own chapels. Mr. Graham seems to have acted very moderately during the whole affair. Indeed, in the County Wexford they were nearly all in favour of the measure, but he humorously remarked, that "the poor stewards and leaders found it difficult to release all the circulars and letters," as postage was very high at that time. Surely, one might imagine that *now*, at the end of fifty-two years of Methodistic history since then, the subject might be very gravely and prayerfully considered again, and we would add, may it be speedily, and satisfactorily, and for ever settled. The signs of the times demand it. Charles Wesley prayed thus for a similar object—

> "But wilt Thou not at last appear?
> Into Thine hands *this matter* take;
> We look for no protection here,
> But Thee alone our refuge make.
> To Thee, O righteous Judge, appeal,
> And wait thine acceptable will."

During this year the missionaries prosecuted their perilous duties with great ardour and success amidst great discouragements. One of the honoured band broke down under the weight of numerous but gloriously successful toils, namely, the Rev. William Hamilton, the companion of Ouseley for some years. He was compelled to retire, and died triumphantly on the 8th of October, 1843. Some of his last expressions were :—" If I could shout so that the world might hear, I would tell of the goodness and love of God my Saviour. Not a cloud! Not a cloud! Victory over death! The sting is taken away! Glory, glory to God!"

But while one and another of the standard-bearers thus fell now and again, there were always those around who rushed forward to lift the falling banner, and baptized unto the dead, cried again, "Behold! behold the Lamb!" The Conference record is :—

"While we rejoice in the success of missionary exertions abroad, it is still further ground of gratitude that our own Irish missionaries have been blest in their labours at home. In the course of last year new ground has been broken up, the Word of God widely distributed, many sinners awakened, and some, who were the ripe fruit of the mission, have escaped away to the mansions of light. In one sense we are all missionaries; and our prayer is, that we may possess more of the true missionary spirit, and that the kingdom of Christ may spread till the whole earth is filled with his glory.

"SAMUEL WOOD, *Secretary*."

Mr. Graham was removed this year to superintend the Carlow Circuit, with Mr. Archibald Campbell as his colleague. Shortly after the Conference he wrote to his son. The following is an extract from the letter:—

"CARLOW, *October 4th*, 1817.

"MY DEAR CHARLES,—I received your letter, which has given me great comfort to find that you have joined the people of God at last. Blessed be the Lord for all His mercies. There is a young lad* near Athy, who was a rigid Roman Catholic. He left the mass since I came to this Circuit, and is now converted. He is from the County Sligo. I have some hope that he will become a preacher. He is a young man of fine abilities, can read and write and speak the Irish. I hope if the Lord call him out, he will be useful to that class (Romanists). May the Lord raise up some who will show them the light, for they are in a deplorable state, and few care for their souls. I am often led to believe that I should again take the streets; but having a Circuit to attend, I know I would not be adequate to standing out. The weary wheels will soon stand still: oh, that I may be prepared to give up my accounts. What is life?

"Your ever affectionate father,
"CHARLES GRAHAM."

Mr. Graham was also cheered this year by the receipt of an interesting letter from Mr. Fossey Tackaberry. We will

---

* Afterwards the Rev. John Feely, of whom more again.

introduce an extract from this also, which will, we are sure, be read with great pleasure :—

"TOMAGADDY, *Dec.* 15*th*, 1817.

"MY DEAR AND NEVER-TO-BE-FORGOTTEN FATHER AND FRIEND,— I received your welcome letter, which I have read many a time, and many a time I have longed to see you, even for one hour. How much I needed your conversation, I did not know until you were gone. Mr. Douglas is worthy the character you gave of him in your letter. He is an honest man and useful, especially in discipline. But I never could feel free to open my mind to any preacher since I saw you. When I think of the way I used to speak to you, and how little afraid of you I was, I wonder; and never did I need your advice more than since you left. But, thanks to my loving Lord, I was never so happy as I have been for some time past—never such access to God—such close union and communion with Him; nor yet felt I my own weakness and helplessness as now. Without Christ I can do nothing. Temptations have driven me closer to the Lord, and led me to cast my care upon Him who is able to save. Still I long to see you, I would willingly go every foot to Carlow to spend one night with you. Our people here are doing well. Many in our class are increasing in holiness, especially the young men. They are also increasing in zeal, activity, and usefulness. A few have been put out of the class at Ballycanew, but we have gotten five or six ornaments in their stead. The members of our class are really a wonder to us, they have made such progress in the Divine life. There is an increase and earnestness in a class, which I asked you if I should give up. Ten young men of us meet once a week in band, to watch over each other in the Lord, and our souls have been wonderfully strengthened, comforted, and knit together; and thanks to the Most High that while Zion is torn in other places, we are determined to follow after holiness. Remember me to dear Mrs. Graham. I felt at home with her on the day I spent in Newtownbarry. Remember me at the throne of grace.

"Your unworthy son and servant in the Gospel,

"FOSSEY TACKABERRY."

The Rev. C. Mayne was the representative to the English Conference of last year (1816), and the circular which he sent to the brethren on his return now lies before me. The following extract may be interesting :—

"I arrived in time in London to enjoy a very blessed Sabbath, previous to the sitting of the Conference. Dr. Clarke and Mr. Moore preached. In the Love Feast, at 3 o'clock, a spirit of prayer and earnestness prevailed, which was truly delightful. Mr. Reece was chosen President, a wise and steady man; and Mr. Bunting, Secretary. I can truly say, that the English brethren are a body of pious ministers, and their sermons are plain and evangelical. A young gentleman of great piety, and large property, who had just taken the degree of Master of Arts at Cambridge, offered himself to travel. He was received and placed on the list of reserve. We had a very interesting visit from two Prussian clergymen, sons to the Bishop of Berlin, young men of piety. They came to England by the desire of their aged father, and by permission of the Prussian Court, to inquire into the state of religion, charities, and education of England. They were admitted. The President gave them an account of our origin, and Dr. Clarke of our doctrines, and Mr. Moore of our success. They retired deeply impressed with the importance of Methodism, which is a mighty work, and is spreading from shore to shore. I pray the Father of Mercies, to pour out His Holy Spirit on us, as on the sister kingdom. Wishing you a very happy and prosperous year,

"I remain your truly affectionate brother,

"C. MAYNE."

The above shows the spirit of piety, and the talent for observation which characterized this truly devoted man of God, himself a well-educated Christian gentleman, and a member of a highly-respectable family, and one who bore no small share of "the burden and heat of the day," even in the public streets, and in the depth of winter. It was some contrast to find him one day in the street of Gorey, proclaiming Christ in the midst of a stone-throwing mob, and, perhaps, in a short time after, sitting with his brother, Judge Mayne, on the bench, in some county town. A preacher gives the following graphic account of such vicissitudes in Ireland :—" At Mrs. Tighe's we conversed with senators, ministers, and ladies of rank and talent, we were attended by liveried servants, and cheered with the sound of the organ ; perhaps in the next place our lodging was on straw, in some outhouse or newly prepared dwelling, of those who had recently suffered the loss of all things. In a word we might say, " Our life was in our hand."

The following is the epitaph of the Rev. Charles Mayne, on a marble tablet in the Wesleyan Chapel at Kingstown, near Dublin :—

> In Memory
> OF THE
> REV. CHARLES MAYNE,
> Who for upwards of 42 years,
> As a Wesleyan Minister,
> Successfully preached the Gospel
> Throughout most of the
> Cities, Towns, and Rural Districts
> Of Ireland, and in
> This Town,
> After a short illness, died in the
> Faith of Christ,
> May 4th, 1838, aged 66.
>
> This tablet is erected by his bereaved Widow, as a small *Memento* of his worth And her sorrow.

During this Methodistic year, 1817, the Rev. James Rutledge writes to Mr. Graham, from Sligo, the following brief but cheering note :—

"Thank God, we have a good work on this Circuit. We have very large congregations. Sinners are being converted, and our Societies increasing."

Having travelled for a year (1835) with this devoted servant of the Most High, the writer feels much gratification in introducing the high estimation in which he was held by his brethren in the ministry. "He entered the army in 1793, and in that situation was enabled so to honour God, that he was made the instrument of great good to many of his fellow-soldiers. He was a man of strong understanding, great prudence, and immovable fidelity. He entered the Methodist ministry in 1802, and spent thirty-seven years in the active itinerant work, and nine as supernumerary, and died in the full assurance of eternal rest on the 5th of September, 1848." There is also a circumstance told of him, which is said to have occurred in 1798, the year of the rebellion in Ireland. Mr. Rutledge was a sergeant in the Leitrim Militia, and a local preacher in the Methodist Society. He was a terror to evil doers; and it appears a conspiracy was concocted against him, and, like Daniel, it was no doubt said of Rutledge, " We shall find no occasion against him, except we find it against him concerning the law of his God." Accordingly, they watched Rutledge returning several times from outside the camp, to which they alleged he went for the purpose of holding communication with the rebels. A charge was drawn up and sent in against him. A court-martial was summoned, and Rutledge and his accusers appeared. The case was tried, and all the accused could say in defence of his frequent absence from barracks was, that he retired for devotional purposes, which was disbelieved, and he was sentenced to be shot. The whole examination, the accused's statement, and the judgment, were laid for confirmation before Lord Cornwallis, then Commander-in-chief in Ireland. His Lordship thought the plea to be rather singular, and he sent for the prisoner, saying—

"Rutledge, you state that the purpose for which you so frequently retired beyond the camp was to pray?"

"Yes, my Lord," said Rutledge.

"Well," said his lordship, "if that be so, you must be pretty expert at that business now. You had better, therefore, kneel down, and give us a specimen of your devotional powers."

Rutledge knelt, and poured out his soul in such marvellous strains, in which he prayed for the king, for his lordship, for the British army, for his country, that before he was half through his lordship interrupted him, and said to Rutledge—

"Quite enough. A man of such intercourse with God could never be a rebel."

It is also said, that his lordship took him into his own *special* confidence; and, for anything we know, he may have often heard Rutledge pray again, and, perhaps, the means of his lordship's conversion.

We may truly, in this case, adopt the following lines:—

> "When one that holds communion with the skies,
> Has filled his urn where these pure waters rise,
> And once more mingles with us, meaner things,
> 'Tis even as if an angel shook his wings;
> Immortal fragrance fills the circuit wide
> That tells us whence his treasures are supplied."

Coming to the close of this Methodistic year, Mr. Graham's cup of joy was filled to overflowing. On the occasion of his son's conversion to God, an event long prayed for and earnestly anticipated, his rapturous emotion is expressed in the following communication:—

"CARLOW, *February* 24, 1818.

"MY DEAR CHARLES,—Your last letter was greatly blessed to me, seeing the Lord in mercy has looked upon you again, and brought you into His fold. May He, of His great mercy, keep you the residue of your days near His wounded side. He loved you, and gave Himself for you. "O to grace how great a debtor." While I live, may I live to Him. Two Catholics have been lately converted.

"Your affectionate father,
"CHARLES GRAHAM."

CHAPTER XVII.

REAPPOINTED TO MISSION WORK.

"Our field is the world, and our work is before us;
To each is appointed a message to bear;
At home or abroad, in the cottage or palace,
Wherever directed our mission is there."

AT the Conference of this year, 1818, Mr. Graham was appointed to the Newtownbarry Circuit as *a new* mission field. Now, within a month of the sixty-ninth year of his age, he entered on his labours here with all the animation of a young man. He seems to rejoice that the closing years of his eventful life were likely to terminate as they began, on the mission field, which was actually the case, and a fitting termination it was. It was not with him "a youth of labour and an age of ease." Immediately after his appointment to this mission, he says, "I had to supply Circuit work for the Rev. Andrew Hamilton for a short time, who was laid aside by a sore leg." He refers to this event in the following extract of a letter written to his son:—

"Thank God, my health has been good since I left Dublin. Mr. Hamilton cannot travel, and I have been confined to this Circuit for him. I have been preaching in the streets and in the markets. The poor people are sunk in superstition and idolatry. Heaven alone can relieve them. Many of them give me a patient hearing, and seem to be greatly affected ; but having to do with their priests does not admit of their judging for themselves. Perhaps their deliverance may be at hand. May the Saviour who redeemed them open a door for them, and deliver them from the galling yoke they labour under. We have a great work on this Circuit, near Gorey. Mr. Reilly and a local preacher and myself held forth lately at a field meeting to some thousands, who were greatly broken down. They said they never saw such a day. I hope this will be a year of great blessing. May the great Head of the Church assist us.

"Your affectionate father,

"CHARLES GRAHAM."

Shortly after this the Rev. Samuel Steele wrote to Mr. Graham on the subject of missionary labour, and about keeping his journals regularly, and forwarding them to the London Mission House. Mr. Steele was representative to the English Conference this year, and after his return he thus writes to Mr. Graham, to Newtownbarry :—

"ROSCREA, *September* 16, 1818.

"MY VERY DEAR BROTHER,—You are to write to London at least once a quarter, giving the committee a circumstantial account of your success and mode of your proceeding. They wish to be able to state to their friends and the public what their missionaries are doing in Ireland. Nothing interests them so much as a particular account of the conversions of Roman Catholics. By so doing you will make the Irish Mission interesting to the English. Thank God we have a prospect of doing good in several parts of this Circuit. Our congregations in this town are increasing. Let us be zealous and faithful, and our path will be like that of the just that shineth more and more to the perfect day.

"I am, my dear brother, affectionately yours (with love to Sister Graham),

"SAMUEL STEELE."

The following is from his son about the same date:—

"DUBLIN, *September* 23, 1818.

"MY VERY DEAR FATHER,—On last Sabbath I, and indeed the whole Society, attended the remains of Mr. Arthur Keene to 'the Cabbage Garden' (an old burial ground), where he was buried, and very near the spot where my mother lies. Mr. Averell came from Cork to see him, but was too late. He died before he came, but he spoke at the grave; and I went to hear him in the evening. I bless God my face is still Zionward, and I trust, by the grace of God, to continue so. I feel no desire to turn back, and I can truly say, 'I hate the sins that made Him mourn.' I earnestly long for and desire purity of heart. This, I believe is my privilege to obtain, and which I trust I shall never rest until I possess it. I beg an interest in your prayers that I may obtain the desire of my soul, and that I may be enabled to serve God acceptably, with a perfect heart and a willing mind. I offer up my feeble prayers to God for your success, and that God may give you many seals to your ministry, and preserve you to a good old age, to be a blessing to thousands.

"I remain, dear father, your affectionate son,
"CHAS. GRAHAM."

During this year—from July 19, 1818, until February 24, 1819—he seems to be in labours more abundant in the fairs, and markets, and fields of the County Wexford. His records are very brief, but sufficient to show that the *ruling passion* for saving souls did not decline with age. His journal runs thus:—

"February 2, 1819.—As I came to the fair of *Ballycanew* I heard that John Gowen had been murdered the night before, and, from the appearance of the times, I was tempted for a moment to think it dangerous to preach in the fair; but I considered—whether I should be the next to suffer or not—I should do my duty and sound the alarm to misguided perishing sinners. The Lord sent me help. John S. Wilson stood by me (afterwards the Rev. J. S. Wilson), and delivered a faithful warning. We had a patient, and, I am persuaded, a profitable hearing. February 3, I preached in the market of Gorey, and the Lord stood by me. It was a solemn time; God grant the impressions may be lasting. February 10, preached in Newtownbarry, from Acts iv. 12, 'Neither is their salvation in any other,' &c. This subject bore down on the Popish doctrine of priestly absolution, the intercession of angels and of saints, dead or alive. One cried out, 'What then shall we do?' I said I would set him right. I then opened the way of salvation through our Lord Jesus Christ, and soon after he went away quietly. February 17, came to the market of Gorey. A drunken priest,* a day or two before, made a great noise, and blasphemously cried out that he would put Graham down, as he did in Newtownbarry, but he took good care not to meet me in either place. I had a great hearing on this day. Some of the Catholics thought to drag others away, but they would not stir until they heard me out. February 24, preached in Newtownbarry. A man at a distance made a great noise, but I continued to alarm the people, and to warn them to be prepared for death and judgment. They seemed to feel much. A woman, with tears in her eyes, took me by the hand and thanked me."

Thus this aged veteran continued, both in winter and in summer, his exhausting labours for the five years he was stationed on this mission; and when it is considered that one street service requires a larger expenditure of bodily strength than half-a-dozen of sermons inside—at least in Mr. Graham's style, with a voice of thunder—we are utterly amazed how he held out so long. But surely there must have been supernatural strength afforded according to his ministerial "day." Nor was he without singular fruit to his incessant labours. It was on one of those occasions of street preaching in Gorey that young John Byrne was

---

* The writer feels pleasure in acknowledging the vast improvement of the present times in regard to the habit above alluded to, when compared with what it sometimes was with the clergy of both Churches, fifty or sixty years ago.

convinced, and afterwards converted to God, and became a minister in our connexion, and travelled for three years, when his health failed and he had to retire, but finished well, as we shall see hereafter.

The following letter is from Mr. John Feely, to whom reference was made by Mr. Graham to his son in Dublin, when he travelled the Carlow Circuit in the year 1817 :—

"ATHY, *Oct.* 1, 1818.

"MY DEAR SIR,—I have a few moments to disburden a mind full of thought. I hope in our God your soul and body prosper, and that you enjoy the full assurance of hope; also that the work of God is prospering in your hands in that country (County Wexford). Here in Athy we have a prospect of a revival of the 'undefiled religion' of the Lord Jesus. The great Husbandman is seemingly determined to ingraft new branches in the room of those who have fallen off. Oh, pray that He may even here raise up a people to His name. Providence has fixed me here. I have opened a school, and have tuitions in the country. My mind, after all, is not easy. I fervently implore my heavenly Father to circumcise my heart and lips with power Divine, and send me to call poor, perishing sinners to repentance. Oh, if He would deign to do this one thing for me, I would be perfectly easy. I am well aware of the greatness of the work, of my own unfitness, but also of the Lord's omnipotence. My clay is in the hands of the potter. I lay me down at the feet of the Almighty Jesus, in whom dwells all the fullness of the Godhead bodily. Thy kingdom come. O Lord God Almighty, Fountain of love, take pity on a perishing world. May the unspotted spouse of Jesus (His Church) daily flourish, and be adorned in the beauty of holiness. God bless you, Mr. Graham.

"Your son,
"JOHN FEELY."

The following is the first letter from Mr. Graham to the Rev. Joseph Taylor, Methodist Mission House, No. 74 Hatton Garden, London :—

NEWTOWNBARRY, *Oct.* 17, 1818.

"MY DEAR BROTHER,—I have undertaken the work of this mission with fear and trembling, knowing that I have not only the infernal powers to contend with, but also the leaders of those poor deluded sheep. As I was the first called out to this work after the rebellion, Mr. Ouseley was then appointed to travel with me. We laboured for six years together, and, thank God, it was not in vain. The day of judgment only will be able to tell the results. I had no idea of being sent to the mission work again, being now in the sixty-ninth year of my age. I have taken to the streets since I came, and had a good hearing. Those who understand the Irish say I speak the truth, and seem to be much affected. Their clergy are crying out against us in their chapels, as 'false prophets,' &c.; but I trust the light will break in upon them, and raise up from among themselves some who will be able to instruct them, such as John Feely, who fled and sought mercy, and found it, under the first sermon he heard me preach. The Lord has raised him up to be useful. Also, David O'Hanlon, and a drum-major and his wife (a Catholic), have been all lately converted to God, and three other Catholics converted last year ; and now a blessed work is going on here.—I am yours affectionately,

"CHARLES GRAHAM.

"*To the Rev. Thomas Taylor, of London.*"

We also find the following letter from the same place :—

"GOREY, *Feb.* 13, 1819.

"MY DEAR BROTHER TAYLOR,—Since you heard from me last, I have been preaching in markets and fairs, until I have been so exhausted as to be forced to take my bed ; but I trust my labours have not been in vain in the Lord. I had rigid opposition in one of the fairs—nothing like it since the rebellion. They thought to have conquered. Some of them said, 'they would have but one religion.' It was in Gorey. Mr. Mayne was put down, and I could scarcely be heard, the noise was so great. Satan and his angels disputed the ground with us, but the rioters were confounded, and many of the poor Catholics were ashamed of their conduct. I published I would preach there again the following week. I did so, although the day was very cold. I had a blessed hearing. The Lord sent a young man to my help. He was as bold as a lion. He sounded an alarm indeed. [We suppose this to be John S. Wilson.] The truth triumphed. I preached lately at a funeral, where I had many Catholics. The Lord attended the Word, and many were convinced. I endeavoured to undo the doctrines of purgatory and priestly absolution by proclaiming a *free* and full salvation. Our Churches (Established) in this country are greatly corrupted with a limited redemption. I told some of them that I feared they would undo their Church, as the mass will undo the Roman Catholic Church. Mr. Ouseley told me that between Dublin and Cork about one thousand members have joined Society. About two hundred have joined us here lately, and many of them Catholics. Feely is preaching, Owens holds on his way, and O'Connor is taken up by the Church (Establishment). God be praised for this glorious work.

"Your affectionate brother,

"CHARLES GRAHAM."

He writes again as follows, to the Rev. Joseph Taylor of London :—

"NEWTOWNBARRY, *March* 21, 1819.

"MY DEAR BROTHER,—When I came to this mission I had but two places which I could call my own, and therefore I went through the fairs and markets until places opened to me, where I am now fully employed, independent of the places where the Circuit preachers labour. And still the prospect opens. I may say I labour more than when I was on a Circuit. The outside work is very heavy. Our preaching-places are crowded, and many forced to stand outside. The Most High has come to our help this year. We have a blessed revival on every hand. When we were at the lowest ebb, He hasted to visit us. It would not be easy to tell the numbers who attended Messrs. Ouseley and Reilly. These blessed men are indefatigable, and the Lord is mightily with them, and blessing their labours; and both missionaries and Circuit preachers are working in this revival. All glory to God for ever and ever. He helps me in the decline of life, and I feel grateful and humble, that he enables me to do anything to bring glory to His great name. In this revival some of the Catholics have been awakened. One was persecuted for joining us, and was branded as 'a heretic.' Poor man! he took ill, and died;

but I hope the Lord has taken him to Himself. The Romans reported he was mad. A woman (a Roman Catholic) also died lately; she heard me attentively, and was most anxious to see me in her last moments. O Lord Most High, have mercy on this people. Burst their bonds. How many of them would be blest, if they were at liberty to hear the truth; as they say themselves, 'if they knew the right way, they would walk in it.'

"I am yours affectionately,
"CHARLES GRAHAM."

This letter was written in answer to certain inquiries relative to the missionaries occupying Circuit ground.

We must now introduce a very interesting letter from Mr. Graham to his son. It is dated from the residence of Mr. Tackaberry:—

"TOMAGADDY, *April* 25*th*, 1819.

"MY DEAR CHARLES,—This has been a good year with me in every sense of the word. I am loudly called upon to look forward and be prepared whenever it pleases the Lord to call upon me. May He grant me grace to have my work done! The blessed work of conviction and conversion is still going on in the Society and congregations. Much of the power of the Lord attends the Word in every direction, and much of heaven is found in our meetings. This was a glorious morning—to see young and old broken down, and then rejoicing in God, was truly affecting. Blessed be He that directed me here again (previously there three years as a Circuit preacher). I find this fourth year to be the best; they are so far from being tired of me, that they only fear I shall be taken from them. May I be humble and thankful. 'O what hast Thou for sinners done!' I preached yesterday week in the market of Gorey. I had a blessed hearing, although the ballad-singers thought to annoy me. Blessed be the Lord, even those who were open enemies are become friends. In fact everything seems to give way to the work of God. Perhaps the Lord will make my last days my best and happiest. While other preachers are laid up with infirmities, I have health to eat and drink, and sleep and labour. Marvellous are Thy works, O Lord; and above all, to see the fruit of our labour! A young woman who was converted three years ago prayed this morning, to the astonishment and edification of all. Perhaps in the kingdom you would not meet with such young men and women as are on this Circuit. Most of them are not only justified, but in the possession of sanctification. This work is spreading and deepening. I am a wonder to myself, now going into my seventieth year. All the priests can do cannot prevent some of them (the Catholics) from hearing.

"As ever, your affectionate father,
"C. GRAHAM."

He writes again to the Rev. Joseph Taylor of London:—

"NEWTOWNBARRY, *June* 25, 1819.

"MY DEAR BROTHER,—I bless God for your prosperity. Our God will do great things. We had to hold our meeting last Sabbath in a Roman Catholic chapel, which our people have obtained. It is now a preaching-house. The priest of this chapel was killed in the last rebellion. *His name was Murphy. He was shot on the bridge of Arklow while professing to catch the balls of the heretics, and exhibiting them to the unfortunate rabble.* We had *John Feely*, the converted Roman Catholic, to preach in it. Brothers Reilly and Barber also preached, and we had much prayer. The place was well watered. Brother Feely is recommended by the district to travel. A clergyman of the (Established) Church strove to persuade me against preaching in the street, but I had a patient and profitable hearing! The power of the Lord fell on the crowd. Thus we leave the truth in public places. It is mighty, and will prevail. Some of the Catholic servants, who hear us where we lodge, have been greatly persecuted and injured, but they are faithful. Oh, the mercies of the year!

"Yours affectionately,
"C. GRAHAM."

CHAPTER XVIII.

SPIRITUAL CHILDREN—LETTERS.

"Who," I ask in amaze, "hath begotten me these?"
And inquire from what quarter they came;
My full heart, it replies, "They are born from the skies;"
And gives glory to God and the Lamb.

Mr. Graham, in writing to his son, says:

"Newtownbarry, *August 20th,* 1819.

"My dear Charles,—Fossey Tackaberry helped me in Gorey market. The Lord gave us a wonderful hearing. The Protestants wondered at the attention of the Catholics, although their Bishop charged a man and his sister 20s. for hearing me near Arklow. A schoolmaster was reported as having heard us, and had our books in his house. He was denounced, and all his scholars dispersed. He was to be excommunicated on the following Sabbath, but he slipped off to church—(the Established.) It is hard to get one soul out of their hands. Fossey Tackaberry's servant boy has left the mass. It is amazing to think how long this delusion lasts; and how they can dream of having religion, and at the same time committing all manner of sin, I cannot divine. But error is infatuating, and 'she has made the nations drunk with the wine of her fornication.' Hence they are unable to judge for themselves. But nothing should concern myself so much as to be ready to leave when I am called. Kempis says, 'It is vain to desire to live long, and not desire to live well.'

'O that the world might taste and see
The riches of His grace!'

Although my feeble voice can extend to few, my prayers can extend to many. Lord help me to be found more fervent and more earnest than ever. I have been warning S——, lest she should be hardened through the deceitfulness of sin. We hear bad news from England. No doubt Popery is at the bottom of it. 'Tis not unlikely but they have some devilish scheme on foot, for they are always working in the dark. Remember me to Mr. and Mrs. Dale.

"Ever your affectionate father,
"CHARLES GRAHAM."

How Mr. Graham secured time to write journals and long letters we are at a loss to know, except by a marvellous redemption of time from sleep, and other interruptions. He writes again to London, in the following terms, continuing his reports as requested :—

"NEWTOWNBARRY, *August 4th*, 1819.

"MY DEAR BROTHER,—Last Sabbath we had John Feely again, and hundreds of people flocked to hear him. He was once a determined enemy to this way, but now 'a workman that needeth not to be ashamed.' He has the salvation of souls very much at heart. All the Catholic converts are delighted with him. William Byrne, from the County Wicklow, came to see him, and converse with him, also George Miller. These men have been proclaimed and deprived of all subsistence. I hear there were forty candles put out, and all horrible curses pronounced by the bishop and clergy in excommunicating John Feely and Francis Cavanagh, and likely George Miller also, for what they call *heresy*. [This was surely *canon law*.] It requires no small share of resolution to leave that apostate Church. A young man refused to obey his father in going to mass, and the priest came and asked, 'Why he disobeyed his father?' The young man answered, 'If any man love father or mother more than me, said Christ, he is not worthy of me.' The priest said, 'Let him go; he is full of heresy.' The lad escaped, and said to a friend, 'That portion of Scripture comforted me, *Greater is He that is for you than all that is against you.*' The youth had by some means obtained one of Mr. Ouseley's tracts, which first unhinged him. A Roman Catholic girl, to whom I spoke at one of my lodging-places lately, is now a member of our Society. Several schoolmasters have left; and next to the priest the people look up to them as men of understanding. May the great Head of the Church prepare us for, and assist us in, this glorious work!—I am, yours affectionately,

"CHARLES GRAHAM.

" *To the Rev. Joseph Taylor, of London.*"

The following is an extract from a circular forwarded to all the Wesleyan Missionaries employed under the British Conference, and sent to Mr. Graham by the Rev. Joseph Taylor, with the annexed note :—

"WESLEYAN MISSION HOUSE, 77 HATTON GARDEN,
"LONDON, *October 5th,* 1819.

"MY DEAR BROTHER,—I beg to acknowledge the receipt of yours, and to thank you for the regularity of your communications. We rejoice to hear of the prosperity of your work in Ireland. May the Lord increase it!—I am, yours truly,

"JOSEPH TAYLOR."

EXTRACT.

"DEAR BRETHREN,—We have just concluded our Annual Conference at Bristol. The form of receiving brethren into full connexion, on the Monday and Tuesday evenings of the second week of the Conference, was rendered peculiarly impressive by the experience of Mr. Hawtry, formerly a captain in the army,* and now appointed a missionary in Paris; and also by the presence of Mr. Harvard, whom Providence has safely brought to this country from Ceylon. The ardent missionary feelings and just views of the honour, importance, and peculiar sanctity of missionary labour discovered in his address, raised all our hearts in thankfulness to God for having raised up such men among us for His own purposes!

---

* This Captain Hawtry was converted in Ireland, through the instrumentality of Mr. Graham's street preaching. He was in the Irish Conference in 1824. When the obituary of Mr. Graham was read, he rose and said,—"It is far below his worth;" and alluded to the time of his own conversion, and when he first heard him preach in Ireland.

The increase in our Societies this year is 6,905, of which the increase in Great Britain was 1,700. In Ireland, 3,528—*(more than half of all!)*—and in the Missions, 1,677. The increase in America is upwards of 11,000. You will rejoice with us in the goodness of God to our brethren in Ireland, in cheering them under the recent troubles they have suffered, in consequence of the lamented divisions of their Societies in that country, by rendering their ministry eminently useful throughout the year. The fruit of your missionary labours during the last year will never be fully estimated but in eternity! It is from your living in Christ, and under the efficient influence of His grace, that a sense of the inestimable value of souls will be preserved in your minds, for 'out of the abundance of the heart the mouth speaketh.'

"Dear brethren, bear with us whilst we remind you, not in the spirit of suspicion, but in that of watching over each other in love, that, as missionaries, you have peculiar temptations, and will need not only to put on, but to wear *daily* the whole armour of God. Against a *slothful disposition* let us affectionately exhort you to make vigorous efforts. Almost everything depends upon the personal exertions of a Missionary; for, from his example, all subordinate agents will take the measure of their own duty, and however willing they may be to labour, yet they need the constant and vigilant superintendence of their ministers. Look at the example of all distinguished missionaries, of **Wesley, Coke,** Swartz, Elliott, Brainard, and others. Imitate their labours, love, and patient zeal.

It is necessary for the Christian missionary to spend as much time as public duty will allow in *retirement*, not merely for purposes of study and mental improvement, but to cultivate a full acquaintance with his own heart, to hold intercourse with God in prayer, and fully to obtain the promised supplies of the Holy Spirit, read books on practical divinity, and also the lives of good men. Of the former we commend Wesley's *Christian Library;* and of the *latter, The Life of the late Rev. Henry Martin.*"

We are, dear brother, yours affectionately,

J. Bunting,
J. Taylor, Jun., } *Gen. Secs.*
R. Watson,

We may observe that this year (1819) was very remarkable for its increase of new members in the sphere of Mr. Graham's labours, and on his mission. Between the new mission just formed and the Circuit around, the increase was 270 members.

Mr. Graham was appointed again—from July, 1819, to July, 1820—to the same mission as last year, and on which he appears to have laboured with the same arduous toil and success as during the former; indeed, each succeeding year, as his life nears the goal, appears to be more abundantly honoured with the richest conversions, all solid and pillar-like, as his allusions will justify anon. The following is another interesting extract of a letter from his endeared son in the Gospel, the Rev. John Feely, to whom allusion has been made again and again:

"CROSSABEG, *February* 9, 1820.

"MY DEAR MR. GRAHAM,—I am happy to have an opportunity of writing to you—I wished for it. The Lord sent me where I believe he had work for me to do. Athy is remarkable. There I met two young men who were *inquiring*. One heard me on New-Year's morning on Philippians iii. 3, 'We are the true circumcision,' &c. His heart became divinely determined never more to go to the mass. The other came and had his remaining doubts removed. Mr. Guard, a young preacher (on reserve), preached, and we prayed with this young man. The Lord heard, and next day he returned home rejoicing. He is a very sensible young man. Next day I went to a Mr. Wesley's, near Baltinglass, where I delivered a short sermon on purity of heart. Brother Guard preached the next evening on love. We were happy; but at family prayer the Lord manifested Himself to us. The Divine blessing descended, and a young man cried out for mercy, and confessed his sin of backsliding in a most lamentable way. He retired, and found peace while praying. Glory to God. This young man was lately married. I asked his wife if she found peace; she said not. We sang and prayed, and God blessed her also. In fact, the whole family was moved, and also the servants. We cried to God, and He heard from heaven. Our parting was very affecting. God be glorified; He was my portion all through and my instructor. We had large congregations in several places, and good has been done during this missionary tour.—I am your affectionate son in the Gospel,

"JOHN FEELY."

Thus the Lord was training this young evangelist, and a better companion he could not meet to stimulate his zeal and confirm his faith, than the Rev. William Guard, then a local preacher, and on the list of reserve for our ministry, and afterwards an indefatigable Irish missionary for many years. He fell in harness on the Donegal mission, but his lamp was well trimmed. The writer had the privilege of knowing him for many years, "a faithful man above many." We have now his three honoured sons in the Methodist ministry: one in Africa, the other two in Ireland; and long may they be spared to the Church of God. This would have been the highest ambition of his large fatherly Wesleyan heart, had he lived to see it; but on his beloved relict has fallen that honour. She had been long a full sharer with him in that oft, but submissively prayed-for and mutually anticipated consummation.

The next letter is from Mr. Graham's son—now doubly such, not only in the flesh, but also in the spirit:—

"DUBLIN, *April* 23, 1820.

"MY VERY DEAR FATHER,—We should aim at being as perfect as possible. If we never set the prize in view, we shall never attain to it. May God help me. I cannot attain to half the perfection I know it is my privilege to enjoy. I daily see not only my weakness and imperfections, but the seeds of evil still cleaving fast to me, and sometimes they show their heads over ground, and it requires much labour, perseverance, and self-denial to keep them down. God only can root them out.

"I am, dear father, your affectionate son,

"CHARLES GRAHAM."

The above extract reminds the writer of a letter which he saw lately (Feb., 1868), when he was at Swanlinbar, in the County Cavan, on general mission work, and which Mr. Wesley wrote at one time, to Mr. James Copeland, of Lisbellaw, County Fermanagh, on the very subject, namely, "*Sin in believers*," to which young Mr. Graham refers. Mr. Wesley writes as follows :—

"GLASGOW, *May* 4, 1786.

"MY DEAR BROTHER,—There is no reasonable doubt but you had, at the time you mention, a *real* blessing from God. I make no doubt but He did then give you a taste of His pardoning love ; but you were not then thoroughly convinced of inbred sin, the sin of your nature. God is now convincing you of this, in order to give you 'a clean heart,' but Satan strives hourly to drive you to despair. Regard him not. Look to Jesus. Dare to believe. On Christ lay hold ; wrestle with Him in mighty prayer. Yea,—

'A sigh can reach His heart,
A look will bring Him down from heaven.'

He is at hand.

"I am your affectionate brother,
"JOHN WESLEY.

"*To Mr. James Copeland, Lisbellaw, Ireland.*"

Mr. Graham writes to London as follows :—

"NEWTOWNBARRY, *March* 31, 1820.

"MY DEAR BROTHER,—Thank God I am still preserved, and endeavouring feebly to witness for the Saviour in public and in private. I lament I do not see a real breach made on the errors of the day. Oh, that I could see more of the travail of the Redeemer's soul. Still it is cause of praise to see any making their escape. May I finish my life and labours to the honour and glòry of God. But, alas ! how little have I done for Him who did so much for me! John Feely's labours are greatly blessed, although not yet called out. He is well acquainted with the Irish language, and is willing to give up all to warn sinners, and his own countrymen especially. William

Byrne is still an ornament; and although John Byrne has not yet left the Mass, but is almost persuaded, my soul is drawn out after him. John Brophy is preparing for America, to escape. A poor woman (a Catholic) joined us in prayer. She said the priest would have nothing to do with her, for she went to him to church her and put his hands on her; but he would not, as she had no money. I told her of the Great High Priest, who would not reject her. I hope she may obtain mercy. She joins in family prayer. I had to pray twice with and for her. O Lord, hasten Thy coming, and kingdom, and glory, among all men; and that 'the priests themselves may believe, and put salvation on,' for they are a great stumbling-block in the people's way, and are at present most rigidly opposing the work of God.

"I am, yours truly,

"CHARLES GRAHAM.

"*To the Rev. Joseph Taylor.*"

He writes next from the metropolis:—

"DUBLIN, *July 1st*, 1820.

"MY DEAR BROTHER,—I am pained when I consider the awful effects of sin, and how the 'blind lead the blind,' and are instrumental in their destruction. But, notwithstanding all the vigilance of those teachers, the Lord is at work, convincing and converting some among them. John Feely has passed this Conference. Oh, that the great Head of the Church may call and qualify many more who without reserve will give themselves to the work, and not be afraid or ashamed to stand in the streets and market-places, to publish the tidings of salvation to perishing sinners. I know this has a good effect. The people now expect me to preach at every fair and market when I come round. It is delightful to see the crowds that attend in the open air, and 'faith comes by hearing.' I met a young man in coming to Dublin who heard me preach two years ago, and he is now truly converted, and a praying member of Society. A woman whose life was threatened stands fast. Thus we have many faithful witnesses who have fled from Babylon. O Lord, hasten her downfall. All glory to God. Amen and Amen.

"I am most affectionately yours,

"CHARLES GRAHAM.

"*To the Rev. Joseph Taylor.*"

Writing again from Newtownbarry, to which he returned after the Conference of 1820, he says :—

"NEWTOWNBARRY, *Oct. 21st,* 1820.

"MY DEAR BROTHER,—Many wonder at me, and I wonder at myself, that at my time of life, having passed seventy years in the world, I am enabled to attend my places both in public and in private houses. Thank God for all His mercies to me, who am so unworthy of any favour from His hand. But He is good and 'His mercy endureth for ever.' Hitherto He has helped me. Many desire to hear me. Others call me 'a devil,' and curse me most bitterly. If I take this patiently, as I ought to do, I should have much cause of rejoicing seeing I am not only called 'to believe,' but also 'to suffer for His sake.' O, may He grant me patience and resignation to do His divine will, so that I may 'finish my course' to the 'praise and glory of His name.' The converts from Rome are doing well. Some of them preaching in public places. The Lord has given us another schoolmaster lately. May kind Heaven increase the number daily. I hope before I go home to see some of these men able to fill even more than my place. I am going this day to the market, to proclaim to the listening throng salvation through a Saviour's name. May the great Master of assemblies send His own Word with Divine power to every sinner's heart.

"I am yours affectionately,
"CHARLES GRAHAM.

"*To the Rev. Joseph Taylor.*"

He writes again from Newtownbarry :—

"NEWTOWNBARRY, *January,* 21st, 1821.

"MY DEAR BROTHER,—I find we have no other way in getting at Roman Catholics but by street preaching at fairs and markets. They are watched close by their clergy, and they leave nothing undone in order to keep them from hearing us. They even prevent servants from going to hire in Protestant houses, especially where we lodge. But in the markets we have a full hearing. I said in the open street lately, 'We need no other place for cleansing the soul than the blood of Christ. We may sing that Jesus' blood—

> 'Through earth and skies,
> Mercy, free, boundless **mercy cries.**'

"Blessed be God for this open fountain. I don't fail **to warn** them even at the expense of my health, and all **that is dear to** me. I trust I shall live to **see better** days. The work of the Lord is prospering in convincing, converting, and sanctifying. I trust the Lord will avert the malice of men and devils. I cannot but admire the fortitude of **the converts** from Rome. Two of them went lately to warn their friends. The **mother of** one of them (a female) struck her with the tongs, and blackened her arm. The other was near being murdered, but escaped with his life. The country is disturbed. I hear that two cartloads of pikes have been taken near Dublin, and lodged in the Castle, and that many delegates have **been taken.** If **the present disturbances** subside, I hope the word preached will have greater power, as their minds would be more tranquil. May **they** see their danger and **speedily return.**

"Yours affectionately,
"CHARLES GRAHAM.

"*To the Rev. Joseph Taylor.*"

CHAPTER XIX.

ENLARGED MISSION—LETTERS AND RESULTS—1821.

"Enlarge, inflame, and fill my heart
With boundless charity divine;
So shall I all my strength exert,
And love them with a zeal like Thine;
And lead them to Thy open side,
The sheep for whom their Saviour died."

THE following letter affords strong evidence of the truthfulness of the Divine record in a spiritual and ministerial sense—"He bringeth forth fruit in old age." It unfolds much of his labours during the greater part of the year, as indeed the whole of this marvellous chapter of incidents does; at his age almost passing strange, and yet gloriously true:—

"NEWTOWNBARRY, *March* 24, 1821.

"MY DEAR CHARLES,—Thank God, we are all in health, and want for nothing, unless more gratitude and love to our Maker; and we may have these blessings also for asking. Oh, what a mercy that heaven is so free of access! Encouraged, yea commanded, to come and receive out of His fulness. Alas! how little faith we possess. It appears there is a total stop put to the schemes of the disloyal in this country. There was much night-work among them; but the Lord reigns, and blessed be our Rock. I am still preaching to them, and, notwithstanding all the prohibitions of their clergy, I have a hearing. 'Tis of the Lord I am left so long in this country. Before I leave, it would appear the Lord will raise up young men who will more than fill my place. Two of these blessed young men took their station **by my side on the** last market-day of Gorey. It appeared very formidable to see three men, set in battle array, preparing to open a battery upon the ramparts of Babylon. It was a glorious time. Many rejoiced to see it. After we had done speaking, a Catholic came to one of the young men **and** said, 'I heard the truth, and **will** embrace **it.**' We shall soon have him amongst our people. It is astonishing how my health has been **preserved with so much** work through the winter, and what has transpired **of** the spring. I have been every week at some market or other, **when it** was dry overhead ; and it seemed to harm me **less** in winter **than in summer.** I wonder at the goodness of the Lord. Perhaps He will let me see another Conference. I hear Doctor Clarke* is to **be over in the** month of May to **open your new house in** Abbey Street ; and if I am spared, mercy **only knows where I** shall spend **the next year.** But I leave it all to Him who has hitherto directed me. If I could lie passive in His hands, all **would be well.** Oh, **for faith** and **patience,** resignation, gratitude, **and humility !** How **many** are my mercies and obligations ! 'Surely goodness and mercy have followed me.' I see his **hand, and I adore the riches of His** redeeming love. I hope young Charles (*grandson*) is growing good. If he bends his mind to serve God it will make him dutiful, and he will be a blessing. Oh, to bear the yoke in youth ! May parents and children so live and act as not to be separated at last.

"I am, as ever, your affectionate father,

"CHARLES GRAHAM.'

---

* The **writer cannot** allow Doctor Clarke's name to pass without adverting to his experience, as expressed **in the following lines a** a short time before his death, in 1832 :—

"I have enjoyed the spring of life,
I have endured the toils of summer,
I have culled the fruits of autumn,
I am passing through the rigours of winter,
And I am neither forsaken of God, nor abandoned of man.
I see at no great distance the dawn of a new day,
The first of a spring that shall be eternal ;
It is advancing to meet me ; I haste to embrace it ;
Welcome, welcome, eternal spring. Hallelujah !"

The following letter from his son refers to a great many stirring events, as indeed our whole history, both national and ecclesiastical, seems always to have been eventful; it also shows what a keen observer of men and things young Mr. Graham had been :—

DUBLIN, *April* 8, 1821.

"MY VERY DEAR FATHER,—You will have the Doctor at the Conference. He is to open our chapel in Abbey Street at the end of June. He will also administer the sacrament of the Lord's Supper on that day. The Catholic Bill has passed the House of Commons by a majority of nineteen, and has gotten the first reading in the House of Lords; and there is little doubt entertained but it will obtain the royal assent. Peel and Ellis were the only members who opposed it in the Commons, and succeeded in getting a clause inserted that disqualifies Roman Catholics from filling the office of Lord Chancellor of Ireland; and it is supposed the Lords will insert a clause to exclude them from being judges. There were two bills brought in—one to emancipate the Roman Catholics generally, and the other to regulate the intercourse of the clergy and people with the See of Rome. To the latter their clergy are strenuously opposed, for by it all their correspondence with the Pope should be submitted to Government. There is another measure in contemplation, which is to pay all the clergy out of the Treasury, and take the expenses off the people altogether. . . . I wrote the above three weeks ago, and I have now to tell you that, notwithstanding the strenuous efforts made, and the strong expectation created for the bill to pass, it was thrown out in the Lords by a majority of thirty-nine. The Duke of York was against it; and he is the heir to the crown. The majority of the Lords went with him. It has created a great sensation amongst the Catholics. It is said that the king's ministers will bring it forward again. God only knows what is best. How thankful and devoted should I be! May God enable me to put my whole trust and confidence in Him, who has fed, and clothed, and preserved me all my life—far above what I could expect. May I devote the remainder of my days to His service, so that I may at last inherit eternal life, for the sake of Jesus Christ. You will not go to any one from me at the Conference. I have a house and a heart to entertain you.—Your affectionate Son,

"CHARLES GRAHAM."

From the above we see what efforts were made to remove the disabilities of the Roman Catholics at that time; but it was not until 1829 the Emancipation Act was passed, in reference to which Lord Eldon remarked—"If this Act pass, the sun of England's glory **sets.**" It is said that a solemn oath was taken that there never would be any effort made to injure the Church of England in this country. What the present stirring events (1868) about its disendowment may bring to pass, it would be difficult to tell. "May the Lord defend the right." At the Conference of 1821, the sphere of Mr. Graham's labours was somewhat enlarged by taking in the whole county of Wexford. His **Mission was** now called "**The County** Wexford Mission," very likely for the purpose of keeping him **the** longer **in** this part of the country, to mature the work so auspiciously begun. The following was the first letter **after** this Conference to his son:—

"NEWTOWNBARRY, *August* 8, 1821.

"MY DEAR CHARLES,—I have gone round my mission since I returned, and preached in the market of Gorey to a vast crowd. Fossey Tackaberry helped me: a most blessed young man. We held **field-meetings for** the last three Sabbaths, when crowds flocked to hear. **What a** mercy that we are privileged to preach *when* and *where* we please. **God** bless King George IV. May he long live to sway the British sceptre, and defend **his** loyal subjects! **What a** mercy that we are not driven into corners, **and sent to prison for** preaching the Word. We have many mercies **to be** grateful for that our forefathers had not—having so **few to explain to them** the **word of life.** I was to see Mr. Feely. He is greatly lamented by the inhabitants of Athy. He had a most commodious place to live in; but the dear man seems willing to forsake all, and give himself to the work. What a mercy when one is about to give up his account, others are ready to take his place. Since I began this letter, I heard of the Queen's death. I must confess I feel concerned. Perhaps the Lord has taken her away from the evil to come. 'The Lord sitteth on His throne judging right,' and 'His judgments are a great deep.' In the day of His coming all will be brought to light. Lord help us to watch and to do all things in reference to that day. It will be a serious thing to meet the Judge. Happy are those who have their doubts removed, and their peace made. Oh, Charles, strive to be ready!" I need not tell you what opposition I feel in my mind against going out upon my mission this year. I doubt not but much of it may come from the powers of darkness, who contend with all who resolve to be on the Lord's side; but he has been often better to me than my boding fears! I am in his hand, to make use of me or lay me aside, as seems good to Him. If the Queen is dead, I suppose all expectation of the King's coming to Dublin will be dismissed. May we learn from all these things to keep looking unto Him, 'who shall come, and will come, and will not tarry.' May the Most High bless and prosper you for time and eternity.

"So prays your ever affectionate father,
"CHARLES GRAHAM."

While Mr. Graham was thus pursuing his hallowed and successful toil in the south-east of the kingdom, God was carrying on His work in the far north, through the instrumentality of Messrs. Langtree and Hill,* on the Ards Mission. The following records a specimen of their work. It is from a communication sent to the Mission House, London:—

"Respecting the spiritual state of our people I can say, to the glory of God, I never saw more genuine piety in any part of Ireland. Lately, at a Love Feast, as many spoke as time would admit, and all were happy. Shortly after, at the Lord's Supper, in Portaferry,

---

* The Rev. John Hill still lingers amongst us, a saint indeed. I had the great pleasure and privilege of travelling with him for three years on the Tullamore Circuit, 1846-49; and also of seeing him at Belfast Conference last year (1867), and after that of spending part of a day with him in Donaghadee, and, oh, such power as he had with God in prayer!

such was the holy influence, that I could scarcely perform the sacred office. At this sacrament we had two converted Roman Catholics —one of whom is now a leader—both the fruit of this mission. Many have been converted from a state of great profligacy, and some of them from infidelity, one of whom is now beginning to instruct others with considerable success. There is a remarkable spirit of hearing, and the improved morals recommend the preaching by which that improvement has been effected. While the season remained favourable we held large meetings almost every Lord's day in the open air, which have been exceedingly owned of God.

"MATTHEW LANKTREE."

Mr. Lanktree also wrote the address on the subject of uniting to ours a branch of the Methodist body in England, who had separated many years before. This body had a few congregations in this country. His views we consider very appropriate and applicable to a union of the Primitive and Wesleyan Methodist bodies in Ireland, towards which some efforts have been already made by the Irish Methodists of New York, two years ago. We feel pleasure in inserting the document :—

"BRETHREN,—I anticipate the happiest consequences from a candid, serious, and liberal discussion of the matter thus providentially brought under your consideration. It is evident that there can be no earthly, interested, or selfish motive to influence this proposal. The spirit of Christ can alone effect this union, which would be conducive to the best interests of our common cause. Were not the Methodists raised up, as a people, to magnify the riches of divine grace, by diffusing 'scriptural holiness' throughout the world? Why, then, should we be separate bodies—we who are one in *doctrine*, experience, design, and even general *economy?* Oh, let our hearts and hands be indissolubly one, and wholly engaged for our God and Saviour. Satan strove, by dividing, to destroy us. He raised up mountains of prejudice, and barriers of human expediencies between us, in order that we might never reunite. But the God of peace is confounding Satan's devices. The principal difficulties are already removed. Our affections are again flowing together, like mingled streams of a mighty river, to stop the mouths of our enemies, and once more to revive the ancient proverb, 'See how these Christians love one another.' Let judicious deputations of brethren be appointed on both sides, and let the result be known to all parties. This appears to be a favorable season for consolidating our interests, which if now lost, may never return with the same advantages. May its final consummation bring glory to God, and the Psalmist's language be realised—'Behold how good and pleasant it is for brethren to dwell together in unity.'

"MATTHEW LANKTREE."

We trust those observations may now meet the eye of some influential lovers of our common Zion in Ireland, and England also, especially those of the Wesleyan and Primitive Wesleyan Methodists in Ireland. God Himself has given us indication already of what may be done in this way by the spirit of true unity, which has been lately poured out so abundantly on both demoninations, on the Manorhamilton Circuit, during this year, 1868.

"How good and how pleasant it is to behold,
The union of brethren who dwell in the Lord;
Like odours from ointment poured out on the head,
The fragrance of love all around them are spread.
Like the dripping of myrrh on the beard running down,
As the dew drops that Zion and Hermon do crown,
When the Lord gave the blessing of life without end,
So sweet is the union of Brother and Friend."—Ps. 133.

During the year 1821 Mr. Ouseley was zealously working away in the south and south-west part of the kingdom. He writes:—

"Our congregations were principally Romanists. They refused to be hindered by the priests. One young man in Kerry, a Romanist, who had been an atheist, was providentially led to hear us, and became so deeply convinced as to fall on his face and cry aloud for mercy. A Roman Catholic gentleman said to the priest (who allowed him to read the Bible), 'Why do you keep the cup from the laity in the sacrament?' He replied, 'Don't you know we are very poor and very numerous, and the expense of the wine would be very heavy.' 'But,' said the gentleman, 'you make them pay for baptism, confession, masses, and extreme unction,' &c.? 'Yes, certainly we do,' said the priest. 'Then, why do you not make them pay for the wine also, as it is enjoined by our Lord, who said " *Drink ye all of this*," &c. ' Really, Sir,' said his reverence, blushing, 'this is certainly an error in our Church.' That was true, but the real cause of withholding the cup was this, that it would prove too much, whereas the body and blood, &c., are said to be in the wafer already; it would be useless to repeat it. But still to make the practice *apostolic*, the priests themselves partake of both kinds!!"

On Mr. Ouseley's return to Dublin, the Rev. Matthew Tobias related the following circumstance to cheer him in his Missionary toils:—"A Roman Catholic man had heard him and Mr. Graham in the streets of Ballyshannon, when they first commenced their general mission labours—was deeply convinced of sin, but strove by every method to resist the impressions, and quench the Spirit's operations. At length he entered the army, and fought in the battle of Waterloo. Multitudes were falling on every side. All his former convictions returned with tenfold force, and fearing he might be the next called off, and remembering some of the expressions made use of in the sermons and prayers of the missionaries twenty years before, he began to plead with God for mercy, and asked Him for the sake of Christ to forgive his sins. On the spot, and in the midst of shot and shell, he found peace. He escaped unhurt, returned to Dublin, and was then walking in the ways of the Lord."

"I hope," says Mr. Ouseley, "this will be the case with multitudes, who are deterred from making an open avowal of what they believe."

Perhaps it was so with Obadiah in the court of Ahab, and "those of Cæsar's household" of whom St. Paul speaks.

Mr. Graham writes the following letter to his son:—

"NEWTOWNBARRY, *Nov.* 22*nd*, 1821.

"MY DEAR CHARLES,—My strength and sight are failing, although I have cause to bless God that I have not been 'labouring in vain nor spending my strength for nought.' The people seem to love me as much as ever, and would be pained to think of my sitting down. I am in the hand of the Lord. He knows what to do with me better than I know myself. But 'tis likely I must desist from the mission; and whether I shall be equal to a Circuit, time will tell. I have only to live for the present, and leave the rest to the Lord. If I must sit down, I have some thoughts that Dublin would be my place. I have been doing a little in the fairs and markets, and meet with no opposition. The *Antinomian* ministers used to do all in their power to annoy us, by going to some of our preaching places, and holding lectures; but the bishop, at the last visitation, has interdicted them, and the (Established) Church is now at war with itself. The world will soon discover who is right and who is wrong. Calvinism was formerly the death blow of Methodism wherever it had influence. *I have been long apprized of their combination against us, and our people are so simple, that when they meet with anything like religion in those (Established Church) ministers, they think there are none such, but time will tell.* Truth alone will bear the test, and all false systems shall fade away, and come to nought. Peace and safety are only found in the way of holiness. I hope you are going forward. There are few to help; many to hinder.

"Your affectionate father,
"CHARLES GRAHAM."

During this and the following year (1821–22), the Rev. John Feely was appointed to travel with Mr. Ouseley on the General Mission. We regret that Mr. Ouseley's biographer was not aware that this young man was the direct fruit of Mr. Graham's ministry when he was stationed on the Carlow Circuit, in the year 1817. Mr. Reilly merely says, at page 239—" Mr. John Feely, a young man, who had been converted by the Irish missionaries from the Romish creed, in which he had been educated." The fact was, Mr. Graham was on a Circuit at the time, and first met him at the house of a Mr. Large, on the Carlow Circuit, where he was employed as a tutor in the family. He ventured to hear Mr. Graham preach, and the results were several conversations, or rather stern controversies, on the disputed tenets between the Reformed and Romish Churches. The writer remembers Mr. Feely to say, that what decided his mind was, the emphatic manner in which Mr. Graham concluded the last controversial conversation by quoting so authoritatively Rev. xviii. 4, 5,—" Come out of her my people, that ye be not partakers of her sins, and that ye receive not her plagues. For her sins have reached unto heaven, and God hath remembered her iniquities." The Spirit of God accompanied this passage with such power to the young man's conscience, that he literally trembled, and from that day forward never attempted to defend his system. He sought the mercy of God, and soon found it; and did indeed become, as we have already seen, and as the sequel will still further confirm, "a burning and a shining light."

Mr. Ouseley speaks of him in terms of high respect and affection thus :—

" He is quite in his element, when he stands or rides in the street to address his countrymen in their own tongue, which he speaks with great facility. And as they learn that he had been of their own Church, they are the more eager to hear him."

Mr. Feely also speaks of Mr. Ouseley with admiration and respect thus :—

"I found him a man of deep devotedness to God, and, if possible, of still greater missionary zeal. As a minister of Christ, he was indeed 'instant in season and out of season;' endeavouring at all times, and by all Christian means, to lead sinners to the one all-sufficient Saviour. He often encountered things of an unpleasant nature while engaged in open-air work, which was almost constant. And, oh! how did he labour in prayer both before and after these exercises! Often have I heard him weep, and agonize, and wrestle with God. In coming into a town, he stood on the most convenient spot he could select, and commenced forthwith to sing a hymn in English and in Irish. In a short time a goodly number might be seen around him—of all creeds—attentively listening to the Word of Life, although sometimes one and another would, in turn, mimic or indulge in malice. It is not in my power to describe him as a preacher. He clearly expounded the moral law in its spirituality, extent, and requirements; and then the depravity of the heart as a fountain, sending off seventeen streams of corruption continually. (See Gal. v. 19—21.) Then the meritorious cause of human salvation, by the redeeming work of the Lord Jesus; and then presssd the present acceptance of pardon through faith in His blood. He was a great enemy to Popery, *as a system*, but not to its unhappy subjects. These he greatly pitied, but blamed their teachers.

"JOHN FEELY."

Mr. Graham writes to his son early in 1822, as follows:—

"BALLYCANEW, *January* 18*th*, 1822.

"MY DEAR CHARLES,—Thank God, I have seen another year, and am in good health at present. I have an increase of hearers on my mission, and some new places, which are likely to do well. I am preaching in the fairs and markets, as usual—which proves a blessing, in stirring up the people and increasing our congregations. I was violently opposed on the day I preached in Enniscorthy market. There was an uproar. They began at last to throw whatever came to hand, and resolved to prevent me being heard. This was the great market day before Christmas-Day. The Mayor of the town came forward and put a stop to the confusion, and let me loose at them. Many of them stood pale-faced and confounded before I had done. On yesterday week I had a real hearing. The

Mayor attended, and the Protestants were roused by the conduct of the Romanists on the former day. I know nothing better calculated to stir up ignorant Protestants, lukewarm Methodists, and backsliding sinners, than this outside work. They will not come to our houses, but here we find them out. I wonder how my health stands under this heavy labour. When Mr. Banks saw the attention of the Catholics in the market of Newtownbarry, he said—'That he had no hope for years to come to see such results of the Mission.' I hope the Lord has something in store for it. I am never happier than when I deliver my message, and then leaving it with the Lord to give the increase. We had a great watch-night in the market-house of Gorey, and I preached in the fair next day. John Wilson (I suppose John S. Wilson,) a local preacher, mounted my horse when I had done, and we had (both) a blessed hearing The people were attentive. Perhaps I was never loved or respected so much as I am at present. The Lord is good, 'and his mercy endureth for ever.' Others are being raised up for this warfare when I am no more. I had my day, and I am thankful. All glory to God! my peace abounds. I know nothing put peace at present It may be that my last days shall be my best. May the Most High bless and keep you all. Amen. Amen.

"CHARLES GRAHAM."

Mr. Graham again writes to the Secretary of the Missionary Society in London :—

"NEWTOWNBARRY, *April* 20, 1822.

"MY DEAR BROTHER,—Although the minds of the people are disaffected, and many are alarmed, yet, through all I have an attentive hearing, and many are melted into tears under the Word. My health is greatly impaired, and I find myself inadequate for the work. Mr. Banks and others think I ought to sit down at present; but if I could struggle on until Conference, I would be unwilling to do so. I am in the hands of that wise Being who knows what is best to do with me, and I leave it all to Him. 'Through waves, and clouds, and storms, He has gently cleared my way.' Hitherto He has helped me. I feel this an important period of my life—just finishing my course, and desisting from that blessed work, wherein He has so long supported and kept me from departing from

His ways. My heart is full. I could say much, but I forbear. I have a pleasing account to give of my Mission. The work is deepening and spreading. I met thirty in class in Newtownbarry, on last Sabbath morning. It was like the opening of heaven. The progress they are making in the Divine life is astonishing. One of these was a late convert from Rome, a young man, named T. B——. His father enjoined on him, when dying, to pay ten shillings quarterly to get him out of purgatory; but his mother, who was a Protestant, dying shortly after, left Thomas her Bible, with a dying request to read it. The young man felt as much attached to his mother and her safety as to his father, and brought five guineas to the priest to pray for her also. The priest refused, saying 'She was hopelessly lost as a heretic; but as he was so anxious, he would write to the bishop.' The bishop was of the same mind as the priest, and poor Thomas was in a state of black despair, when some one invited him to come and hear me. He did so, and asked my advice. I told him by no means to give the priest another penny, and pointed him to Christ. He sought and found, and now rejoices in God exceedingly, as do two females, formerly Romanists.—Yours, &c.,

"CHARLES GRAHAM.

" *To the Rev. Joseph Taylor, London.*"

Shortly before the Conference of 1822 he writes to his son, thus:—

"MY DEAR CHARLES,—It appears my travelling will be over at the next Conference, if spared. Mr. Banks thinks I should sit down at present. The last month has been hard upon me. A swelling in my legs, a violent cough, a lightness in my head, loss of sight, and loss of appetite. My time cannot be long. I feel this an important period of my life. The finishing of my course and of the ministry which the Lord committed to me, and in which I had a name and a place so long. Thank God, I have not turned aside from the path of duty until I can labour no longer. I have been long afraid of sitting down too soon; but now I am convinced that I can no longer fill up the place of an active man; and as the Lord is raising up men who are willing and able to work, and supply my lack of service, why should I not submit? Oh! what a mercy that our ministry is not failing, but is gloriously increasing, both in gifts and in grace. We have a number of most blessed young men on this mission, and a number of holy men and women who are alive to God. Their cups are full and flowing over. Among these is a young man who has fled from the Mass, and, for his time, is an ornament to religion; and, notwithstanding the danger he is exposed to for having left the Mass at such a time as this, he neither fears priests nor people! There are females also belonging to that system, who are striving to make their escape; but they are watched by their parents or other friends. I hope they may be steady! I am going out to the Circuit to-morrow, please the Lord, to try how far I can go. The good Master can yet strengthen me, if He has any work for me to do.

"Your affectionate father,

"CHARLES GRAHAM."

CHAPTER XX.

FIFTH APPOINTMENT TO THE COUNTY WEXFORD.

"These are precious, golden moments,
　　Kindly lent us to improve :
Are we faithful to our calling—
　　Earnest in our work of love?
Ever at our post of duty,
　　Whereso'er our call may be,
Let our lamps be trimmed and burning,
　　And the world their glory see."

AT this Conference, July, 1822, Mr. Graham was appointed the second year to "the County Wexford Mission," and wrote the following letter to his son within one day of the seventy-second year of his age :—

"NEWTOWNBARRY, *August* 19*th*, 1822.

"DEAR CHARLES,—I was brought very low since I returned from Dublin. I had to return from the mission very unwell, and spent eight days at home, after which I set out to meet Messrs. Ouseley and Feely in the market of Gorey. As they were late in coming, I took to the saddle and faced the crowd, and then a local preacher held forth. But before he had done, the men whom we expected came up, and you would imagine that there was scarcely a particle of antichristian superstition but was exposed and swept away for ever. The field meetings were astonishing. The Lord is paying those two men well for their labour of love. We had a great breaking down. The places are well watered. You would wonder to see so many Protestants in a country place as we had at the field meeting. The Lord be praised, Methodism is likely to drive all before it. We have had those good men two days. I feel no desire at present to desist from the blessed work of warning sinners 'to flee from the wrath to come.' ''Tis worth living for this.' May the Lord ever save me from growing weary or faint in my mind. There is nothing I dread more than that lukewarmness, which the Lord so much abhors. I feel grateful to my Saviour for what He has done and is doing. The people are blessedly alive. Some are joining our classes and some getting converted. Oh, what a mercy that any are making their escape from the world and the devil. 'The kingdom of heaven suffereth violence, and the violent take it by force.' Therefore strive for as much religion as will make you happy. I am joined by Mr. Feely in love to you and all the family.

"Your affectionate father,

"CHARLES GRAHAM."

He writes to the Mission Secretary in London early in 1823, in the following terms :—

"NEWTOWNBARRY, *Jan.* 18*th*, 1823.

"MY DEAR BROTHER,—I have lately enjoyed a good degree of health, and was enabled to take the streets. Although every effort is made to prevent the Catholics from hearing, yet they do *hear*, and I believe *feel* the truth of what is declared. And although the seed may appear for some time to be under the clods, it will spring forth and bear fruit at last. On last Christmas morning, a dispute arose between the priest and one of his parishioners, which led the priest to attempt to strike him, and would have done so, only that another prevented him. The priest then turned his vestments to curse this man, and opened a book to close it on him, when another came and swept the book out of his hand, and a scuffle ensued. It appears the secret was that the man whom the priest struck keeps a Bible. The priest had to beg pardon from this man, to his great mortification, but the other declared he would never hear him again. This priest told another man to burn a Testament he obtained from a friend. The Bible is opening the eyes of the people, and I am resolved they shall hear in the streets. Crowds are hearing now. Tears flow apace. The power of God is falling on them. Errors are exposed, truth enforced, and none daring to contradict now.

Many say it was in the street they were convinced of their lost condition. Oh, why have we not more street preaching. Oh, let us give them—both Romans and careless Protestants who will not come to our houses—warning from the Lord, whether they will hear or forbear. I hear six priests have left the Mass. I wonder why the Lord has kept me so long in this country. The end will be glorious. The prospect is good. Lord help me to finish my course well.

"I am yours affectionately,
"CHARLES GRAHAM.
"*To the Rev. Joseph Taylor, London.*"

The next letter to his son is also dated at the opening of the year 1823, and contrasts with his state of health when he wrote to Mr. Taylor:—

"*January 31st, 1832.*

"MY DEAR CHARLES,—I am unwell at present, and it is high time to attend to that admonition, 'Set thine house in order, for thou shalt die, and not live.' My time must be short. Thank God I have lived so long! During the latter part of the past year and the beginning of the present, my soul has been *happier than usual.* I sometimes thought the Lord was preparing me for a better world. Oh, that I may be ready! This should engross my attention above all things else; for no past experience—no matter how precious—would do for the present. But I bless God, He makes me happy, especially in the path of duty. The weary body would say,—''Tis time to give up!' but the Lord knows what is good for me, and I hope He will give me strength for my day. I am leaving home to-morrow, please the Lord, as I am well. I expect to be at home next week. Write during that time, if you have anything of interest to communicate. After that I shall have the full round of my Circuit or Mission to take, which will take me nearly three weeks. May the good Lord guide and bless you and your family is the prayer of your affectionate father,

"CHARLES GRAHAM."

In this letter he refers, no doubt, to the rich baptism of the Spirit to which the Rev. R. Huston alludes in his *Life of the Rev. Fossey Tackaberry*, thus:—"When Mr. Graham was on the Newtownbarry mission, and at the close of his career, Mrs. Morris, sen., of Ballycanew, at whose house he was wont to make a monthly pastoral visit, mentioned to the writer, that the last time he called, there was such an extraordinary power and unction in his prayer, she inquired—'Mr. Graham is your soul nearer to God than usual?' 'Oh, yes,' he benignantly replied, 'much nearer.'"

This venerable Christian lady still lives; she went to America some years ago, and has lately returned. The writer heard her pray a few days since in Ballycanew. Oh, such access to the throne of grace! It might be well said of herself now, that "her soul is much nearer to God than usual." She is like another Anna—"a widow of four score and four years," and like her also, "serves God with fastings and prayers night and day;" and as well "speaks to all them (in that neighbourhood of Ballycanew) who look for redemption;" that is, for a glorious revival of God's hallowed work, such as she has seen in America. Nor is her devoted son less to be admired for his filial attachment, and for the interest he takes in Zion's prosperity. A good motto follows:—

> "More fully moulded to Thy will,
> Let, O Lord, Thy servant be;
> Higher, and yet higher still—
> Liker, and yet liker thee."

CHAPTER XXI.

JOURNALS—GREAT OPPOSITION.

"Soon my journey will be ended,
　Life is drawing to a close;
I shall then be well attended :
　This 'my Father knows.'

"Home in prospect still can cheer me,
　Yes, and give me sweet repose,
While I feel his presence near me;
　For 'my Father knows.'"

AT the Conference of July, 1823—his last—Mr. Graham was appointed to "the King's County and County Westmeath Mission," and to reside in Athlone, where he had his wish gratified, namely, "a quiet place and a short time to prepare for flight." How he parted with his dear friends and his spiritual children on the Wexford Mission, we may judge from the following extract from Huston's *Life of Tackaberry*.

"He was held in the highest veneration and esteem by those among whom he laboured; and his parting from them bore an almost literal resemblance to that of Paul from the Ephesian Elders. 'And they all wept sore, and fell on Paul's neck and kissed him, sorrowing most of all for the words which he spake, that they should see his face no more.'" And this was literally true of Mr. Graham; but many of them have seen him since in that spirit land where friends in Christ shall part no more.

With these sentiments he closed his five years' mission labours in the County of Wexford.

The following letter is the first from Athlone to his son:

"ATHLONE, *October* 30, 1823.

"MY DEAR CHARLES,—This day I feel a little better, thank God; and I hope, if spared, to go to my Circuit to-morrow. Mr. Banks has been very ill, and I hear Mr. Steele is not well. We old preachers must expect shortly to be removed, so as to make room for others to take the field. May the good Lord help us to finish our course well, and may He send more faithful labourers to enter the list. We had the Rev. Valentine Ward here, who gave great satisfaction to all who heard him. I hope our cause will get on well in this town and country. I have been preaching a good deal of Irish in some of my places. There is a Roman Catholic young man who hears me. He has bought a Bible, and now doubts the Popish doctrines. If he were converted, we would have hope of him, as he is a young man of abilities. It is not easy for any one of that Church in such times as these, to make their escape. Perhaps the Lord is giving them the length of their chain; and may shortly stop them. The army seems much on the alert. All these things call upon us all to be ready, for 'in the midst of life we are in death.' But we are in His hand, who hath the sole control, and who can say to all His enemies, 'hitherto shalt thou come, and no further.' May our confidence be such that we 'may not fear what man can do unto us.'

"Your affectionate father,
"CHARLES GRAHAM."

The following sympathetic letter, of nearly the same date, is from the well-known pen of Mr. Graham's dear friend and companion for many years "in the kingdom and patience of Jesus," the Rev. G. Ouseley:—

"21 GREAT SHIP STREET, DUBLIN, *Nov.* 8, 1823.

"MY MUCH ESTEEMED AND GREATLY BELOVED BROTHER GRAHAM,—By a letter from brother Reilly, which Mr. Ward received yesterday, I learn, with no small concern, that you are so unwell, that it is not advisable for you to travel until your strength shall return.

If it please God, it shall return. Be satisfied; it is all of God. Take a little rest for the remainder of your time. It is singular I was telling Mr. Ward (the Rev. V. Ward, Superintendent of Missions) of your illness before Mr. Reilly's letter arrived. I dreamed a few nights ago that a number of the preachers were together, and some unusual ordination was about to take place. I thought you were the person first to be ordained, and that I was fixed on to pronounce your character. I spoke aloud, and said—'Brother Graham's character is, that he did always promptly, and with all his might, everything he conceived right to be done to promote the glory of God, and the good of the cause he was engaged in; this ye all know.' Methought the Divine power and blessing fell upon us all, and that a shower of tears of gratitude and love burst forth from your eyes and mine, and from the eyes of all. Giving glory to God, I awoke, and my soul was very happy. Yes, Charles, my good brother, as we have seen many happy and prosperous days together, and many times were thus refreshed together of God, so that we were 'filled with joy unspeakable, and very full of glory,' which, when I now think on, my eyes begin to overflow, I have a hope that, after a little, a short time indeed, we shall meet in the everlasting joy, in the presence of our ever blessed Lord, in our Father's house above, never more to be severed again. Be of good comfort, my brother; wait with joy your appointed time. How delightful is that saying, 'The blood of Jesus Christ his Son cleanseth us from *all sin.*' God upbraideth not. 'I will never leave thee; I will never forsake thee.' Give my love to good brother Dowd and his family. He flinched not in the day of rebuke. My Harriet, who loves you much, and looks to be with us for ever after a little, joins me in affectionate regards to you, sister Graham, and Ann.

"Your ever affectionate brother in Christ,
"GIDEON OUSELEY.

"P. S.—We have a prospect of a blessed work on our mission (Meath). Thank God, my health continues as good as when I was a boy."

The following short extract is from the first of the last three letters which Mr. Graham wrote to his son. It is dated—

"ATHLONE, *Dec.* 3, 1823.

"MY DEAR CHARLES,—It pleases me before I go hence, that the Lord has put into my power to be of any use to my family. They have been long the subjects of my prayers, and I hope He has, in some measure, answered me. How soon I may have done with prayer I know not, but the Lord affords me much time for that duty. I get but little rest at night, about three hours, when the pain returns, and continues until morning. The weary wheels at last stand still, except what little I do in the old preaching-house. The good Lord sent me a man to take my place, and to travel the mission, just at the nick of time. He is well liked. I hope the Lord will make him a blessing. Let us watch and pray, for the time is hastening when you will be as I am now; and how awful would it be for me to come to the borders of the grave, and have no prayer answered. The Lord be praised, He gives me comfort in my affliction. I can cast myself and all my concerns upon Him. God grant this may be the best year we ever spent if preserved. Amen.

"CHARLES GRAHAM."

The following is from the second :—

"MY DEAR CHARLES,—The Lord may have something still for me to do. Although I cannot put my foot out of doors, I can pray for the people who have been committed to my care, and direct him who is labouring in my place. And blessed be the Lord, the work is prospering. There is a good appearance. ''Tis not by might, but by my Spirit, saith the Lord of Hosts.' He gives, and who can stay His hand? How few have faith in prayer; therefore instead of making 'their requests known to God,' they strive to live independent of him. But some will say we are not worthy to be heard, as we are sinners; but let this cursed cause be removed, and then the effect will cease. Let every one cut off the right hand sin, and pluck out the right eye sin, and give themselves sincerely and unreservedly to seek and serve the Lord; and we have His word for it —'Prove me now herewith, saith the Lord of Hosts, if I will not open the windows of heaven, and pour you out a blessing, that there shall not be room enough to receive it.' Let these words leave a lasting impression on your mind. You may hear from me again before I go hence, and be no more; but there is nothing certain, for if you knew what I pass through, you would wonder I am alive this day. Mother joins me in love to you and all the family.

"I am your affectionate father,
"CHARLES GRAHAM."

The above observations on prayer are worthy the last days of such a man, whose whole religious life was a life of prayer. To this we may attribute the great success of his ministry. How true are Miss Lutton's beautiful lines—

"When torn is the bosom with sorrow or care,
Be it ever so simple, there's nothing like prayer;
It seizes, it soothes, softens, subdues, yet sustains;
Gives vigour to hope, and puts passion in chains.
Prayer! prayer! sweet, sweet prayer;
Be it ever so simple, there's nothing like prayer."

We now come to the last letter which this venerable servant of the Lord wrote, but wrote with a tremulous hand, and just waiting until his change came. And oh! what a scene follows—

"ATHLONE, *April* 2, 1824.

"MY DEAR CHARLES,—I am advised by my family to send for you to come down as soon as possible, for I may say with the patriarch, 'I know not the day of my death.' The Lord has spared me to a good old age, but from my great weakness, and my want of rest and appetite, it is not possible that I can hold out much longer. I will not say what the Lord can do. I did not expect to see this time; but He knows what is best, and what He is doing, therefore all I want is to wait His time. My affairs are mostly settled. Perhaps there will be something due at the Conference, after my debts and funeral expenses are paid, which may be of use to somebody. The will is ready to be signed. I can say little more, but expect to see you shortly. My strength is failing, or I would say more. Farewell, my dear children. May that God who blessed me and kept me, bless and keep you all forever, is the prayer of your ever affectionate father,

"CHARLES GRAHAM."

After this the *hand* forgot its cunning, and the *pen* the readiness of the ready writer. "The keepers of the house (hands) trembled, and the strong men (legs) bowed themselves," and only a short time was now to elapse until this venerable patriarch gathered up his feet to die; and nobly was he enabled to meet the final foe, proving that he could realize the truth of what he long preached, "For so an entrance shall be ministered unto you abundantly into the everlasting kingdom of our Lord and Saviour Jesus Christ." —(2 Peter i. 11). He verified the following lines:—

> "Tranquil amid alarms,
> It found him on the field,
> A veteran slumbering on his arms,
> Beneath his red-cross shield."

CHAPTER XXII.

SICKNESS AND DEATH.

> " Soldier, rise—the war is done ;
> Lo ! the hosts of hell are flying :
> 'Twas thy Lord the battle won;
> Jesus conquered them by dying.
> Pass the stream—before thee lies
> All the conquered land of glory ;
> Hark ! what songs of rapture rise,
> These proclaim the victor's story."

THE following sketch of his last illness and death was written by Mr. Pilch, the assistant, to whom Mr. Graham referred as having supplied his place on the Circuit, and who was made so useful. He afterwards removed from this country to New York, where he occupied a very useful ministerial position, and died some years ago, happy in the Lord. He has met his companion and friend :—

"*December* 4, 1823.—On my arrival in Athlone, Mr. Graham came in from Firbane scarcely able to ride. I wondered at seeing him so reduced, and concluded he had done with the labours of the harvest field."

[Here we see a remarkably special providence. This friend was on his way to take charge of one of our mission schools at Firbane, and had just arrived in time to meet the emergency of Mr. Graham's illness. He was advanced in life, but talented, and very acceptable. Mr. Graham asked him to take his place, saying, "If you don't go I will go myself, if I should fall in the ditch in the attempt."]

"I saw," continues Mr. Pilch, "that he could not attempt it again, but such was his love for souls, and his unflinching regard for regularity in being at his places to the very last, that nothing but absolute incapability could prevent him from setting out. Mr. Graham concluded the interview by saying, 'I had a heaven on earth while engaged in the blessed work, and I never had it nearer my heart than now.'" He always wept with joy when I told him of any conversion. He lived in the old rooms connected with the preaching-house in Athlone, and would, when able, lean over the bannisters of the stairs and pray at the conclusion of the service, but his strength soon failed, and he had to decline even this slight service. When speaking of death he only smiled at the thought of soon getting away, but not impatient to be off. He was perfectly resigned to the will of God, and said, 'I have not a doubt of joining the blood-besprinkled band, and I have that assurance now for fifty years, and I could not now be deceived. I neither fear the devil nor his blood-men, nor all the powers of darkness; Christ is my stronghold, and I defy their hellish rage; I had many conflicts with the enemy, but now the victory is won, I could not but be happy.'"

"*Friday, February* 26, 1824.—I was surprised," says Mr. Pilch, "to see the change which had taken place in one week. He said to me, 'I am going home fast, and I will never leave this bed-chamber until carried out.' On the next morning I called and found him asleep, but he awoke in about an hour, and smiled as if on the wing for flight. He was all praise. I asked him how he was. He said, 'I am the same in body, but happy in my soul.' The tears ran copiously down his weather-beaten cheeks, while he was exclaiming, 'Precious Saviour, loving Saviour: praise the Lord, O my soul, and all that is within me bless his holy name.' When I prayed, it appeared as if heaven was let down into our midst. This was glory begun."

"*Sabbath*, 28.—We held our Love Feast in the chapel, after which several of the friends visited him, to their unspeakable joy."

"*Tuesday, March* 1.—I called and asked him 'how he felt.' He merely said, 'breathing;' but immediately asked 'How is the Lord's work going on?' I told him of a Roman Catholic family who had renounced the errors of Popery. He smiled and said, 'Many times I have both warned and wept over them, but it is not easy to get disentangled from that yoke.' It appears he was instrumental in convincing this family of the errors of Popery before his last illness, as if God would crown his last public effort with another rich trophy from that dark system, for the destruction of which he spent his life!"

"*March* 3.—His son arrived from Dublin, which was a source of much comfort, for he greatly loved him. Mr. Graham then took me by the hand, and, with his eyes heavenward, prayed for me, and then said 'All is well; I am delivered from the sin of doubting. After preaching the Gospel to others for fifty years, how could I doubt? Jesus is mine and I am His.' I said, 'You seem to be happier than you were a few days ago.' He said, 'I was so tortured with acute pain that I could not converse much, but I have not followed a cunningly devised fable.' I said, 'The Brethren above will be glad to see you, and welcome you home.' 'O, yes,' said he, and wept. We were all melted into love. I left him on the 5th of March, and did not expect to see him again, so Mr. Lemaistre and I prayed with and for him. I heard Mr. Feely came to see him, and that it was a rich season, and a time of mutual blessing, and even of rejoicing. They partook of the Lord's Supper before he left, which was a source of unspeakable satisfaction to Mr. Graham,—Mr Feely was his own loved son in the Gospel, as already recorded. Their parting was truly affecting. Again we see the kind providence of God, in placing Mr. Feely in a station which made it convenient to visit his spiritual father on his death-bed. They have long since met to part no more for ever."

[Here we will digress for a moment to introduce a few observations on our venerable Brother Feely. The writer knew him for about forty years. His last Missionary appointment was the Antrim Mission, in the year 1858-59; here the Lord granted him the comfort of witnessing one of the most remarkable revivals of religion he had ever witnessed,—at least in connection with his own ministry,—as if the Lord would honour him in age as well as in youth. A letter now lies before the author, written in Mr. F.'s hand, referring to that auspicious event, and of which the writer was, to some extent, an eye-witness, and in which he co-operated with his venerable brother. The following is an extract:—

"ANTRIM, *October*, 1858.

"MY DEAR BROTHER CAMPBELL,—We have been getting on pretty fairly since you left. Our meetings (now at 6½ a.m.) are well attended. Our young professors hold on their way delightfully. I have not heard of one drawback. I account for the revival in this wise:—Subordinate to the mercy of God, we were engaged in prayer in our daily morning prayer-meetings, for some months, imploring the Lord—the Head of the Church—to grant us a more abundant effusion of the Holy Spirit on ourselves, and to extend the work. We did not dictate or specify. The Lord granted us some (immediate) tokens for good, and at length directed your steps amongst us. Our friends here are most desirous you should return immediately. I told them they were indebted to your study of the Irish literature for your visit. Were the whole affair at my disposal I would say *return*; make something of the language; and promote, through the Divine blessing, this hopeful revival just now.

"Your Brother,
"JOHN FEELY."

In the above revival,—between backsliders restored, believers sanctified, and penitents pardoned,—there could not be less than at least one hundred who professed to receive tokens of the Divine favour; and the writer has always thought that John Feely's prayers had more to do with what was called "The Great Ulster Revival of 1859," as far as instrumentality is concerned, than any other agency, although this agency was hidden, whilst others were blazoned abroad through the land. Antrim is close by to Connor, where the bodily manifestations first commenced; but the writer remembers distinctly the old Methodist class-leader coming over from Connor to see about the revival in Antrim, and telling us that one or two young men from America and himself were holding prayer-meetings. When the old leader returned, he told what he had witnessed and heard in Antrim; and immediately the work began, and resulted in what brought spectators from England, Scotland, and America, namely, to see this great *Ulster Revival,* of which John Feely, under God, was the first originator. But the Lord oftentimes thus hides pride from man!

Mr. Feely finished his glorious career a few years afterwards, in Hollywood, near Belfast.

These observations are written for the *Third Edition* of this work, in the City of **Toronto**, Upper Canada, February 25th, 1869. The writer is on his way to Hamilton, where he expects to see the daughter of the above venerable minister, who was also brought to God in that revival. She is now a teacher in the Female College in Hamilton.]

"*March* 13.—I returned to-day, and found my venerable friend still lingering on the shore, but ready to launch away,—

> '**Nearer** the bound of life,
> Where we lay our burden **down**
> Nearer leaving the cross;
> Nearer wearing the crown.'"

"*March* 14.—Found him still very happy in God, but patiently awaiting the will of the Lord."

"*March* 15.—Found him scarcely able to breathe."

"*March* 16.—Found him cheerful and without pain. He said, 'When I was going round my mission before my last illness, my soul was, at some times, so happy, and so filled with the love of God, that I could scarcely refrain from crying aloud, and shouting the praises of the Lord; and since my affliction my joy has been beyond expectation.'"

"*March* 18.—Found Mr. Graham, to all appearance, on the brink of eternity; his eye quite sunk. He could only speak in a whisper. He gently and humorously said, 'It takes a great deal of affliction to kill an old man;' referring to the agony he endured all night with a racking cough. But how soon a reverse, even for the better, came. Found him yesterday evening quite cheerful, he conversed about the work of God, and about the time he went to travel, and about his being nearly upset by erroneous teaching, but, said he, 'The Lord delivered me.' He spoke of Fletcher and Benson, and of their interview with Lady Huntingdon, and of their fidelity on behalf of the truth. This conversation was too much for him, but he rallied again and again, and even after this sat up in his chair."

"*Sabbath, March* 29.—Visited my aged friend to-day, and, oh! how sweetly did he speak about the beauty of the Sabbath, and about the day when all shall be brought home to enjoy an eternal Sabbath around the throne above. He was very happy, but next day worse, still rejoicing. My next visit found him much composed. We conversed about the establishment of Wesleyan day-schools. He rejoiced that the teachers would be like so many missionaries. He next referred to Satan's temptations, that he thought to tempt him to doubt his acceptance, 'But,' said he, 'he was discomfited, and should be so, for the Lord filled my whole soul with love divine. The endurance was hard for a time, but I considered Christ as enduring such.'"

"*April* 6, *Sabbath*.—Found him in some heaviness through manifold temptations (bodily afflictions), but he said, 'Though He slay me, yet will I trust Him. I had long contemplated death, but never thought it was so difficult to get through it; it is a great mercy that these afflictions cannot follow beyond the gate of death. It is now nearly over; it is too sharp to tarry.' Some good brother alluded to God's unchangeable fidelity, and that He would never leave or forsake him. Immediately Mr. Graham broke out in faltering notes—

> 'The voyage of life's at an end,
> The mortal affliction is past;
> The age that in heaven they spend,
> For ever and ever shall last.'"

"*Sabbath, April* 13.—On yesterday he gave me directions about the mission, and committed me and all to God in prayer. This day he said, 'I hope soon to be out of the reach of the spoiler; I can rejoice with joy unspeakable.'"

In this happy and triumphant state of mind he continued to the last, but sometimes unconscious: whether in the body or out of the body, he knew not. He had passed through what Pope calls "the pain," and was now entering on "the bliss of dying." Fond nature had almost "ceased its strife," and he was about to "languish into life." Already he could sing—

> "Lend, lend your wings, I mount I fly.
> O grave! where is thy victory?
> O death! where is thy sting?"

In this rapturous state he continued for eight days, sometimes unconscious of everything around him. Like Bunyan's Pilgrim, he was in the land of Beulah, and on the "Delectable Mountains"—"viewing the landscape o'er." Nothing but "Jordan's stream" rolled between. On the 23rd of April the final scene arrived, and, to the astonishment of all around him, he broke forth into the most thrilling strains of praise. The room seemed filled with a flood of light and glory, and it is even said that sounds seraphic were heard by his wife and daughter, as if a convoy of angels were in waiting—"the chariots of Israel, and horsemen thereof"—to convey his happy and sanctified spirit "to the realms of the blest" the moment the weary wheels of life stood still; reminding us of the following lines which seems so very appropriate:—

"How calm his exit!
Night dews fall not more gently to the ground,
Nor weary, worn out winds expire so soft.
Behold him in the evening tide of life—
A life well spent, whose early care it was,
His riper years should not upbraid his green.
By unperceived degrees he wears away,
Yet, like the sun, seems larger at the setting."

The writer should here state that his eyes beheld that placid countenance in death at Athlone. It indicated all the appearance of one anticipating, and even almost participating, the glory which its spirit companion had already realized. It was truly "the lovely appearance of death," if ever that expression could be justified.

The description of Mr. Graham's happy death brings to our recollection the account which records the death-bed scenes of the Rev. Messrs. Mather and Pawson, Wesleyan Ministers of England, as almost similar. Of Mather it is said he exclaimed, in his last moments, "Why did you call me back? I have been in paradise as surely as I shall go there again. I have been in heaven this morning. I long to be gone. Oh, proclaim Jesus. Glory to God and the Lamb. Amen. Amen. Amen." Of Pawson it is said he cried out, "Oh, bring near the joyful hour! I think I'll get the start of you," said he to an old friend, "and show you the way to the regions of bliss and immortal glory. I am dying, but my death-bed is a bed of roses. I have no thorns in my dying pillow. Heaven already is begun. Everlasting life is won, is won, is won: my God, my God, my God."

It also reminds us of the death-bed scene of Dr. Payson, of America, who died in 1827, three years after Mr. Graham. On being asked, "Are your views of heaven clearer and brighter than ever before?" he said, "Why, for a few moments I may have had as bright, but formerly my joys were tumultuous; now all is calm and *peaceful*." In a letter which he dictated to his sister, he says:—'Were I to adopt the figurative language of Bunyan, I might date from the land of Beulah, of which I have been for some weeks an inhabitant. The celestial city is full in my view. Its glories beam upon me. Its breezes fan me. Its odours are wafted to me. Its sounds strike upon my ears, and its spirit is breathed into my heart. Nothing separates me from it but the river of death, which now appears but as an insignificant rill, that may be crossed at a single step, whenever God shall give permission."

But it is not only to the death-bed, but to the battle-field of life to which we must principally look. A celebrated minister once visited an humble member of his congregation, and found him at work as a tanner. He gave him a pleasant tap on the shoulder. The good man started, and, looking behind him, exclaimed, "Sir, I am ashamed that you should find me thus employed." "Let Christ, when he cometh," said the minister, "find me so doing." "What!" said the good man, "doing thus?" "Yes," said the minister, "faithfully performing the duties of my calling."

"Herein," says John, "is our love made perfect, that we may have boldness in the day of judgment: because as He is, so are we in this world." Yes, the believer's growing conformity to his Maker's image, imparts a "boldness" which naturally springs from the assurance that he has "passed from death unto life." It was this led General Havelock to say to Sir James Outram, "For more than forty years I have so ruled my life, that when death should come, I might face it without fear." This was in no spirit of pride or of self-confidence. Caleb did not boast although he said, "I wholly followed the Lord my God." It was so with Havelock, the Christian warrior, when about to

"Rest from the two-fold strife—
The battle-field of India and the battle-field of life."

"Schooling the heart," says Cecil, in his "*Remains*," "is the grand means of personal religion, acting from the *occasion*, without recollection and inquiry as to motive is the death of personal piety. Such acts may be called moral intoxication; and the man is only sober when he begins to 'school his heart.' We may appear to be occupied with magnificent purposes, and yet some obliquity may contaminate its motive—like the celebrated Dean Kirwan, who said on his death-bed—'I have been for years holding forth the lamp of charity to others, but walking in darkness all the time myself; and like another Nero, 'fiddled while Rome was in flames.' It is said, however, that he got a saving view of Christ before he died. But what a warning! How few can say with the venerable Wesley,—'To candid, reasonable men, I am not afraid to lay open what have been the inmost thoughts of my heart.' And again he states, 'Genuine humility is to think and speak the truth of one's self.' Faith and holiness are inseparable, not only to look into the perfect law of liberty, but to continue therein; then we can 'rejoice evermore, pray without ceasing, and in every thing give thanks,' for the bitter as well as for the sweet. Then we can pray—'search me and try my ways; prove me and know my heart, and lead me in the right way.' Let us never make the atonement of Christ a cover for our sins, as the Antinomians do,—

"'Rather I would in darkness mourn,
The absence of Thy face,
Then e'er by light irreverence turn,
Thy grace to wantonness.'"

CHAPTER XXIII.

CHARACTER OF MR. GRAHAM.

"Of life's past toils, the fading trace
　Hath given that aged patriarch's face
　Expression holy, deep, resigned;
　The calm sublimity of mind.
　Years o'er his snowy head have passed,
　And left him of his race the last;
　Alone on earth, but yet his mien
　Is bright with majesty divine.
　And o'er his features poured a ray
　Of glory, not to pass away—
　One to sublimer worlds allied,
　One from all passions purified—
　Even now, half mingled with the sky,
　And all prepared—oh, not to die,
　But, like the prophet, to aspire
　To heaven's triumphal car of fire!"—HEMANS.

OUR venerable father in Christ is now gone; not lost, but only gone a little before, to be "for ever with the Lord" whom he loved so long and loved so well on earth. He will be had in everlasting remembrance. His name is still embalmed in the memory of many who linger behind, and who will be his (increased) crown of rejoicing in the day of the Lord Jesus. The writer saw his remains in Athlone forty-four years ago, and his prayer then was, and still is, that his mantle and a double portion of his spirit might fall upon him.

"Oh, may we in his footsteps tread, and follow him to heaven."

His death was more like a translation than a dissolution. Like Payson, of America, he "swam in a sea of glory, long before he plunged into the Godhead's deepest sea." The secret of his unbounded labours and usefulness, as well as of his persevering stability to the end, may be attributed, next to Divine influence, to the genuine character of that "faith which works by love, and purifies the heart." This was the vital current which flowed continually through the moral system. It was not a sentiment; it was Christian principle. It entered into all the sanctifying duties of his life, both towards God and man. Hence the stability of his zeal, the magnitude of his labours, and the unbounded character of his usefulness. He had, no doubt, his infirmities, and he may have had faults too; but if he had the latter, we never heard of them. There may appear to some that there was an unjustifiable roughness of manner in his earlier days; but we might as well blame John the Baptist or Martin Luther for calling things by their right names, as to blame Charles Graham. If he employed rough implements, it was because he had rough work to do.

The Rev. John Hartley, in speaking of John the Baptist, says:—"His words were often as rough as his garments, and piercing as barbed arrows; but such will be borne, when spoken by thorough and consistent men, and spoken in real love. His preaching stirred like a clarion, and woke many an echo in the depths of men's hearts and consciences; still eager thousands hung upon his lips." So it was with Graham. It is said, that in the latter years of his life a peculiar sweetness and amiability of disposition was manifest to all; still he blendid the "son of thunder" and the "son of consolation" into hallowed combination. If the writer was requested to write his epitaph he would select that on Sir Christopher Wren's monument at St. Paul's, London. It is this—

"SI QUÆRIS MONUMENTUM
CIRCUMSPICE."

"If you enquire for his monument, look around;" and if he was called on to throw Mr. Graham's character into suitable lines of poetry, he would select those written by Cowper on Whitfield. They are as follows, and almost to life :—

"He loved the world that hated him, the tear
That fell upon his Bible was sincere;
Assailed by scandal and the tongue of strife,
His only answer was a blameless life.
And he that forged, and he that threw the dart,
Had each a brother's interest in his heart;
He followed Paul, his zeal a kindred flame,
His apostolic charity the same;
Like him he laboured, and like him content
To bear it, suffered shame where'er he went."

His ministerial appointments stand thus :—Kerry, 1790; Limerick, 1791; Enniskillen, 1792-93; Birr, or Parsonstown, 1794-95; Mountrath, 1796-97; Longford, 1798. General Missionary :—Province of Connaught, and Counties of Meath and Louth, 1799; Province of Ulster, 1800, 1801; South and West of Ireland, 1802; Munster, 1803; Counties of Limerick, Tipperary, Mayo, Galway, and Clare, 1804; Provinces of Connaught and Leinster, 1805; the Limerick and Athlone Districts, and country in their vicinity, 1806; the Cork District, 1807; Athlone Circuit, 1808-9; Mallow Circuit, 1810; Longford Circuit, 1811; Cavan Circuit, 1812-13; Mountrath Circuit, 1814-15-16; Carlow Circuit, 1817; Newtownbarry Mission, 1818-19-20; County Wexford Mission, 1821-22; King's County and County Westmeath Mission, 1823.

The following is the Conference record of Charles Graham, in the Minutes for the year 1824:—"He was born near Sligo, where he lived as a respectable farmer during a period of forty years. At an early age he heard the Gospel by some of the Methodist ministers. He was soon after converted to God. In the commencement of his Christian course, he was led to entertain the doctrine of particular redemption; but he afterwards had more scriptural views, and he continued to the end of his life testifying that God is loving to every man in Christ Jesus. He was actively employed for twenty-one years as a local preacher, calling sinners to repentance. In the chapels of our connexion—in the fairs and markets—'in season and out of season'—he was abundant in labours, beseeching men 'to be reconciled to God.' As a preacher, his abilities were highly energetic and useful. His powerful appeals to his street congregations in the Irish language, were pathetic, and sometimes overwhelming. The multitudes heard, trembled, and fell before him. When no longer able to proceed on his mission, he was favoured with more than ordinary influences of the Holy Spirit, as if the great Master had already said, 'Well done, good and faithful servant.' During his confinement, he endured much pain with patience and fortitude. Near the close of his life he spoke little, yet his whole soul was wrapped up in the 'blessed hope of immortality.' And he was often heard to repeat these words—

'The age that in heaven they spend
For ever and ever shall last.'

He gently fell asleep on the bosom of our Lord, in Athlone, April 23, 1824, aged seventy-four."

The next testimony is from his dear Charles, his only son and namesake, with whom he corresponded so familiarly and affectionately for twenty-four years:—" It would far exceed my feeble powers of description, to give an adequate idea of the happiness, resignation, and divine confidence, possessed by my dear and lamented father during his long and painful illness. He never discovered a doubt, or even a temptation, on the subject of his acceptance with God through Jesus Christ. Of him it might frequently be said, as of the ancient patriarch, that he literally 'worshipped leaning on the top of his staff' [Alluding to his efforts to perform family devotion, while either lying or sitting up in the bed]. He made it a matter of prayer, that God, before He removed him to his eternal rest, would be pleased so to reveal Himself and the invisible world, that he might have some just idea of the ineffable glory of that heavenly kingdom, into which he felt persuaded he was about to enter. And it appeared that God, in infinite condescension, answered this prayer of His dying servant, for on the night previous to his dissolution he had such a discovery of the eternal world made to his mind as caused his prayer to be turned into the most rapturous praise. 'Glory, glory be to God: glory, glory be to God,' were his continued expressions. In the course of the night he lifted up his hands three times and repeated the words, 'Amen, amen, amen,' [Perhaps in allusion to the language of the four beasts in

Rev. v. 14, who are represented as saying, Amen]. We could not ascertain the immediate reference to these devout ejaculations. He was totally abstracted from the world, and from all earthly concerns. About half-an-hour before he expired he said to Mrs. Graham, 'I am going to depart; I am going to depart. Livy, my dear, I am going to sleep;' and in a few moments he literally fell asleep in Jesus, without a sigh or groan, or the least distortion of a muscle of his countenance. He had the use of all his faculties to the latest hour of his life, and his sight, hearing, and understanding were as perfect as in the time of his health. For these also he expressed his constant thanksgiving to God, thus proving the truth of the declaration, 'If any man serve me, him will my Father honour.'"

The above documents were read by Rev. Wm. Stewart, after he preached his funeral sermon, on the 26th of April, 1824, in the Wesleyan Chapel, Abbey Street, Dublin, his remains having been brought from Athlone and then to the chapel, previous to interment. The audience was deeply affected. The preachers, stewards, leaders, Strangers' Friend Society, and many of the members and friends of the Dublin Society, followed him to the grave, reminding us of what is said of Samuel's sepulture :—" And Samuel died ; and all the Israelites were gathered together, and lamented him, and buried him in his house at Ramah (1 Sam. xxv. 1); and under the Christian dispensation in which life and immortality are more fully brought to light, we have the tenderest sensibilities of our sanctified nature called forth, thus, " And devout men carried Stephen to his burial, and made great lamentation over him " (Acts viii. 2). One is sometimes led almost to ask, when great and good men die in these latter days, whether we are as much affected as we ought? Surely—

"Nature unreproved may drop the tear."

The following is from the pen of Mr. Graham's affectionate and long-tried friend, the Rev. William Ferguson.* It is found, as supplied by him, among "Recent Deaths," in the July number of the *Wesleyan Methodist Magazine* for 1824:—"The Rev. Charles Graham, one of our oldest, most laborious, and most successful Irish missionaries. In the

---

* It affords the writer great pleasure to record here the high estimation in which the venerable Wm. Ferguson was held by his brethren in the ministry. The following is the epitaph on the marble tablet which is found in the Wesleyan Chapel, Stephen's Green, Dublin :—

THE
REV. WM. FERGUSON,
Departed this life,
IN THE FAITH OF CHRIST,
on the
26th of July, 1854,
In the 84th year of his age,
and
64th of his ministry.

This Tablet is erected by his brethren of the Wesleyan Methodist Conference of Ireland, as a memorial of the esteem in which they held his eminent piety, practical wisdom, and the many virtues that adorned his character.

year 1790 his appointment to the County Kerry was made by the express desire of Mr. Wesley, by whom Mr. Graham was personally known and approved. He had much opposition from the Catholics, yet his ministry was to many of them 'the power of God to their salvation.' After seven years of Circuit work he was again appointed to the General Mission in 1799, to preach the Gospel *in the native tongue* to his benighted countrymen, for which he was eminently qualified.

"The sweetness and fluency with which he spoke the Irish language, and his pronounciation of it, afforded more general satisfaction than that of any other Irish speaker I have ever known. His morals were unblameably correct; his piety was sincere and fervent; and his talents as a preacher truly respectable. I have often seen hundreds, yea, thousands, hang upon his lips, still as night, whilst the tears, streaming from their eyes, gave ground of hope that they were not hearing the word of life in vain. My acquaintance with Mr. Graham commenced in 1793, and, during a period of thirty-one years I have invariably found him the same pious, laborious, ardent, and faithful minister of the Gospel of our Lord Jesus Christ."

The Rev. Mr. Lanktree writes,* "I had a letter from my old friend and brother Ouseley, which gives such a testimony to his former colleague, Mr. Graham, lately called to his eternal rest, as should comfort and cheer the servants

---

* So many references having been made to Mr. Lanktree, the writer feels great satisfaction in introducing the following sketch of his character from the Minutes of Conference for the year 1850. "His public ministrations were eminently spiritual, rich in evangelical truth, and accompanied by the unction of the Holy Ghost. He was specially a son of consolation to the sick and the dying. In

of our Lord, who are still in their state of probation. It is this:—

"MY DEAR BROTHER LANKTREE,—I have just come from the country, and heard that our good and greatly beloved brother Graham has a day or two since fled to that fair world of light and love, after which he had so long panted, and to arrive at which he laboured day and night. And what a labourer was he! But the time of rest is come. Yes, he has just gone a little before us. Oh, what days of the Son of Man have he and I seen together! But a blessed eternity is at hand, and there all the ship's company meet, never again to part. I am still supported as when young, thank God. I labour much in the streets also. Yesterday I rode twenty-two miles, preached in the morning in Cavan—in Ballyjamesduff market at one, to a vast crowd—and last night in Kells. This day I rode to Dublin, thirty-two miles, and am not a whit the worse.

"G. OUSELEY."

The next is selected from a lecture, entitled "*Ouseley and Graham*," delivered by the Rev. R. Huston, in Armagh, about five years since, and afterwards published by request. He says,—

"Mr. Graham was the most remarkable of Ouseley's co-evangelists, and was born in Connaught, as were several who were endowed with popular talents.

"*First*—He was remarkable for *high-toned spirituality*. An humble, serious, and holy man; entirely devoted to God.

"*Secondly*—For *marvellous answers to prayer and singular revelations from God*. He made it a matter of prayer

---

his latter days, when a supernumerary, he sought to save souls. His last ministerial act was to pray at the bedside of a poor man, who was dying of cholera; shortly after which he died himself of the same disease. His last words were, 'To die is gain.' He died in Belfast, in the seventy-ninth year of his age, and the fifty-fifth of his ministry."

that God would reveal the ineffable glory of the invisible world to him before he entered it, and He did so. For some days before he departed, he shouted, again and again, 'O, the glory! O, the glory!'

"*Thirdly*—For *moral courage*. This was seen from the beginning of his career, especially when preaching in the open air; and more especially in his defiance of Romish opposition. It was tested frequently in the County Kerry, and in the streets of Clones, when opposed by the magistrate and the army.

"*Fourthly*—For his yearning pity for perishing sinners, such as in the case of the culprit at Longford, for whom he pleaded with God on the morning of his execution, and had hope in his death.

"*Fifthly*—For his perception of the morally sublime. This may be seen in his graphic description of some of those expressions which female converts from the Church of Rome used after they found peace with God: one exclaiming in Irish, 'A thousand praises to Thee, my Saviour.'

"*Sixthly*—For his pungent and apposite wit, as when he was preaching from—' Why stand ye here all the day idle?' he said, 'Just like the boy gallopping for the priest; he was idle, although in haste!' It is so with many still: *idle*, although apparently *labouring* hard.

"*Seventhly*—For pathos and unction as an Irish speaker, the Rev. W. Ferguson said of him,—'The commanding sweetness and fluency with which he spoke in the Irish language, eminently qualified him to preach the Gospel to his benighted countrymen. I have seen hundreds, yea, thousands, as still as night, listening to the pointed and powerful appeals to their consciences, whilst the flowing tears proved they were not hearing in vain.'

"*Eighthly*—For convincing argument and persuasion. Holding a lengthened debate on the tenets of Rome with a shrewd controversialist, Mr Graham at length turned on the sanctity of the Church as a mark of apostolicity, and said, 'If I went next Sabbath to your place of worship and took out all the rogues, liars, drunkards, swearers, Sabbath-breakers, &c., how many, think you, would I leave behind ?' 'Why, Sir,' said the man, 'If you went so close to work as that, you would pull the priest himself off the altar !"'

Mr. Huston forgot, however, to mention another prominent feature of Mr. Graham's character—that of *great meekness under provocation*, especially when arising from ignorance. It was this which arrested that young man in Gorey of whom mention was made more than once in this biographical sketch. Mr. Graham was preaching as the people were coming out of mass, when a miscreant took some of the mud of the street and flung it in Mr. Graham's face ! Mr. Graham, with dignified meekness, said nothing, but took out his handkerchief and wiped off the mud. Young Byrne was passing by, and witnessed the scene. He said to himself, 'That is a man of God,' and he soon after left the Church of Rome.

> "Teach us to bear the taunt, the scoff,
> The hour when timid friends fall off ;
> In meekness tempered best.
> Teach us to witness for the Lord,
> And still to wield the two-edged sword,
> And then 'remaineth rest.'"

"Graham's portrait," says Mr. Huston, "*physically* and *morally*," and we would add, *mentally*,—" may be thus drawn :—A muscular frame, a penetrating look, a commanding voice, an authoritative bearing, a strong understanding, a heart overflowing with love to Christ and the souls of men. Bold as a lion, mighty in the Scriptures, antagonistic to error, pastoral in his spirit and habits. [And we would here add, conscientiously scrupulous in all his appointments, especially ministerial.] Fatherly in his manner, energetic, self-denying, candid, prudent, instructively witty, prayerful, unwearied in toil, and faithful unto death.'

We strongly commend Mr. Huston's lecture which, for its size, is the best characteristic description extant of the two great men on whom he lectures. It is well written, and abounds with anecdotes. See end of Chapter XXIII.

Another description, taken in part from Mr. Reilly's account of those two 'Great Hearts,' will be pleasing :—
' Mr. Graham was *naturally* gifted with persuasive powers; Mr. Ouseley with reasoning powers. Mr. Graham's voice was soft and musical; Mr. Ouseley's rough and sepulchral. Mr. Graham brought the Scriptures, with a mind filled with holy truth, to bear upon errors and prejudices convincing to all; Mr. Ouseley, by logical arguments and varied research, would stop the mouths of gainsayers. Both were perfect masters of the Irish language, and each felt inspired with a pure zeal for the truth of Christ, and burned with an unquenchable zeal for the glory of God and the salvation of sinners. They were sons of thunder."

The Rev. Richard T. Tracy, of Limerick, kindly sent the following, unsolicited, a few days ago, relative to Mr. Graham's person and labours :—" The last time I saw him (Mr. Graham) was at the Conference [most likely 1820], in Dublin. His figure was compact, firm, and erect. I saw him leaving town. He seemed dead to all around him, and alone in the midst of the multitudes. I thought,—What a noble herald from the courts above! An ambassador of Christ, having delivered his message of mercy to thousands, who were subdued beneath the shadow of the cross. And as my last glance fell on this venerable man of God, my very heart sighed, 'Let my last end be like his.'"

The last is from the poetic pen of the Rev. Mr. Byrne, who is mentioned in a former part of this Memoir, as being the fruit of Mr. Graham's ministry, in the street of Gorey. He became a preacher in our connexion, and travelled with great acceptance for three years. When his health declined he had to give up the ministry; but he was very useful wherever his lot was cast. He died of cholera, in the year 1848, in Tralee, where he was greatly respected. He published a volume of poems, in which the following is found to the memory of Mr. Graham :—

"LINES ON THE REV. CHARLES GRAHAM.

" To tell where sleeps the brave,
  The column lifts its head ;
How grateful on the patriot's grave
  A nation's tears are shed.

But there's a holier spot
  Where dust more sacred lies ;
The hoary veteran's rest, who sought
  The triumphs of the skies.

Such this aged warrior was,
  Who in his armour died ;
A valiant soldier of the cross,
  In hottest conflicts tried.

The high commission came—
  He heard, he rose, he went,
The Gospel trumpet to proclaim,
  To all, wherever sent.

Wherever men would hear
  The story of 'the Cross,'
He nobly stood, unmoved by fear,
  In mercy's glorious cause.

Then, then, with tears bedew
  The dust where GRAHAM lies;
'Look up, look up,' he cries to you,
  'Come! meet me in the skies!'"

CHARACTER AND ANECDOTES OF MR. OUSELEY.

WE here introduce a more succinct account of the character of Mr. OUSELEY and his remarkable labours and successes, principally from the pen of the Rev. R. Huston :—

All through life, Mr. Ouseley was emphatically a man of prayer. This was the secret of his power. His custom was to go from his knees to the street or the pulpit. "His devout breathings when alone," says his memorialist, "were often most affecting. It was difficult, on such occasions, to determine whether the love of lost men or the love of Christ predominated. 'My gracious Master! my gracious Master!' had usually this accompaniment: 'Oh, poor lost sinners! Oh! my deluded countrymen! O Lord, save my country!'" Mr. Noble, who was his companion on the Mission for eight years, says,—"Oh, how often have I known him to spend hours together, wrestling with God in mighty prayer for the conversion of lost souls!"

In preaching, it was his wont, after the example of the great Apostle of the Gentiles, to relate the manner of his conversion, and his present religious experience. Such testimonies to the Divine mercy and power were often signally blessed to the salvation and edification of others. Of this his biographer gives the following remarkable instance :— "On Sunday, 24th December, 1837, he preached in the town of Mountmellick at 10 o'clock in the morning. In the course of his sermon he gave, what afterwards produced a wonderful effect, the relation of his own experience. A young gentleman, a native of Scotland, who had recently come to reside in Ireland, went to hear him preach, from a motive of curiosity. The word was quick and powerful. He believed what Mr. Ouseley declared, that God gave his Son for all. He loathed himself and sin, and went as a penitent to the footstool of mercy. His prayer had power with God through Christ. After a severe conflict he was led to the Saviour in whom he was enabled to rejoice with joy unspeakable and full of glory. Now, he has a place in the Methodist ministry, preaching the great truths by which he himself was made free." This gentleman is now the gifted, pious, and loving John Hay, of the English Conference, and the constant friend of Ireland.

Mr. Ouseley's piety retained its freshness and fruitfulness to the last. Amid the intense pain which he endured on his death-bed, no murmur escaped his lips. His cry was, "Oh, my Father, my Father God, support thy suffering child. Thy will be done, my Father God!" And when just to the margin come, he bore this refreshing testimony —"I have no fear of death. The spirit of God sustains. God's Spirit is my support!"

His attainments in classical and in mathematical knowledge, proved that he was a hard-working student. He acted on the maxim all through life, that "What was worth doing at all, was worth doing well." As the result of such close application, he had learned to love " the sweet-toned romances of Virgil, the cold and exquisite lyrics of Horace, and the living deeds and men of Homer,"— carried much of their contents in his memory, and often made use of them in after life, as occasion required. Apposite quotations from classic authors often gave weight to his controversial publications ; but he never was guilty of the disgusting pedantry of those who make a display of their learning in the pulpit. His acquirements in this department often proved of great advantage in his epistolary correspondence with the Romish clergy. Of this, his visit to England on one occasion, where he endeavoured to check the alarming progress of Popery, furnishes an example :—"As I went along," he says, "I wrote to the Priests a short letter in Latin, and enclosed a printed paper to each in defence of the Gospel, and against their fatal creed of Trent, or Pius the Fourth. Glory be to God! Amen." Thus did he ascribe glory to God that he could encounter and defeat the Priests with their own weapon— their boasted Latin.

The work which is now a text-book for Reformation Societies, which will hand down his name to posterity as one of the best informed, most acute, and unanswerable opponents of that system—and would that a cheap edition of it were published, placing it within reach of "the million."—is his book entitled, "Old Christianity against Papal Novelties." Such was the estimate in which that work was held by the late excellent Lady Farnham, and the value she attached to it as a book "for the times," that she requested liberty to reprint it at her own expense.

He possessed most uncommon powers of reasoning and illustration. These powers, sanctified by the Divine Spirit, will account for the deep convictions which generally seized his hearers, and for the strong emotions which followed. Out of numerous illustrations of these powers, take the following:—Riding along one day, he saw some men cutting turf. "What's that you're doing, boys?" he enquired. "Cutting turf, Sir." "Why don't you leave it till Christmas?" "Till Christmas, Sir! musha, it would be too late, then." From their answer he took occasion to shew them the folly and danger of postponing their salvation to a future time, when it might be impossible to attain it.

"I had," says Mr. Huston, "the privilege of hearing him once in the town of Granard. The preaching-place was an untenanted house in the main street. Every apartment on the first floor was crowded with eager hearers—many of them Romanists. His text was Mark xvi. 15, 16, 'Go ye into all the world, and preach the Gospel to every creature.' His leading divisions were:—

I. What sort of men did Christ send to preach his Gospel?

II. What was it they preached? The Gospel.

III. The effects that followed.

In discussing the first head, he dealt unsparing blows at immoral teachers of religion, without naming those of any Church. "The preachers our Lord sent out—were they swearers? No. Were they liars? No. Rogues? No. Sabbath-breakers? No. Drunkards? No. Sensualists? No. To all such, God says, What hast thou to do to declare my statues?"

In explaining what it was they preached, he levelled his artillery against the Romish dogma of *Tradition* without once naming it. " It was the *written* Gospel they preached." To illustrate and enforce his argument, he supposed the following case :—" If your child were dangerously ill, you'd send for the doctor, wouldn't you ? I know you would. Well, the doctor comes, and you say, ' Oh, doctor, my child is very bad.' After making some enquiries, the doctor prescribes, ' Give him this ; ' after a while, give him that ; then after so long a time, give him the other.' But you'd say, ' Oh, doctor ! I'm afraid I'll forget it. Please, doctor, *write it down.*'" The drift was perceived, as bearing against the doctrine of *tradition.*

When in Cork, he mentioned an incident which took place in Kilrush some years before. " I knew a lady in the County Clare"— and, turning suddenly round to me, he said, " Brother Reilly knew her, too. One day she took a vial off her sideboard, and, mistaking it for another, she poured out a glass of its contents, and swallowed it. She felt herself indisposed immediately, rang the bell most violently, and when the servant came, she cried out, ' What was in that bottle ?' ' Laudanum, ma'am,' was the reply. Laudanum !' she said ; ' I'm a dead woman ! I have swallowed a dose of it !' She ran to the office of her husband, and exclaimed, ' P——, my love, I'm a dead woman ! I have swallowed a dose of poison ! Send for Dr. Elliott immediately.' The doctor was sent for, administered a strong emetic, and the poison was dislodged ; but she had not an easy moment while the poison remained. And yet," he added, " *you* will eat, and drink, and sleep ; you will laugh, and sing, and dance ; take your pleasure, and transact your business, and the poison of hell in your soul." This was expressed with appalling gravity and force.

Preaching once at Newtownbarry, on Gal. v. 19, "The works of the flesh are manifest," &c., the word did great execution. "Every person under the dominion of the flesh," said he, "is possessed by a monster with seventeen mouths, and every mouth is seeking food suited to its nature." Naming the mouths in the text, the people appeared horror-struck, and many of them roared aloud for mercy.

His argument with Father Glynn, of Killimor, on the Real Presence, furnishes an instance still more characteristic of Ouseley's extraordinary power of reasoning and illustration. Just before the family with whom he and Mr. Reilly stopped went to tea, a tall gentleman of very marked, intelligent countenance, entered the room. His outside coat hung loosely over his shoulders, and by his whole manner he showed that he was on familiar terms with the family. It was no other than the parish priest, who, as is the habit with many of his order, among respectable Protestants, had cultivated an intimacy with the family. He very soon gave indication of dissatisfaction at seeing Missionaries there; and, not knowing Mr. Ouseley, at once threw down the gauntlet, imagining himself secure of victory. "It would be very desirable," he said, "if there were a convention of all the states in Christendom to settle the faith of the world and the true sense of Scripture, and not to have every tinker and tailor that pleased standing up to interpret the word of God." This was too plain to be misunderstood. Although Mr. Ouseley said, "Indeed, sir, if it could be accomplished it would be very desirable." He replied "It is impossible, sir, that the judgment formed by such an assembly could be anything but infallible." Mr. Ouseley then commenced his attack on the system of Popish infallibility already existing, and which had stood for centuries, and said I feel strong and increasing objections to that system. "To what part of it?" the other enquired. Ouseley began with Extreme Unction; showed it could not be a Christian sacrament, as not being instituted by Christ; then went to Half Communion, and from that to the doctrines of Intention and Transubstantiation. At last, so pressed was the priest that he exclaimed, "O, my dear sir, if you were to see all the books I saw when I was in college in France on that one subject, the *Real Presence,* you would be afraid to speak a word upon it all the days of your life." "My dear sir," said Ouseley, "there are some things which a child can understand as well as an archbishop. For instance, how many panes of glass in that window?" "Poh," said the priest, "that's a physical fact. Any one can tell that." Ouseley retorted, "Is it not equally a physical fact that John the Baptist was not the son of the Virgin Mary?" "Very true indeed, sir," said the priest. "Why," inquired Ouseley, "was he not her son?" "Because," said he, "John the Baptist was not born of the Virgin Mary." "Could any man," asked Ouseley, "that had never been born of her by any power, ever become her son?" "Certainly not," said the priest. "Could any *thing* that never was born of her ever become her son?" "Indeed, I think not." "I have you now, my good fellow! Can the corn which grew up last year, which was ground by the miller, baked by the baker, and consecrated by the priest, become the son of the Virgin Mary by any power of God or man?" "O," said Father Glynn, "all things are possible to God." "No," said Ouseley, "all things are not possible to God; for it is impossible for God to lie or work a self-contradiction, which would be necessarily involved in the doctrine of your Church. Besides there are, according to your canon, twelve cases in which defects may occur in the Eucharist—defects in the bread, the wine, the form, the ministry, &c., so that according to your own doctrine it is utterly impossible to know when there is a true sacrament. How can any rational being believe that the accidents to which the Host is liable can happen to the Son of God? It can be carried away by the wind, totally disappear, be devoured by a mouse or a rat; and the wine can be poisoned. Now, sir, can you believe the doctrine of your own Church? Can any man in his senses think that any of the above circumstances can take place with regard to the true Christ?" The priest was confounded. The young gentleman said, "But what did you think of your own argument, Father Glynn?" "If it were not for the *bit of bread*," he replied, " I would never celebrate Mass as long as I live!"

Ouseley was remarkable for meek endurance of injuries. At Kilkenny, on one occasion, the infatuated mob seemed resolved to murder him and Graham in the open street. " Brother Graham was not hurt," says Gideon; " but I got several bruises. The mayor and commanding officer came forward and escorted us out of the town; but some went on, and from behind the ditches, after we got away from the town, attempted to stone us again; but they did us no harm, thanks be to God! *I greatly pitied them, for they knew not what they were doing.* Unless the Gospel were thus publicly preached, how should they ever see the light thereof? I wrote to the Catholic Bishop, and laid the barbarity of his people before him, with some *mild* expostulations, and enclosed him a couple of the papers I distributed among the people."

On another occasion, while preaching in the street of Kilkenny, stones flew from all directions around him. A priest was walking up the street, and Mr. Ouseley, just at the moment, stepped down, and said, "Sir, I'll take your arm, for these poor people will injure themselves." Of course no one would now throw, when they saw the preacher and the priest linked together!

One fact more to illustrate this feature. Preaching in the street of a town in Connaught, to a vast crowd, he received a blow on the mouth, which knocked out two of his teeth. He placed the teeth calmly on his hand and showed them to the crowd, while the blood flowed from his mouth, and meekly said, "If you go on in this way you will soon send me to paradise." "The sight," says Mr. Noble, "was truly affecting; and if he had been killed on the spot, I believe he would have offered up that prayer with his latest breath, 'Lord! lay not this sin to their charge.'"

Indifference to human censure was another of Ouseley's characteristics. As he was walking through a town one day, he heard the bellman mumbling the announcement of his sermon, in a low voice and indistinct manner, for fear of the consequences. Mr. Ouseley was indignant. Going over, he took the bell out of the bellman's hand, and, beginning to ring, shouted with stentorian voice,—"This is to give you notice, that Gideon Ouseley, the Irish Missionary, will preach this evening in such a place, at such an hour, and *I'm the man myself!*"

His ingenuity in saving souls is worthy of notice and of imitation. He was "all things" lawful "to all men" that he "might by all means save some." That ingenuity he sometimes evinced in familiar conversation. Meeting a man once returning from a pilgrimage, imposed on him as a penance, the following dialogue took place:—

OUSELEY.—" Where have you been, poor man?"

PILGRIM.—" At the Reek, Sir." (A mountain in Connaught.)

OUSELEY.—" What were you doing there?"

PILGRIM.—" Looking for God, Sir."

OUSELEY.—" Where is God?"

PILGRIM.—" Everywhere, Sir."

OUSELEY.—" How far did you travel?"

PILGRIM.—" Forty miles, Sir."

OUSELEY.—" And would you go forty miles this morning to look for the *daylight*, when it was shining into your own cabin door? And is it not worse to go forty miles to look for God, who made the *daylight* at home as well as at the Reek?"

PILGRIM.—" O, then, gentleman, the Lord pity us; it's *thrue* for you!"

The same character showed itself once at a Mass said by a priest over a corpse, at a private house in the country. Mr. Ouseley knelt with the people, rendered into Irish every word that would bear a Scriptural construction, and audibly repeated it, saying,—" Listen to that!" Those within hearing were deeply affected. The priest was thunderstruck. All were ready to receive what he might say. The service over, Mr. Ouseley and the congregation rose to their feet, when he delivered an exhortation, showing the necessity of having their peace made with God as the result of reconciliation with Him. Mr. Ouseley mounted his horse and rode away. " Father," said they, " who is that?" " I don't know," replied the priest; " he's an *angel*. No *man* could do what he has done." The Missionary was followed by the blessings of the multitude; and afterwards met a man who told him " he had *got* that blessed peace he spoke of, the day he talked to the people at the berr'in" (burial).

Preaching on one occasion in the street, an apple-woman, whose sales he interrupted, bitterly and repeatedly cursed him. "I began," said Gideon, "to speak of the great love of God, in giving his son to die for sinners, for all kinds of sinners—that he gave him to die for cursing and blaspheming sinners. I had not been long speaking, until her heart was softened. At last she came up, and addressing me with altered tone, said, "Arrah! cushla macree, will you take a share of my apples?"

"Before I left the Circuit," continues Mr. Huston, "he came again to Drogheda, preached in the chapel on a Sabbath evening, and published for himself next morning at seven o'clock. He was at the gate by six. 'You're an hour too soon, Mr. Ouseley,' I said. 'No, it is 7 o'clock.' 'You will find, sir, it is but 6.' 'Well, I'll go down to the Tholsell and see.' I followed him down, and found him preaching to the labourers, who were waiting to be hired! Some townspeople passed rapidly by with their fingers in their ears, as if dreading moral contagion. A young man opposite, just out of bed, his night-cap on, opened his window, and hurled a large sea-shell at the preacher with fiendish violence. It fell at his feet with a loud crash. I said, as we walked back, 'Mr. Ouseley, that shell was very near hitting you. I think it fell within half a yard of you.' 'An inch,' he gravely replied, 'is as good as a mile!' He kept his appointment in the chapel at seven. What quenchless ardour—what superabundant labours in advanced age!

"Many waters," *literally*, could not quench this holy flame. "On Monday," says his biographer, "they rode to Manorhamilton, a distance of twenty miles. The day turned out exceedingly wet, but as a meeting had been published for that evening, nothing could induce Mr. Ouseley to rest short of the end of his journey. 'A disappointment to an expecting congregation,' said he to me, 'is a sin of such magnitude, that I would prefer running a great risk rather than be the cause of it.' We were wet, continued Mr. Ouseley, to the very skin. Poor dear Noble now and then cried out, 'What shall we do? My very boots are full of water. I am wet all over.' 'My dear fellow,' said I, 'let us conceit that we are *in* the water—that we are *swimming* through; let us push on!'" Arrived at Manorhamilton, they got dry clothes, and God gave them that night a season of great power and blessing. (They stopped with the writer's uncle, Mr. James Graham, who had to put suits of his own clothing on them).

The ruling passion of hatred to Rome, but pity for its deluded followers, was strong in death. The Rev. John F. Mathews records that, during his last illness, on two occasions he spoke of the " dire apostacy," and said if he had any wish to live at all, it was to do something more towards hastening its destruction. The feeling strengthened as his end drew near. Mr. Wm. Banks, son of one of our venerable ministers, himself a respectable local preacher, mentioned to me that, one day visiting our veteran evangelist, when just " to the margin come," he said,—" Mr. Ouseley would you wish me to engage in prayer before we separate?" " Oh, yes, dear," he replied. Seeing that the closing scene was at hand, Mr. Banks asked the Lord to sustain his suffering servant, and to prepare him fully for his approaching end; when Mr. Ouseley laid his hand on his shoulder, saying, " Stop, dear; pray that I may recover! Pray that I may live to see an *end* of the dire apostacy of Rome."

Ouseley's whole-length likeness, in conclusion may be thus drawn :*—Of middle stature ; strongly built ; rough in his exterior ; sound in his physical constitution ; mentally vigorous and acute ; constrained by the love of Christ ; overflowing with compassion for perishing souls ; an able oppo-

---

* We may here introduce the epitaph on Mr. Ouseley's tomb in Mount Jerome Cemetery :—

GIDEON OUSELEY,

DEPARTED THIS LIFE

MAY 14, 1839,

IN THE SEVENTY-EIGHTH YEAR OF HIS AGE.

He was a
Zealous, laborious, and self-denying Minister
of our
LORD JESUS CHRIST,
Throughout the United Kingdom ;
And during nearly
Half a century he was ceaselessly engaged in his
Master's work ;
In Ireland especially :
In its towns and villages,
Fairs and markets ;
Regardless of personal ease—Fearless of
danger,
Uninfluenced by the policy of those
" Who are prudent in their own sight,"
He persuasively called on men
To " REPENT AND BELIEVE THE GOSPEL."

nent of doctrinal popery as embodied in the Trent canons; chary of politics; ardently patriotic; devotional in his habits; decisive in purpose; fearless of danger; ever on the aggressive; superabundant in labours; unmoved by appalling difficulties, like another "Great Heart;" and withal a refreshing example of patient continuance in well-doing to the last."

His last words were, "God's spirit is my support," and then passed away triumphant home.

> "Servant of God, well done!
> Rest from thy loved employ;
> The battle's fought, the victory's won,
> Enter thy Master's joy.

CHAPTER XXIV.

CONCLUSION—GENERAL MISSION AND IRELAND'S EVANGELIZATION.

" Yes, Erin ! thou nursling of error and feud,
   Though dark and long fitful thy story,
To the meek Prince of Peace shall thy vales be subdued,
   And burst forth with millenial glory."

IN bringing this unpretending volume to a close, the writer humbly hopes that the expectations which he led his readers to indulge, with regard to the historical and incidental character of the materials of which it is composed, have been in some measure realized. The special providence of God, which runs through the whole of Mr. Graham's history, verifies the two following Scripture declarations :— " The steps of a good man are ordered of the Lord ;" and, " Delight thyself also in the Lord, and He shall give thee the desires of thine heart."

Speaking of the joint labours of Graham and Ouseley, Dr. Stevens states :—" They generally rode into towns with hats off, and Bible in hand, when immediately they were followed by a procession. They sung a hymn, or a translation of one of Wesley's, in the Irish. The pathos of the lyric and of the language touched the hearts of the rude crowds, who sobbed aloud and waved to and fro, swayed by the simple music even before the prayer began.'* We may thus tolerate what a certain writer calls music—

"Sweet soother of a thousand ills;"

and what another calls—

"The sweet delusion of a raptured mind."

No wonder a great man was induced to say,—"I care not who governs a country if I am only allowed to make the ballads." Such is the sympathy of sound and song. Dr. Stevens goes on to say, in his description of these marvellous street services, that—"Others fell in the streets on their kneess, calling upon the Virgin and the saints. Some shouting questions of defiance to the preachers; others throwing sticks or stones at them; some rolling up their sleeves in defence of them—others in hostility to them. Frequently the confusion culminated in a genuine Hibernian riot, the parties rushing pell-mell upon each other, roaring and brandishing shillelahs, and only brought to order at last by the intervention of troops from the barracks.

---

* The author is here reminded of the story told of Orpheus, by Virgil, "That when he played on his lute the stones rose from the quarry, and danced till they arranged themselves in the building; and likewise the timbers from the forest came together to their proper places in the roof under its magical tones, till the whole building stood in its completeness, a monument of its power." To this, no doubt, Charles Wesley alludes, when he makes Virgil's dream a glorious reality.

"Thus would I charm the listening throng,
And draw the living stones along,
  By Jesus' blessed name.
The living stones shall dance and rise,
And form a city in the skies,
  The new Jerusalem."

—(See Irish Hymn, in Appendix A.)

"Whatever doubts such occasional tumults might suggest respecting the expediency of the mission, they were borne down by its triumphant results. The Gospel was heard by the Irish masses. How otherwise could they be reached was a question which none could answer, unless it was 'not to go near them at all.' They will not come to Protestant churches. They believe it a sin to do so. Shall they, then, be left to perish? You cannot conduct your elections, or even, in many instances, administer law without tumult. Must we, therefore, argue that government should be abandoned? And shall not the administrators of the Gospel have courage as well to confront the indignities and perils which the magistrates face? In the midst of all such disorders it was frequently seen that incalculable good was done. Not only scores and hundreds, but thousands of the wretched population were savingly converted, and brought into the Methodist and other Protestant Churches. These brave itinerants were evidently grappling with the monster evil of the land. They were doing what Protestantism had hitherto failed to do. Some of the clergy of the establishment, who saw that there was no other way to conquer Popery, began to take sides with the missionaries, and welcomed them to their parishes, and frequently with their congregation stood faithfully round them. M'Quigg's Irish Bible, and Ouseley's Controversial Tracts, especially his 'Old Christianity,' did good service; but the living voice was the grand agency.

>'Truth from their lips prevailed with double sway,
> And those who came to mock remained to pray.'"

"This mission gained strength continually. The Irish Conference saw that it was opening a new and grand field of evangelization before them, and gave it their heartiest interest. It is hardly now a contingent calculation, that Ireland, after so many struggles and sufferings, will yet, and before many years, become one of the most fertile fields of Protestant Christianity. In that day Graham and Ouseley, and their fellow-labourers, will not fail to be recognized as among the chief apostles of its evangelization. Such labourers, together with the hardly less energetic exertions of the regular Circuit preachers, would have rendered Methodism mighty in the island, had it not been for continual emigration to the new world. The Irish itinerants were virtually labouring for American Methodism on the Celtic population. Amidst popular tumult and rebellion, the most wretched accommodation, and the continual drain upon their congregations by foreign emigration; and yet, considering their persistent labours and success, it may, indeed, be doubted whether the energy of Irish Methodism has had a parallel in the history of its widespread denomination. Its blessings, not only to America, but to the Wesleyan Foreign Missions, and to England itself, in the gift of many eminent preachers, entitled it to the grateful admiration of the world."

We will now glance at the future prospects of the General Mission. As to the past, we may truly say, "The half has not been told," nor will the full volume of its records be opened until the day of eternity. Its utility, however, has been fully established as a means of spreading Divine truth throuhout the length and breadth of this benighted country. Had it been continued and carried on with the same vigour, and without intermission, as in its earlier days, it is hard to say what would have been the results. In looking over the dates, it will be seen that it is now seventy years since its commencement. Only thirty of these were occupied by men appointed to what we may call "The General Mission proper." During the other forty we had missions, but they were limited to certain localities, and had all the responsibilities of Church organization—ministerial, pastoral, and financial—to fill. For many years, during the latter period of Mr. Ouseley's life, he was the only general missionary in Ireland. "He assumed," said Dr. Hoole, "the apostolate of all Ireland." Seven years after his death it was resumed for a year, by the appointment of two of our ministers for the South of Ireland—just at the time of the famine, 1846—and God greatly blessed and owned their united labours, as He generally does when we take His own method of sending them out, "two and two, before His face,"—proving that

"Work, divided aptly, shorter grows."

The English Minutes for the following year (1847) have these observations in reference to their labours. In answer to the Irish Address it is said:—"While itinerant friars, in some parts of the world conduct their missions in squares and market-places, and on the high roads, with ostentatious zeal, and thereby work on the passions of the people, and sustain their cause, it cannot be thought unbecoming that you should solemnize your missions throughout neglected districts as our fathers did. Gird on your armour, and hasten to engage in this holy and peaceful warfare, and God will preserve you from every evil."

In fact, Methodism can only exist on the aggressive principle, as was stated a year or two ago in the English answer to the Irish address, on the appointment of the writer and the Rev. J. Wilson to the general mission—"In order to gather in, we must first go out." There are difficulties still, there have been difficulties, and there will be difficulties, very likely for many years to come. But, as in mathematics difficulties are of no weight against demonstrations, so it is here. The carnal mind is the same now as ever, but, as Graham said of Mallow, "The deeper sunk, the greater need to rise." What we want to prepare men for this work is the baptism of fire. In the year 1851 the writer was appointed to the hallowed enterprise, and was shortly after joined by Messrs. Hewitt and Samuel Johnston for a few years. The latter fell in harness, but fell triumphantly, to die no more. The work was then suspended until the Conference of 1865, which was held in Cork, when the providence of God seemed to smile upon it and favour it again. The Lord laid this agency on the heart of an Irish lay gentleman, now in England. He offered to give the Irish Conference £100 a year for four years, if it appointed two men, who were total abstainers, to the work of the General Mission. The Conference complied with the request, not stopping to inquire into the habits of the men in reference to drink, not wishing to infringe on the rights of liberty of action; but it so happened that the choice fell on two rigid abstainers from alcoholic liquors. The keynote thus struck called forth other generous responses—such as a handsome annual offering from the Rev. D. Butler, of the Methodist Episcopal Church of America, who was just returning from India, after establishing a very prosperous mission there, and with spoils of victory, of which neither Lord Clive nor Lord Clyde could ever boast. Bishop Janes, of America, was also at that Conference, and the ever-to-be-lamented Draper, from Australia, who shortly after met with a watery grave by the loss of *The London* steamer. All advocated the re-establishment of the mission, and we would hope the results justify the Conference in so doing.

Two of us were then appointed for north and west. Last year another was added to our ranks, and, we trust in the Lord, a fourth will be sent out with us next year. All thanks to the Methodist Episcopal Church of the United States for the liberal help towards this, as well as towards many other Irish objects, not forgetting their aid towards the splendid Methodist College in Belfast, which has just been opened.

That there is as great a necessity now, if not greater than ever, for some more enlarged aggressive movement, must be patent to any one who seriously looks at the signs of the times. Satan rages; errors abound; Churches are convulsed; and the nation itself seems to upheave with the dread of events which loom in the distance, and cast their shadows so very palpably before them. In fact "men's hearts are failing them for fear;" but it is to the moral aspect of affairs we would direct special attention. The morals of our country are bad. Witness the Sabbath-breaking, the profanity in regard to swearing, the lying, the drunkenness, and blood touching blood. "Shall not my soul be avenged on such a nation as this, saith the Lord?"

The question now arises, What is to be done? or what can we, as a Church, do in addition to what we are doing? That Methodism has done, and is doing a good deal, is not at all questioned. It has its thousands of Church members in Ireland, and its tens of thousands of congregational hearers. It has also a large number of self-denying and laborious ministers; and it may be safely stated, that error rarely meets with more able or temperate antagonists. Yet, it must be understood that its efforts, as far as the masses are concerned, are more casual than direct. All our labour is chiefly expended on one class of the community. But, as it regards the Irish-speaking portion of the population, we are doing little or nothing; and unless this subject is grappled with speedily, and a suitable agency raised up, the present million, to whom the language is vernacular, will be gone. The exclusively Irish-speaking people are, according to the last census, 155,000, and those who speak both English and Irish, are 800,000; but to all the latter it is vernacular, as well as to the former. They think in Irish, and would prefer speaking in it if they could; and who that knows the power and pathos of that language would wish it to be extinguished! It is emphatically the language of feeling and of the heart. For instance, when in the ordinary forms of the English language we would merely express a welcome, in the native Irish the greeting would be, " Cead mille fatha roath,"—*an hundred thousand welcomes before you*, or await you. This may be regarded as hyperbolical, but the meaning attached to it, and the manner in which it is generally delivered, have an influence on an Irishman's heart that the colder English could not convey. When an English mother expresses the full tide of her fondness for her child, it is "My little dear." But how far short does this fall of the expression of an Irish mother to her offspring! She calls it "*A cushla mo chree!*"—("The vein, the pulse, the beating voice of my heart.") Any one can appreciate and admire this: a mother only can *feel* it. It is equally expressive in theology. For instance, the word *reconciliation*, signifies *second friendship*; the word *atonement*, signifies the same. An English reader has the idea of sacrifice attached to it; but it really means the *friendship* resulting from the sacrifice, or, as it has been expressed, *At onement*.

The attachment of the Irish to their own language was frequently proved in successfully quelling a mob. At one time, in Clonmel, a rabble of blood-thirsty men rushed into the Methodist Chapel, at the time of holding an Anniversary Missionary Meeting, while the Rev. Phillip Garrett, the English deputation, was speaking. They interrupted him with all the signs of hostility, and every appearance of murder, until the Rev. John Feely, who was at the meeting, rose and appealed to them in Irish, in such affectionate and powerful strains as completely disarmed them. We had this from Mr. Feely's own lips.

They are also as remarkable for their ready wit as for their attachment to their language. It is stated of one, who sent his children to an Irish school to learn the language, that he was forbidden, on pain of being denied the rites of his church on *his death-bed* if he persevered. "Well, well, your Reverence," said Pat, "it's a hard enough case, to be sure, but plase (please) God, I'll just try to outlive you." When the Rev. Elijah Hoole was superintendent of the Irish Mission schools in this country, he contemplated the translation of the Wesleyan Catechisms into the Irish language, but, no doubt, his short stay among us prevented him from carrying out his purpose. He wrote a very valuable letter on the subject of our young ministers cultivating a knowledge of the language. In it he says—" If, in the course of Divine providence, the people should throw of their yoke, would it not be of importance to have men prepared, by a knowledge of their tongue, to take them by the hand, and guide them to a purer worship and a holier faith. Some of the younger preachers might be assisted and directed to turn their attention to that tongue; and if a deeper feeling and a more lively interest be awakened on the subject, and more prayer offered up, fruit may be expected in this, as in other departments of evangelical labour, in the conversion and salvation of this interesting people." There were then two millions who spoke the language. The population was at least seven millions. One million has passed away—we may say a generation—since he wrote that letter. It will be found in the February number of the *Magazine* for the year 1834, now nearly thirty-five years ago. The writer was then stationed on the Boyle Circuit, and in answer to a communication which he wrote to the Doctor on the subject of his letter, he had a kind, and an immediate reply, of which the following is an extract:—

"LIMERICK, 8*th March*, 1834.

"MY DEAR BROTHER,—I shall be truly thankful if the few remarks I sent to the *Magazine* should induce you and others of our brethren to qualify themselves for usefulness among the Irish. Surely we ought to do something for them; and in what way did we ever exert ourselves for God and fail to gain His blessing? I am persuaded that it would be regarded by the Conference as much to your credit, and worthy of imitation, if you could state that you had read such and such portions of the Scriptures in Irish, and that you were improving yourself in that means of usefulness. May God bless you, and make you a more extensive blessing.

"Yours affectionately,
"E. HOOLE."

This made a deep impression on the author's heart, and he never rested until he could at least read a little, speak a little, and sing a little, in that sweet tongue; and, thank God, many an Irishman has since heard, in his own language, "the wonderful works of God," especially the work of redeeming love and saving grace. The writer records, with gratitude, the kindness and anxiety of the Conference, in granting him, some years after the above letter was written, a few months to closer application for the better cultivation of the language, which, at a late period of life, is not easily acquired. Bishop Bedell was, however, sixty years of age when he acquired a knowledge of it. A little knowledge of it serves greatly, if it only proved to the Irish that we sympathize with them in their national predilections. We may say, also, that the Oughterard mission rose out of this desire to become better acquainted with that language: in that district it is spoken freely. An Irish class is formed there, and the master paid by the Rev. William Arthur. How delighted would the writer be if in the Belfast College this subject were taken up, and some of the young men encouraged to cultivate a knowledge and love for the Irish tongue! If the observations, as recorded in the Wesleyan Missionary Notices for the year 1852, on the subject of the Irish College in Ballinasloe for the sons of the Irish clergy, wishing to learn that language, and what was therein stated, in reference to a Methodist College, had even remotely anything to do with our present one in Belfast, the writer would rejoice greatly. But he does hope and pray that it may contribute its share, at least, in spreading to some extent the knowledge of the truth, in the native tongue, among a large portion of our countrymen. Now is our time for increased action in this and in every department, but in this especially. God can still give the spirit of utterance, and of martyrdom, too, if necessary. Duty is ours; events belong to God. How far the present distracted state of the land may be attributed to the want of fidelity and zeal on the part of the Church of Christ, is only fully known to God. But let us, as Wesleyan Ministers, more than ever, sustain the character given us in what is technically called "The Liverpool Minutes"—"Home Missionaries."

Oh, that I could speak to my fathers and brethren in the ministry, and to all the Churches throughout the land, I would in all plainness and fidelity ask, Are not the signs of the times perilous as well as hopeful? And while cheered by the latter, should we not, like one of old, be "moved" by the former, with "godly" fear, to the *saving* of the nation at large in which we live. There seems to be a respite of delay, as if to give us the opportunity of "warning the ungodly of all their evil deeds," and at the same time of directing them to the only ark of safety, and from a flood more terrific in its elements than that which once swept the world round. Oh, what a time for immediate action on some large scale, worthy of ourselves and of our country. Let us claim it for Christ, whose right it is to reign. Let all our literary institutions, let all our prayerful and financial appliances, be brought to bear on this one object—*The conversion of Ireland.* If this can be accomplished, the world's conversion will the more speedily follow, for its influence is world-wide. And who can tell but that God will soon raise up from the Irish mission field men who would willingly go to the very ends of the earth—regardless of life or death—

> "To plant the tree of Life in fields of ice
> And make it flourish in eternal snow."

And what is to hinder, but unbelief and indecision? Let us, in the Lord's name, be up and doing, while we have such a promise, "Lo! I am with you *alway*," &c. And if we have not mistaken the genius of the Gospel, the command of the Saviour—the spirit and policy of the Church to which we belong—the purity of her faith—the harmony of her principles, and the mutual confidence of her lay and clerical members, as well the character of her resources,—may we not reasonably and scripturally hope for better days to dawn on this " our own, our native land ?" Who would hesitate or delay, if they thought thereby that millions would be excluded from the kingdom of glory and of God who might otherwise be there! and how solemn the thought that millions have passed away, even from our own country, unwarned and unwept, and millions more are swelling the legion roll of mortality, and appearing constantly before a holy God, constrained to exclaim, " No man cared for our souls !" A generation has passed away since the faithful Ouseley used to cry with weeping, and in pathetic tones, " Oh ! my country, my beloved country ; my ruined, my unhappy country !" And a generation and a half gone since Graham's voice, sweet as the music of the spheres, used to proclaim, " And Ireland shall be free !" Here was patriotism of the purest and noblest quality, in comparison with which all the *pseudo* professions of nationality by demagogues sink into nothingness. And we, too, are passing away. Shall the work cease ? If we "come not to the help of the Lord, to the help of the Lord against the mighty," others will. But God seems to lay His burden at our door. If so, let us not only do it, and do it well, but let us transmit it also to hearts in which it shall be steadily prosecuted, and it may be that for them, if not for us, the privilege and the honour are reserved of rejoicing over our country ransomed from error and from sin ; but if we are faithful, we shall be permitted to hear the hallelujah chorus swelling up before the throne—" The kingdoms of this world are become the kingdoms of our God, and of His Christ."

Then the din of carnal weapons, the tumult of deadly battle, the strifes, the discords, and the feuds of earth, shall all retreat to their native hell, and the hymn of angels,— "Glory to God in the highest, and on earth peace and good will towards men," shall again be sung, and responded to by a regenerated earth." "Now is come salvation and strength, and the kingdom of our God, and of His Christ." (Rev. xii. 10.) "The great trumpet shall be blown, and they that were ready to perish shall come;" the banner of truth and victory shall be unfurled; the nations shall gather and press into the Gospel kingdom; and the shout of universal triumph shall be heard "from the rivers unto the ends of the earth." Thus standing high on the mount of prediction, and on the vantage ground of eternal truth, and in "the full assurance of hope," we may look along the vista of the future to a glorious day of millennial freedom for Ireland, yea, and for all the world. "By faith we already behold that lovely Jerusalem here."

> "Then every heart shall be a Saviour's throne,
> And every land Messiah's sway shall own;
> Then from all nations, hymns to heaven shall rise,
> And earth shall join the chorus of the skies—
>
> "'Hallelujah! the Lord God omnipotent reigneth!'"

IRISH HYMN—WITH TRANSLATION.

THE following is one of those Irish hymns to which Dr. Stevens so touchingly refers, as producing the most thrilling effects on the Irish people. It is common measure, and may be sung to the tune called *Martyrdom*. The writer has translated it has literally as he possibly could ; but he must depart from the correct orthography, for the sake of coming as near as possible to the Irish pronunciation :—

IRISH.	TRANSLATION.
Oh, thaw mo chree go dorough a throm,	Oh, 'tis my heart that's weigh'd with
Is sconroo an mo lawr,	Within terrific fear, [gloom ;
Mor thaw an baus eg dhrid a lum,	And death, to lay me on the board,
Is bye me fose er clawr.	Is swiftly drawing near.
Augh fose nee foor, an baus an chad,	But, as full power he has not yet
Dho liggoo uusa grey.	To lay me in the clay.
O yia, mo yia do humpium lath	O God, my God, to Thee I'll turn :
Dheean throughey is 'sauwall mey.	Save, pity me, I pray.
Oh, isagam fein, thaw'n thauwor more,	Just cause have I, and truly great,
Na doriv shil go throm :	To shed the heaviest tears ;
Mur is packho, kinthough donna mey,	I'm sinful, guilty, and undone,
Is thiriought foddoo roine.	In view of boundless years.
Oh, dulling thoo er cron na paush,	O Thou who didst for sinners die,
An baus gach packhough boghth,	A victim on the tree,
Oh, feagh an-ish le throkore,	Look now in mercy, and forgive
'Is inauhoo mo hillia loghth.	My crimes beyond degree.

APPENDICES.

APPENDIX A.

SERMON.

A CONDENSED specimen of Mr. Graham's mode of sermonizing will here be given; and, we must say, one of the plainest of his sketches, of which he wrote perhaps not less than five hundred in a distinct hand.

TEXT—LUKE xi. 21, 22.

"When a strong man armed keepeth his palace, his goods are in peace : but when a stronger than he shall come upon him, and overcome him, he taketh from him all his armour wherein he trusted, and divideth his spoils."

[Here we must remark that he seldom spent more than a minute or two on the introduction of his subject, but entered immediately on the discussion of it : his great object was to deliver "the message" contained therein.]

Division I. The strong man armed; II. The palace in which he rules; III. The armour in which he trusts; and IV. Who the *stronger* is, and his victory.

I. The strong man armed.—Doubtless this is the being whom St. Paul calls "the god of this world," "the prince of the power of the air,"—the leader of the rebel "angels, who kept not their first estate, but left their own habitation, and are now reserved in everlasting chains of darkness unto the judgment of the great day." As to the *strength* of this fallen spirit, we find he had confidence that he would overcome Michael and his angels. Hence it is said he fought with them, "but prevailed not, neither was his place found any more in heaven." But we learn that he has great power on earth, even over the sons and daughters of men, for he is said "to rule in the hearts of the children of disobedience." We find also, in the case of Job, what strength he possessed. He commanded the elements of fire and wind, and called the Sabeans, and appointed them their work of destruction, sparing neither property, servants, nor children. No wonder they are called "Principalities and powers, and spiritual wickedness in high places." But we not only see their *strength*, but their *hatred* as well. Satan smote Job "with sore boils, from the sole of his foot to his crown;" and, having stripped him of all earthly comforts, left him nothing but a wicked wife to torment him—for she bids him "curse God and die." We also see his power over the woman whom our Lord cured, and who had been bound by Satan for eighteen years. Many others were possessed with, and tormented by him in the days of our Lord. His power and his wrath are so great in this world, that were it not he is restrained, he would overthrow the earth itself. I doubt not but that he is at the root of all the wars, and murders, and depredations which are carried on in this sinful world, leading its children captive at his will; who are not only sold under sin, but have sold themselves to work wickedness in the sight of the Lord. We need not wonder, then, that "the dark places of the earth are full of the habitations of cruelty." Like Solomon's madman, "**Casting forth fire-**

brands, arrows, and death, and saith, Am I not in sport?"
"He blinds the eyes of them that believe not, lest the light of the glorious Gospel of Christ should shine unto them."

II. The *palace*.—This he keeps in peace. This is the heart of man, which is the seat of all emotion and feeling. Here he dwells and works. Our Lord states—"For out of the heart proceed evil thoughts, murders, adulteries, fornications, thefts, false witness, blasphemy," &c. As long as these *goods* remain, the devil has *peaceable* possession. There is no struggle, no opposition to him. He keeps his palace. But what an **awful** palace—"deceitful above all things and desperately wicked"—"An evil heart of unbelief in departing **from the living God."** No wonder the warnings—"Take heed," and "Take heed, brethren," &c. Satan not only *keeps* his palace, but *fills* it with his *goods—unbelief, pride, anger, self-will, covetousness,* deceit, envy, hatred, malice, revenge, prejudice, ignorance, darkness, blindness, error, evil surmising, whispering, talebearing, back-biting, evil speaking. While all these "*goods*" remain, the house **or** palace will be at peace; for conscience will not be allowed to speak or disturb the deceitful calm. "They are not in trouble like other men."

III. In what consists his *armour?*—It consists in what first **cast** himself away from God, namely, *pride*. **His** language was and **is**—"I will ascend above the heights of **the** clouds; I will be like the Most High." (Isaiah xiv. 14.) This was a grand piece of his armour, which he abundantly supplies to **his** followers. It has done terrible execution. **No** wonder he *trusts in it*. Another piece of his armour is *wrath*—"great **wrath,"** compared by Saint Peter to the "roaring of a lion," going about "seeking whom he may devour." Another is *malice*—

> "He comes, with hellish malice filled,
> To scatter, tear, and slay,
> And takes up every straggling soul
> As his own lawful prey."

Again, he is armed with *envy*. Having lost his own angelical glory which he had when one of the morning stars, "who sang together," and as one of "the sons of God who shouted for joy," he cannot but now *envy* his former companions their happiness, and envies all the saints on earth also, on account of their love and joy, their harmony, and future hope of glory. He cannot be changed from being "an *accuser* of the brethren." With this armour, and with the above *goods*, he has little trouble in reigning in the *palace* of the human heart. But he will *finally* despise those over whom he now domineers, and when he secures their eternal perdition he may well be regarded as saying to his once willing slaves and subjects thus—

> "Our envy once, ye are now become our scorn;
> In vain for you the Son of God was born;
> That mighty favour, that peculiar grace,
> Too glorious for our fallen angelic race,
> Serves only to exasperate your doom,
> And gives the infernal shades a darker gloom."

IV. Who is "the *stronger*" than the strong man armed? and how does he conquer? This is none other than He to whom, as Mediator, "all power in heaven and in earth is given"—"the seed of the woman," and the serpent bruiser—"He who was manifested to destroy the works of the devil." "Thou hast led captivity captive." "He must *reign* until all

His enemies are put under His feet." "He is exalted a Prince and a Saviour."

> "He conquered when He fell,
> And at His chariot wheels
> Dragged all the powers of hell."

"He came upon him" when he dispossessed the legion, and when He cast out the seven devils out of Mary Magdalene, and loosened the daughter of Abraham, and healed the daughter of the Canaanitish woman, and the nobleman's son. And He *overcame him* when He was seen falling from heaven like lightning, and when, after His resurrection, He gave his disciples "power over devils and unclean spirits," and invested them with that armour which pulled down some of the strongest holds of darkness, such as Gentile vanity and Jewish opposition, and brought all into captivity to the obedience of Christ. They were "to turn men from darkness to light, and from the power of Satan unto God," &c. This was "*taking his armour from him*," wherein he trusted. And now to "*divide* the spoils." That is, Christ *divides* or *scatters* the spoils of Satan. This He does when He *scatters* the darkness by introducing light—*convincing* the spell-bound conscience of its guilt, and *breaking* the power of sin by the *converting* grace of God, and thus *destroys* the very roots of sin altogether by the sanctifying power of the Spirit. The cursing, swearing devil is *cast out*; the *proud* and *angry* devil is dismissed; the *lying* and *cheating* devil banished; the *unclean* and *lustful* devil exterminated. And thus the *spoils* on which the devil revelled are *divided*—completely scattered. The heart, once the hold of every hateful and unclean bird, is become the habitation of God through the Spirit, and all the powers of body and mind are become servants of righteousness unto God—yea, the believer "serves God now in holiness and righteousness before Him all the days of his life." Once "the servant of sin, now the servant of God, having his fruit unto holiness and the end everlasting life;" and in fact the former *palace* of Satan is now the temple of the Holy Ghost.

Permit me now, in fine, to inquire of you—does "the strong man armed" keep your hearts? Are his goods in peace? Are you the willing slaves of sin? Are your hearts the palaces of the prince of hell? Do you bear his mark? Do you plead his cause? Do you wear his livery? Does he work in your hearts? Does he lead you captive at his will? Are you ranked among the children of pride? Are your lives among the unclean? Do you *company* with the workers of iniquity? Has he put out your eyes from seeing your danger? Has he hardened your hearts from dreading everlasting punishment? What shall I say more to open your eyes? What shall I do to alarm your fears? God is angry with you; heaven is frowning; hell in enlarged, and moving from beneath to meet you at your coming; and devils are longing to have you in the lake of fire and brimstone. "Now consider this, ye that forget God, lest I tear you in pieces, and there be none to deliver." "Kiss the son lest he be angry with you and ye perish from the (right) way." Turn, oh, turn to the stronghold, ye prisoners of hope, and the Lord will deliver you, and save you from the hand of all your enemies, and you will see them no more for ever.

We will close in Mr. Graham's words on another text:— "There is help laid on 'One that is mighty to save,' and, believing on His name, with an heart unto righteousness, we obtain pardon of all our sins, or justification through the blood of the covenant; peace with God; power over the world and sin; joy in the Holy Ghost; an interest in all the promises of the Gospel; deliverance from the fear of death and the grave, and from the damnation of hell; and lastly, an earnest of the inheritance 'incorruptible, undefiled, and that fadeth not away.'"

The following may be applied to the preacher of the above:—

> "A father's tenderness, a shepherd's care,
> A leader's courage, who the cross can bear;
> A ruler's awe, a watchman's wakeful eye,
> A pilot's skill, the helm in storm to ply.
> A fisher's patience, and a labourer's toil,
> A guide's dexterity to disembroil,
> A prophet's inspiration from above,
> A teacher's knowledge, and a Saviour's love."
> —Bishop Ken.

APPENDIX B.

AMERICAN CAMP-MEETINGS.

"Blow ye the trumpet, blow,
　The gladly solemn sound,
Let all the nations know,
　To earth's remotest bound:
The year of jubilee is come,
　Return ye ransomed sinners home."

THE following letter is in character with the one to which Mr. Ouseley refers. It was written by Mrs. Anne Cook, of Philadelphia, to her mother, near Sligo. She was the fruit of Mr. Graham's early ministry, and aunt to our venerated friend, Mr. Jackson Hawksby, of Ballymote, County Sligo, who has lived to see nearly three generations pass away :—

"PHILADELPHIA, *Sept.* 13, 1806.

"DEAR MOTHER,—This comes with my love, and to give you an account how the work of the Lord prospers here. About eighty miles from this city, we had one of the greatest camp-meetings that was ever known on this continent. We remained eight days at it. The ground, containing twenty acres, was enclosed with a boarded fence. There were four hundred and seventy tents, besides waggons, carts, and twelve dozen of official guards, and seven persons to blow trumpets to sound round the camp every morning and evening, when reports were made of the number brought to God. You would think the praises of God would rend the heavens. There were about eight thousand of white people, and four of blacks. The preachers were in the middle, of whom there were about thirty-five, besides class-leaders, &c. There was a boarded enclosure round the stand This was called "The Mourner's Aisle." After public worship all those who felt distress were invited to come forward. The crowds who did so were astonishing. Scarcely any who knelt down but were blessed, in answer to the fervent prayers of the people of God. On one occasion the overwhelming power of God came down, and set hundreds of souls at liberty. The *proud*, the *grand*, who came in their coaches, were convinced of sin, and converted to God before their return! Glory be to God forever, that I was born to see this day! What I have seen and what I felt, pen cannot describe, or tongue explain. The number of souls computed to have been blessed with pardon, or purity, at this meeting amounts, in all, to 2,249! Hallelujah! Please show this letter to Mr. Charles Graham, as he was the first instrument in bringing me to God in my young days, at about the age of seven. I would count it a favour if he would write to me.

"I am, dear mother,
"Your affectionate daughter,
"ANNE CROOK."

The following extract, in reference to camp-meetings, is of a more recent date. It is taken from a work by the Rev. James Shaw, formerly a member of the Irish Conference, and now belonging to the Methodist Episcopal Church in

America. We had the pleasure of seeing and hearing Mr. Shaw in this country last season, when he wrote his work called *Twelve Years in America*, the perusal of which will, no doubt, do good to head and heart. The *Irish Primitive Wesleyan Magazine* speaks of Mr. Shaw's book thus:—"This is a charming book. The writer enters minutely, and at the same time with remarkable brevity, into the history of several states, cities, and towns in the States of America; beautifully delineating their origin, increase of population, wealth, literature and Church organization; also the soil, produce, railway communication, natural history, mines, minerals, lakes, rivers, and works of art, are described so fully, so graphically, and in a style so chaste, as to charm and instruct the reader. We have felt unmixed pleasure in reading Mr. Shaw's admirable little book. We strongly recommend it to our readers, and hope it may have an extensive circulation. It is written in an excellent Christian spirit, and is full of interest throughout.

Mr. Shaw, in this work, says,—"It was on a Wednesday evening, in September, 1860, that the carriages and waggons bore several families, with their tents, to the scene of the encampment, in a beautiful grove on the banks of the Sanagamon river, near Illiopolis. Soon the stroke of the woodman's axe was heard felling down trees, and putting up tents, seats, and the preachers' stand. The ground was cleared, the tents were fixed, with the seats and stand in the centre, and aisles were formed for the congregation to pass to and fro. Lamps were hung to the trees, stoves were adjusted, and fires kindled for cooking. About four thousand people assembled to hear the Word of Life. Soon the voice of prayer and song of praise were heard in this 'forest sanctuary.' Brothers Lapham and Honnold assisted in preaching and conducting the meeting. By Friday and Saturday several other families, with their carriages, had come and pitched their tents for the remainder of the meeting, which lasted about eight days. The power of God fell on the congregations. The judgment-day was the theme of discourse.

"When the invitation was given to come to Christ, the wounded, the stricken, and the penitent rushed from all parts of the congregation to the altar of prayer. The slain of the Lord were many; and there were mingled with the voice of song and worship, the cry of distress and the sob of the penitent. Rejoicing parents knelt beside their weeping children; wrestling Jacobs and praying mothers pleaded with God on behalf of their families, and soon one after another emerged out of darkness into marvellous light, and from bondage into liberty."

Our dear friend and deeply-lamented brother Wallace, was most anxious to witness one of those camp-meetings in America. In this he was gratified, and took part in the services of one shortly after his arrival, but soon joined the innumerable host who have crossed the flood. He died of one day's illness at Cincinnati. How suitable the following lines—

> " The voice at midnight came,
>   He started up to hear;
>   A mortal arrow pierced his frame;
>   He fell but felt no fear.
>
> " His sword was in his hand,
>   Still warm with recent fight,
>   Ready that moment, at command,
>   Through rock and steel to smite.

> " It was a two-edged blade,
>   Of heavenly temper keen ;
> And double were the wounds it made,
>   Whene'er it glanced between.
>
> " 'Twas death to sin ; 'twas life
>   To all who mourned for sin :
> It kindled and it silenced strife—
>   Made war and peace within."

His last words were " I leave all in the hands of Jesus."

The writer feels much pleasure in being able to record the following epitaph, which he transcribed August 10, 1868, from the tablet erected in the Centenary Chapel, Stephen's Green, by the stewards and members of that congregation, among whom Mr. Wallace laboured with great acceptance for three years, and by whom he was greatly esteemed :—

To the Memory
OF THE
REV. ROBERT WALLACE,

Whose sanctified talents and devoted service will be long held in affectionate remembrance. Appointed by the Irish Conference of 1866 one of its delegates to the Methodist Churches of America, during the celebration of the Centenary of Methodism on that continent, he was, in ten days after his arrival, seized with cholera, and died in Cincinnati, Ohio, on Sabbath, September 2nd, in the 55th year of his age, and 31st of his ministry. "And he, being dead, yet speaketh."

www.ingramcontent.com/pod-product-compliance
Lightning Source LLC
Chambersburg PA
CBHW021208230426
43667CB00006B/615